CRITICAL STUDIES OF
SIR GAWAIN AND THE GREEN KNIGHT

CRITICAL STUDIES OF SIR GAWAIN AND THE GREEN KNIGHT

EDITED BY

Donald R. Howard and

Christian Zacher

UNIVERSITY OF NOTRE DAME PRESS

Notre Dame   London

Library of Congress Catalog Card Number: 68–12297
Manufactured in the United States of America by
NAPCO Graphic Arts, Inc., Milwaukee, Wisconsin

CONTENTS

PREFACE

In the early 1830's Sir Frederic Madden found, among the manuscripts of the Cotton collection in the British Museum, four Middle English poems—*Pearl, Patience, Purity,* and *Sir Gawain and the Green Knight.* They were bound in a volume with two Latin treatises; and the pages containing them, as one can tell from the numbering, had been removed from another volume now lost. The four poems are all copied in the same difficult hand without notable breaks or titles between them, and until Madden's time were thought to be a single poem. In the old printed catalogue by Thomas Smith (Oxford, 1696), they are so catalogued:

> 3. Poema in lingua veteri Anglicana, in quo sub insomnii figmento, ad religionem, pietatem, & vitam probam hortatur Auctor; interspersis quibusdam historicis, & picturis, majoris illustrationis gratia, subinde additis.

A newer catalogue, published at London in 1802, passed on the same information:

> 3. A poem in old English on religious and moral subjects, with some paintings rudely executed. Sec. XV. Begins, "Perle plesaunte to prynces paye . . ."

Thus they remain catalogued to this day—except that in the Students' Room of the British Museum, along the left margin in the printed catalogue shelved there, someone has written in pencil, "Sir Gawain and the Green Knight."

The poem is thus a discovery of the early nineteenth century. Until then, so far as anyone knows, it played no role in English life or thought and had no place in English literary tradition. There are no references or allusions to it in its own time or thereafter; William Dunbar mentions "the poet who wrote of Sir Gawain," but this could refer to any poem about Gawain, perhaps to one which has not survived. Some have attempted to show that it influenced or was influenced by other poets or poems, for example *Piers Plowman;* but such arguments, based as they must be on similarities of various kinds, are of small moment. We do know that *someone* read it, for the one surviving copy is a scribal copy,[1] and a later poem, *The Green Knight,* seems to be an adaptation. Moreover, a motto added at the end, "Hony soyt qui mal pence," is written in a different hand from the scribe's. If the motto may be taken as a comment on the theme or moral of the work, it is the first piece of *Gawain* criticism, indeed the only one in three centuries.

Although the scribe's hand appears to be of the very early fifteenth century, the language of the poem dates it in the third quarter of the fourteenth century. The dialect is of the West Midlands. This is all that can be known about the poem with any degree of certainty. There is general agreement as to its excellence; it is surely the greatest English metrical romance and among the very greatest of all medieval romances. But its dialect is terribly difficult. The author did not write, as Chaucer did, in the London dialect, which was to become a linguistic norm; and being a learned man he used a highly wrought literary language which borrowed words from other dialects. The result is that for many years scholars concentrated mainly on philological, lexical, and historical problems. Much of this work cleared up the meaning of lines and improved the readings in editions. Much, however, reflected scholarly fashions of an earlier generation and so provided, for example, a genealogy of conjectured

---

[1] The one manuscript is certainly a scribal copy. The hand is apparently later than the language. Moreover the initial capitals were added by an illuminator, perhaps the same person who made the four drawings. In some cases, notably on f. 101ᵛ, the scribe has written a tiny letter to be filled in by an illuminator, a common practice in scribal copying.

sources, the provenance in folklore of the characters and motifs, and demonstrations of influence from and upon other works. In particular there has been the question of authorship. The four poems in Cotton Nero A.x are preserved in the same hand and were written in the same dialect; they are similar in style, although the verse forms differ; they share certain basic medieval ideas; and several are unusually good. A fifth poem, *St. Erkenwald,* though found in another manuscript, has seemed to some observers enough like these to suggest the same author.[2] The case for common authorship really has to stand or fall on these points; almost anything else that can be said is a variation or development of one or the other. The author or authors wrote in an age when authorship was only just beginning to have glamor—it took the printing press and humanism to bestow glory on the man of letters. And curiosity about writers' private lives and personalities does not seem to have been a matter of concern until the eighteenth century. One suspects that attempts to single out one anonymous poet and even identify him are prompted partly by the somewhat nineteenth-century hope of finding an unsung "Master" in the West Midlands. Thus we have been given a hopeful chronology of his works and many conjectures about his life and personality. But the evidence can be interpreted otherwise. Perhaps the poems are by a "school" of poets who imitated one of their number or each other. Perhaps they were collected, with stylistic retouching, by a lover of poetry who wrote them down in his own dialect. They might even be translations of works not now known, all by the same translator. The common author, if he existed, was at all events an enigmatic fellow— learned in theology enough to be a priest (though having a daughter who died), knowing court life and filled with worldly

[2] The notion has been discredited by Larry D. Benson, "The Authorship of *St. Erkenwald," JEGP,* LXIV (1965), 393–405.

zest for clothes, arms, and lovely ladies; a profoundly serious moralist; a good-humored ironist.

In 1961 Morton W. Bloomfield surveyed these and other problems treated by previous critics and attempted to point the way for future critical efforts. Others were thinking along the same lines on many points, so that articles and books which appeared concurrently and in the years following were not all inspired by his article. Those which were not, however, have often addressed themselves to the problems he has pointed up. Using Mrs. Loomis' essay as an introduction, we begin this selection with Bloomfield's article, and follow it with studies which appeared at the same time as his, or since. This has meant excluding some excellent studies written before the 1960's; but these were reported with few exceptions by Bloomfield and helped shape his characterization of the poem. What is selected here makes, we hope, a representative sampling from a recent surge of scholarly and critical work. The poem is among those English works which most deserve such attention, and probably one of the great poetic achievements of all times.

D.R.H.
C.K.Z.

July 1, 1967

PART ONE:

INTRODUCTION

GAWAIN AND THE GREEN KNIGHT

Laura Hibbard Loomis

THE HERO OF *Gawain and the Green Knight* (*GGK*)[1] is likened to a pearl beside a pea (line 2364), and so might the poem itself be reckoned among its contemporaries. It moves over an almost flawless structure as smoothly as supple skin over the bones of the hand. With the exception of Chaucer's *Troilus and Criseyde*, no other Middle English romance approaches its artistic and spiritual maturity, its brilliant realism, its dramatic vigor, its poetic sensitivity to nuances of word and mood, its humor, its nobility of spirit.

This treasure of Middle English poetry exists in only one manuscript (British Museum, Cotton Nero A.x), dated by the handwriting of its one scribe and the costumes of its rather

Reprinted, by permission of the Clarendon Press, from *Arthurian Literature in the Middle Ages: A Collaborative History,* ed. Roger Sherman Loomis (Oxford, 1959), pp. 528–540.
[1] All references to *GGK,* unless otherwise indicated, are to the edition by Sir I. Gollancz, with introductory essays by M. Day and M.S. Serjeantson, EETS, O.S. 210 (London, 1940); bibliography, pp. lxvii–lxxii. Other editions are by J. R. R. Tolkien and E. V. Gordon (T & G, Oxford, 1925, 1930, 1936); and by E. Pons (Paris, 1946, with French translation). For recent renderings into modern English see T. H. Banks (New York, 1929); K. Hare (London, 1946, 1948); M. R. Ridley (London, 1950, 1955); Gwyn Jones (London, 1952); [also Gardner (Chicago, 1965); Rosenberg (New York, 1966); Boroff (New York, 1967)—Ed.].

crude illustrations about 1400.[2] The romance has 2,530 lines written in stanzas running from twelve to thirty-eight long lines of unrhymed alliterative verse, each stanza concluding with a "bob and wheel" of five short rhyming lines.[3] The author's mastery of alliterative phraseology predicates a close acquaintance with antecedent alliterative poems, but the extent of his indebtedness to earlier English verse or of his own influence on later verse is still largely undetermined.[4] However, his poetic preeminence and his outstanding artistry have been searchingly studied and praised since 1839 when, in his *Syr Gawayne,* Sir Frederick Madden first published the poem.

The manuscript contains three other poems which, because

[2] A facsimile of the manuscript was published with an introduction by Sir I. Gollancz, EETS, 1923. For description of manuscript see *GGK,* pp. ix ff.; and R. S. and L. H. Loomis, *Arthurian Legends in Medieval Art* (New York, 1938), pp. 138 f., with illustrations of miniatures (figs. 389–391). On Scribal matters see W. W. Greg, "A Bibliographical Paradox," *Library,* XIII (1933), 188–191, and J. P. Oakden, "The Scribal Errors of the Ms. Cotton Nero A.x," in *Library,* XIV, 353–358.

[3] J. P. Oakden, *Alliterative Poetry in Middle English,* I (Manchester, 1930), pp. 177 f., 218, 251–255, 266. See *GGK,* p. lxviii; T & G, pp. 118–121.

[4] Oakden, II, passim. . . . For theories about relation of *GGK* to *The Green Knight,* see G. L. Kittredge, *A Study of Gawain and the Green Knight* (Cambridge, Mass., 1916), pp. 125–135, 282–289; J. R. Hulbert, "Syr Gawayn and the Grene Knyȝt," *MP,* XIII (1915–1916), 49 ff., 461 f.; Ott Löhmann, *Die Sage von Gawain und dem Grünen Ritter,* Shriften des Albertus-Universität . . . 17 (Königsberg and Berlin, 1938), 24–36. For relation to *Wars of Alexander* see *GGK,* pp. xiii-xviii; for connection of *GGK,* ll. 2414 ff., with *King Alisaunder* see R. W. King, "A Note on 'Sir Gawain and the Green Knight,' 244 f.," *MLR,* XXIX (1934), 435 f. For possible influence of *GGK* on Chaucer's *Squire's Tale* see C. O. Chapman, "Chaucer and the *Gawain*-Poet, A Conjecture," *MLN,* LXVIII (1953), 521–524; B. J. Whiting, "Gawain: His Reputation, His Courtesy, and His Appearance in Chaucer's *Squire's Tale,*" *MedStud,* IX (1947), 230 ff. For the influence of *GGK* on a poem by Humphrey Newton (d. 1536) of Cheshire, see R. H. Robbins, "A Gawain Epigone," *MLN,* LVIII (1943), 361–366; "The Poems of Humfrey Newton, Esquire," *PMLA,* LXV, (1950), 249–281; Cutler, "The Versification of the 'Gawain Epigone' in Humfrey Newton's Poems," *JEGP,* LI (1952), 562–570.

of close similarities in vocabulary, phrasing, style, and spirit to *GGK,* have led to a general belief in their common authorship.[5] From different interpretations of the exquisite, elegiac-seeming *Pearl,* the homiletic *Patience* and *Purity* (*Cleanness*), and *GGK,* conjectural biographies and personalities have been built up for the poet, and several identifications have been proposed.[6] None of them, however, has won acceptance, and the identity of the "Master Anonymous" remains a mystery. Was he a monk, a minstrel, a learned clerk, an official in some lordly household, or himself a man of rank and wealth?[7] In any case he wrote as one familiar with courtly life, its pleasures, luxuries, arts, and ways.[8]

The realistic references in *GGK* to North Wales, Anglesey, and the wilderness of Wirral in Cheshire (697–701) are unu-

---

[5] *GGK,* pp. x-xiii; *Purity,* ed. R. J. Menner (New Haven, 1920), pp. xix-xxvii; Oakden, I, 72–87, 251–253; II, 88–93, 393 ff.; Dorothy Everett, *Essays on Middle English Literature* (Oxford, 1955), pp. 68–96. The attribution to one author has been questioned for reasons more ingenious than convincing by J. W. Clark in " 'The *Gawain*-Poet' and the Substantival Adjective," *JEGP,* XLIX (1950), 60 ff.; "Paraphrases for 'God' in the Poems of 'The *Gawain*-Poet,'" *MLN,* LXV (1950), 232 ff.; "On Certain 'Alliterative' and 'Poetic' Words in the Poems Attributed to 'The *Gawain*-Poet,'" *MLQ,* XII (1951), 387 ff.

[6] For proposed identifications see *GGK,* pp. xviii f. For notably perceptive comments on the poet's nature, learning, and background see *Pearl,* ed. C. G. Osgood (Boston, 1906), pp. xlvii-xlix; and Henry L. Savage, *The Gawain-Poet, Studies in His Personality and Background* (Chapel Hill, 1956), Chap. I.

[7] Despite the poet's piety and knowledge of biblical and theological matters, his secularity has been increasingly emphasized. See *Pearl,* ed. Osgood, pp. lii-liv; T & G, p. xx. Oakden, I, 257–261, thought him a retainer of John of Gaunt; Savage, pp. 206–213, would assign him to the household of John's French brother-in-law, Enguerrand de Coucy, of whose chivalric character and English experiences, 1363–1377, Savage (pp. 99–117) thought he detected some reflections in *GGK.* But the content and genesis of the poem seem best accounted for by the literary sources.

[8] For the poet's knowledge of music see C. O. Chapman, "The Musical Training of the Pearl Poet," *PMLA,* XLVI (1931), 177–181; for courtly manners and sports see discussion below.

sual. The scenic descriptions, the extensive use of words of Scandinavian origin, the dialect, all place the author's home in the Northwest Midland area.[9] The detailed account of the so-called Green Chapel and the great castle nearby have suggested even more precise localizations.[10] The architecture, the costume, the armor, so accurately described, are appropriate to a date between 1360 and 1400, and of the four poems in the manuscript *GGK* is considered the latest.[11] Though no one has succeeded in connecting the green girdle worn as a baldric by the knights of Arthur's household (2515 ff.) with any historic order of chivalry, Gawain's wearing a costume like that of a knight of the Garter (1928 ff.) and the insertion of the Garter motto after the close of the poem have tempted some to think that the author wrote under the patronage of a knight of that order, renowned for chivalry and possessed of estates in the Northwest Midlands, where the poet was at home.[12]

[9] Southern Lancashire, Cheshire, and Derbyshire have been suggested for the poet's home. For bibliography see *GGK*, p. lxviii, and Menner, *"Sir Gawain and the Green Knight* and the West Midlands," *PMLA*, XXXVII (1922), 503–526; Serjeantson, "The Dialects of the West Midlands in Middle English," *RES*, III (1927), 327 f.; Oakden, I, 82–87; Savage, 128–133.

[10] Tolkien and Gordon (p. 94), following Madden, accepted Volsty Castle and the neighboring Chapel of the Grene, Cumberland. Oakden, I, 257 f., proposed John of Gaunt's castle of Clitheroe, Lancashire. Mabel Day (*GGK,* p. xx) identified the Green Chapel with a small, rocky "cave projecting from a hillside" at Wetton Mill, Staffordshire, but confused it with Thor's cave (Thursehouse), a huge cavern in a cliff a mile away, which could not possibly fit the poet's description (ll. 2178–83). The supposition that the Green Chapel was a megalithic barrow (*GGK*, note to l. 2172) is questioned by Brewer in *Notes and Queries,* CXCIII (1948), 13. See the reply by R. T. Davies, ibid., p. 194.

[11] *GGK,* p. xiii; T & G, pp. xx-xxii; Cyril Brett in *MLR,* XXII (1927), 451–458; Savage, pp. 8, 141 f., 222.

[12] Connection of the poem with the Order of the Garter was maintained by I. Jackson, "Sir Gawain and the Green Knight Considered as a 'Garter' Poem," *Anglia,* XXXVII (1913), 393–423; Oscar Cargill and Margaret Schlauch, *"The Pearl* and Its Jeweler," *PMLA,* XLIII (1928), 118–123; and by Savage, passim (see especially pp. 146 ff. for a list of Garter knights with West Midland holdings). For those opposed to the

The romance, according to 31–36, was heard "in toun," but was also known to the author in a book (690). He proposes to tell it in "letteres loken," that is, in alliterative verse.

I. SOURCES AND ANALOGUES

The main framework of the plot is known as the Challenge or the Beheading Game, and into this has been skillfully fitted a second major element called the Temptation. The earliest version of the Challenge is found in *Bricriu's Feast* (*BF*), a composite Irish saga of the eighth century extant in a manuscript antedating 1106.[13] The saga contains, in fact, two variants of the Challenge (*BF*, p. 99) and refers to other book versions. The first, or "Terror," version is shorter and more archaic; the second, the "Champion's Bargain," is more elaborate. In each a shape-shifting enchanter challenges Cuchulainn and two other Ulster heroes, likewise contending for the championship, to exchange with him a decapitating blow. Twice the challenger is decapitated but walks away with his head and returns the next day, his head restored to its place. Cuchulainn alone keeps his part of the bargain, and after receiving one or more pretended blows from the challenger's axe, he is acclaimed the champion. When this legend passed out of Ireland, it lost its most primitive and savage elements, and, somewhat rationalized and simplified, it passed eventually into several Arthurian romances. Of these, *GGK* has preserved by far the largest number of features which go back to some form of the Irish saga.[14]

In a fundamental study Kittredge summarized the Challenge

Garter connection see Menner, *Purity*, pp. xxvii ff.; Hulbert in *MP*, xiii, 710–718; T & G, pp. xx, 117.

[13] *Fled Bricrend* or *The Feast of Bricriu* (*BF*), ed. George Henderson (London, 1899), with English translation; Kittredge, pp. 9–26.

[14] Alice Buchanan in "The Irish Framework of *Gawain and the Green Knight*," *PMLA*, xlvii (1932), 328 f.; R. S. Loomis, *Wales and the Arthurian Legend* (Cardiff, 1956), pp. 77 f.

as it appeared in these romances.[15] The earliest extant French version forms part of the so-called *Livre de Caradoc*,[16] included in the First Continuation of Chrétien's *Perceval*. . . . Though the hero of the Challenge is Caradoc, not Gawain, it presents the closest correspondence to *GGK*. Both poems transform the court of Ulster into that of Arthur and refer to his custom of waiting for a marvel to happen;[17] alike they mention the queen's presence and describe the challenger, not, as in the Irish, as a huge and hideous churl (*bachlach*), but as a tall knight who rides into Arthur's hall. Both offer parallels to the Irish challenger's grim proposal, his taunting the courtiers with their hesitancy, his decapitation, and his departure. Both tell how the challenge is accepted, not by three successive heroes as in the Irish, but by one, who is described as Arthur's nephew and who modestly speaks of himself as the most foolish of knights. Both romances remark that anyone accepting such a challenge would be mad; both speak of the grief of the knights and ladies for the hero; both add to the Irish hero's protest against the challenger's delay in striking a taunt as to his cowardice; both change the interval of a day between the challenger's decapitation and his return to a year. Long before the Irish antecedents of the Challenge had been discovered the likeness between the episode in the *Livre de Caradoc* and *GGK* led to the belief that this French romance was the immediate source of *GGK*.[18]

[15] Kittredge, pp. 26–74. . . . His argument that the "Champion's Bargain" was the sole source of the Challenge was refuted by A. Buchanan, pp. 316–325.

[16] For texts of the Challenge see *The Continuations of the Old French Perceval of Chrétien de Troyes*, ed. William Roach (Philadelphia, 1949–1955), i, 89–97; ii, 209–219; iii, 141–156.

[17] Sixteen romances tell of this custom. Chrétien's *Perceval*, ed. A. Hilka (Halle, 1932), p. 668; John Reinhard, *The Survival of Geis in Medieval Romance* (Halle, 1933), pp. 182–195. The reference in *Caradoc* may well have been borrowed from a more original part of the *Perceval*. See *Continuations*, ed. Roach, i, 232; ii, 371; iii, 196.

[18] M. C. Thomas, *Sir Gawayne and the Green Knight, A Comparison with the French Perceval* (Zurich, 1883), pp. 34–68. See criticism in

But Kittredge's conclusion that they were independent versions of a lost French story seems justified, for only thus could those Irish features which are found exclusively in one poem or the other be accounted for.

Among the Irish elements to be found in *GGK* but not in *Caradoc,* Kittredge (pp. 32–34) and others have noted the following: the challenger's size, his fierce eyes, silence as he enters the hall, his great axe (in *Caradoc* a sword), his high praise of the court, his exit carrying his head, not, as in *Caradoc,* replacing it on his shoulders. To these Irish elements, still preserved in *GGK,* another may well be added. In *GGK* alone the Challenger is named Bercilak (2445); as the Green Knight he plays the *same role,* is the *same character,* as the Challenger in the "Champion's Bargain." There he is repeatedly called a *bachlach* (churl), a trisyllabic word in Irish.[19] Changed in transmission, its meaning lost, the Irish common noun seems to have survived in the English name and best explains its origin.

Though so much in *GGK* was thus ultimately derived from the "Champion's Bargain," other elements came from the "Terror" version, also found in *Bricriu's Feast.*[20] In this tale the hero and his two rivals are not tested at the royal court but, journeying into a wild region, stop at a house and receive a

Romania, XII (1883), 376. Also, J. L. Weston, *The Legend of Sir Gawain, Studies upon Its Original Scope and Significance,* Grimm Library 7 (London, 1887), pp. 88 ff.

[19] Hulbert, in "The Name of the Green Knight," *Manly Anniversary Studies in Language and Literature* (Chicago, 1923), pp. 12–19, established the manuscript reading as Bercilak, and identified the name with that of Bertelak, Bercelai, emissary of the False Guenièvre in the Prose *Lancelot.* The reading was accepted by T & G, p. 114. R. S. Loomis in *Celtic Myth and Arthurian Romance* (New York, 1926), found its origin in the Irish *bachlach.* Roland Smith in "Guinganbresil and the Green Knight," *JEGP,* XLV (1946), 16 ff., questioning this derivation, proposed a hypothetical Irish form *Bresalach,* meaning contentious, and sought to relate the Green Knight to figures outside the Ulster cycle and without any connection with the head-cutting episode.

[20] Kittredge, pp. 97–101; D'Arbois de Jubainville, *Cours de Littérature Celtique,* VI (Paris, 1892), pp. 132–135.

guide from their host. They go to Terror, a shape-shifter, who proposes the head-cutting test. Three times, like the Green Knight, he makes a feint with his axe at the hero's neck. The corresponding features in *GGK,* especially the placing of this testing episode away from Arthur's court, establish the influence of the "Terror" version upon the romance.

Besides the *Livre de Caradoc,* only one other French text provides a version of the Challenge which is significant for *GGK,* namely *Perlesvaus*[21]. . . . The Challenge is here set not in a palace hall, but in a Waste City, and its hero is Lancelot. Though differing widely in other respects from *GGK,* it offers three noteworthy resemblances: the challenger whets his axe with a whetstone (1. 6674) as the hero approaches to fulfill his bargain; the hero shrinks from the blow; he is sharply rebuked.[22] These parallels, supplemented by resemblances in phrase, again argue for literary borrowing, whether directly by the English poet or through a French intermediary.[23]

Thus we have three closely related Arthurian versions of the Challenge or Beheading Game. Since they do not agree as to the name of the hero, there is no certainty as to whether Caradoc, Lancelot, or Gawain was the first of Arthur's knights to meet a head-cutting challenger. It is remarkable that the challenger in no version antedating *GGK* appears as a green giant, clad in green and riding a green horse.[24] Explanations for

[21] *Perlesvaus: Le Haut Livre du Graal,* ed. W. A. Nitze and others (Chicago, 1932), I, 136–138, 284–286; discussed II, 281–283.

[22] Kittredge, pp. 52–61, noted the weakening in this episode of the supernatural element.

[23] See *GGK,* pp. xxxi ff., for phrasal parallels. Nitze noted (*Perlesvaus,* II, 3) that the Bodleian manuscript of *Perlesvaus* was once owned by Sir Brian Fitzalan of Bedale, Yorkshire. Possibly this very manuscript was read by the *Gawain*-Poet.

[24] No extant French text before the prose *Perceval* printed in 1530 (Roach, *Continuations,* I, p. xxxii) supports Kittredge's belief (pp. 32, 140) that the challenger wore green in an early form of the *Livre de Caradoc.* For him, as for Hulbert (*MP,* XIII, 456 ff.), the challenger was green because in folklore green is often a fairy color. R. S. Loomis in *Arthurian Tradition and Chrétien de Troyes* (New York, 1949), p. 279,

this greenness have been sought in mythology, folk ritual, and folklore;[25] but since the ultimate sources of the Challenge —the two tales incorporated in *Bricriu's Feast*—provide no support in the way of hints of vegetation rites or concepts, and since in *GGK* the Green Knight and his other self, Bercilak, have only midwinter associations, his greenness there can hardly be due to vegetable traits.[26]

n. 7, explains the color as due to the ambiguity of the Irish and Welsh adjective *glas,* meaning either grey or green, and points out that Curoi, the Irish prototype of the Green Knight, was repeatedly referred to as "the man in the grey mantle," though the word *glas* is not the word chosen. See Buchanan in *PMLA,* xlvii (1932), 327–330. No historic person seems to have been called the Green Knight, but two fourteenth-century Englishmen, Sir Ralph Holmes and Simon Newton, were known as the Green Squire. See H. Braddy, "Sir Gawain and Ralph Holmes the Green Knight," *MLN,* lxvii (1952), 240 ff.; J. R. L. Highfield, "The Green Squire," *M Æ,* xxii (1953), 18–23. Highfield studies an important West Midland family of Newtons of the type which might have produced the author of *GGK.* See R. S. Loomis, *Arthurian Literature in the Middle Ages* (Oxford, 1959), p. 528, n. 4, for the Cheshire Humphrey Newton (d. 1536) who used *GGK.*

[25] E. K. Chambers in his *Medieval Stage* (Oxford, 1902), i, 117, 185, and Nitze, "Is the Green Knight a Vegetation Myth?" in *MP,* xxxiii (1936), 351–366, derive the Challenge from vegetation ritual or myth. John Speirs in "Sir Gawain and the Green Knight," *Scrutiny,* xvi (1949), 270–300, urged that a ritual underlying the story and "the poet's belief in its value as myth is what gives the poem its life." This ignores both the power of individual genius and the evidence of the Irish stories of the Challenge, the sources of *GGK,* which are not easily susceptible to interpretation as vegetation ritual. Even more reckless is the statement of. Francis Berry in "Sir Gawayne and the Grene Knight," *The Age of Chaucer* ed. Boris Ford, Pelican Book A290 (London, 1954), p. 158, that the poet's awareness of "the generic forces of life . . . realizes itself in the Green Knight; . . . his reckless vigor and amorality of life . . . testify to an assumption that moral behavior . . . is subservient to and dependent on something more primary—creative energy. Gawain and his society humbly come to terms with the Green Knight."

[26] Loomis, *Arthurian Tradition,* pp. 208 ff., 230 ff., 280 ff., derived certain episodes in Arthurian romance from Irish texts preserving mythic concepts of sun- and storm-gods. These sometimes survived as dramatic or picturesque features, but it is to be doubted whether the French authors or the *Gawain*-poet who introduced such elements were conscious of their mythical origin and significance.

Fitted into the framework of the test by decapitation is another test—the three successive temptations to which Gawain is subjected by the wife of the Green Knight. Though the finesse with which these scenes were developed was the poet's own contribution, yet the situation itself, the aggressive wooing of a reluctant young man in bed by a lovely lady—was already employed by romancers in the twelfth century. It is easily recognizable in the *Lanzelet* of Ulrich von Zatzikhoven,[27] which . . . he translated from the Anglo-Norman shortly after 1194.

Lanzelet and two companions are welcomed at the castle of Galagandreiz, a rich forester. Their host's daughter arrays herself sumptuously and at night tempts each of the three knights in turn in the most wanton manner. The story anticipates *GGK* in its emphasis on her elaborate dress and her young beauty, in the way she sits beside each sleeping knight and wakes him, in her offer of a gold ring and its rejection, in her urgent plea to hear talk of love, and in her frank proposals. The outcome of the temptation scenes differs from that in *GGK* since, though Lanzelet's companions repel the lady's advances, Lanzelet himself is easily persuaded. Nonetheless, the lady's behavior and conversation are similar enough to those of Bercilak's wife, though on a much lower level, as to suggest that the two poems were following the same original pattern. The Anglo-Norman source of *Lanzelet* also anticipated *GGK* in making Galagandreiz, like Bercilak, a notably human figure; despite warnings of his cruelty, he performs kindly services for his guests, and has almost nothing of the supernatural, gigantic, or imperious qualities of other notable hosts in Arthurian romance.[28] Of special interest is the challenge which he issues to Lanzelet the morning after the temptation scenes—a challenge to throw knives at each other in alternation. It is as truly a *jeu parti* as

[27] Trans. K.G.T. Webster (New York, 1951), pp. 34–43, and notes 37, 43.
[28] For these figures, see Kittredge, Index, Imperious Host; Loomis, *Arthurian Tradition,* Chap. XLVII.

the beheading by alternation in *GGK* and *Bricriu's Feast,* and provides the earliest instance of the combination of the Challenge theme with that of the Temptation.[29] The *Lanzelet* version did not include the strange feature which Kittredge (pp. 79 ff.) pointed out in other Arthurian romances as well as in *GGK,* namely, that the temptress was the wife of the host and that she wooed at her husband's wish.[30] One of these, *Yder,* offers a striking parallel, representing the lady of the castle as making violent love, at her husband's order, to the hero as he lies in bed in the hall.[31] In other analogues cited by Kittredge her role is passive; she is constrained by her husband or father to admit the guest to her bed in order to test him. This situation presents, as Mabel Day has remarked, but a shadowy likeness to *GGK.* Equally remote from it are two repellent Temptation tales in Latin and French versions of the *Vitae Patrum.*[32]

A significant analogue to the Temptation occurs in the Vulgate *Lancelot* and has been proposed as perhaps "the immediate cause for the insertion of Morgain la Fée into the English poem."[33] This enchantress, who in the course of the French narrative thrice attempts to seduce Lancelot in vain, sends her damsel, a younger self as it were, to effect the same end.[34] Three times the girl employs her amorous arts on the recum-

---

[29] Kittredge, pp. 21–23, 219–221, mentioned the combat in *Lanzelet* only as an instance of duelling by alternation and said nothing of the related Temptation.

[30] Kittredge summarized (pp. 83–101) analogues to the Temptation in *Ider, Carl of Carlisle, Chevalier à l'Epée, Hunbaut.*

[31] *Ider,* ed. H. Gelzer (Dresden, 1913), vss. 185–510, and p. LV.

[32] Else von Schaubert, "Der englische Ursprung von *Syr Gawayne and the Grene Knyȝt,*" *ES,* LXII (1923), 330–446. These tales have been widely but uncritically quoted as true analogues. The author's low estimate of the English poet's skill is almost unique. See *YWES,* IV (1923), 52.

[33] Hulbert in *Manly Anniversary Studies,* p. 18.

[34] H. O. Summer, *The Vulgate Version of the Arthurian Romances* (Washington, 1908–1916), IV, 123–128; V, 91–93, 215–218; R. S. Loomis, "Morgain La Fee and the Celtic Godesses," *Spec,* XX (1945), 186.

bent hero. From this episode, with the instigating background figure of Morgain and the foreground figure of the young, active seductress, it is but a step to the two figures in *GGK*, the aged Morgan, prime mover in the plot, and the agent of temptation, Bercilak's young wife.[35] She was, no less than Bercilak, a servitor of the resident goddess who sat highest at their table (1001), who had already forced him to enact the Green Knight's cruel part, and who, presumably, also forced him to order his wife to tempt their guest (2446–2463). No wonder that the young wife was at heart Gawain's "enmy kene" (2406). Despite his moral sensitivity, the poet imputes no moral obloquy to the lordly pair who yet were helpless in the power of that malignant goddess. The might of Morgan le Fay (2446) was, for Gawain himself, a sufficient explanation and exculpation for all that he had endured and made him able to part from the Green Knight on most friendly terms.

The concept of Morgain as an evil enchantress, a witch, had appeared in Hartmann von Aue's *Erek* by 1190; her origin in Celtic mythology and the amazing diversity of her roles in medieval romance have been studied by Lucy Paton and R. S. Loomis.[36] Her wanton traits reappear in many amorous and

---

[35] Kittredge (pp. 131–135) and Hulbert in *MP*, XIII, 454, regarded Morgan as a late and poorly integrated element in *GGK*, mainly because she, though a supernatural person, failed in her purposes and did not foresee her failure. But in medieval romance enchanters often suffer defeat. Baughan in "The Role of Morgan le Fay in Sir Gawain and the Green Knight," *ELH*, XVII (1950), 241–251, defended Morgan's role by the untenable argument that she had sent the Green Knight to purge Arthur's court of moral evil, and that the Beheading Game was "an apotheosization of chastity." Likewise unrealistic is the conclusion of J. F. Eagan, S. J., in *The Import of Color Symbolism in Sir Gawain and the Green Knight*, St. Louis Univ. Studies, Ser. A, Hum. I, 2 (St. Louis, 1949), p. 83.

[36] L. A. Paton, *Studies in the Fairy Mythology of Arthurian Romance* (Boston, 1903), Chap VII, on the Chapelle Morgain in the Val sans Retour; R. S. Loomis in *Spec*, XX (1945), 183–203; reprinted in *Wales*, pp. 105–130; Loomis, *Arthurian Tradition*, index *sub* Morgain; Hulbert, in *Manly Anniversary Studies*, pp. 16 ff.; T & G, notes on ll. 2452, 2460.

related Arthurian figures; as we have seen, there are the temp-
tresses in *Lanzelet* and *Yder,* and the splitting of Morgain's
personality into two selves in the Vulgate *Lancelot.* The author
of *GGK,* apparently familiar with this older dichotomy, has
effectively contrasted the goddess, grown old and wrinkled, with
the young beauty who is at once Morgan's other self and
agent,[37] but who has also a personality of her own.

The earliest example surviving in medieval fiction of a Temp-
tation approximating in curious ways that in *GGK* is to be met
in the Mabinogi of *Pwyll,* attributed to the eleventh century.[38]
Arawn, a huntsman and an Otherworld king, like the Green
Knight himself (992), arranged that Pwyll should be lavishly
entertained in his absence in his palace and lie with his own
wife as a test of his chastity and loyalty.[39] At the year's end
Pwyll, like Gawain, was required to meet a supernatural enemy
at a river crossing. The differences between *Pwyll* and *GGK*
forbid any thought of direct literary connection, but undeni-
ably *Pwyll* offers the oldest example of a traditional story pat-
tern in which carnal temptation, whether passively or actively
offered, and a Hospitable Host who constrains wife or daughter
to tempt a guest, are recurrent themes. It not only anticipates
the conjunction of these and other elements in *GGK* and its

[37] *Sire Gauvain et le Chevalier Vert,* ed. Emile Pons (Paris, 1946),
p. 74, on Morgan as a foil to Bercilak's wife.

[38] *The Mabinogion,* trans. G. and T. Jones, Everyman's Library, no.
97 (New York, 1949), pp. 1–9; for date see p. ix. In *JEGP,* xLII (1943),
170–181, and in *Wales,* Chap. vI, R. S. Loomis detected in *Pwyll* four
features also combined in *GGK:* the royal huntsman-host; the hero's
resistance to the temptation presented by the host's fair wife with the
latter's connivance; the anniversary combat; its localization at a river
crossing. For other cases of the influence on Arthurian romance of
traditions in *Pwyll* see Loomis, *Arthurian Tradition* index *sub Pwyll.*

[39] These are precisely the virtues tested in *GGK.* In *Pwyll* Arawn's
wife, on learning that it was her husband's friend, not her husband, who
had slept chastely beside her, said to Arawn: "Strong hold hadst thou
on a comrade for warding off fleshly temptation and for keeping faith
with thee." Cf. Gawain's fears (ll. 1775 f.) that "he should commit sin
[i.e., lechery] and be a traitor to that man."

analogues, but it at least suggests, as they do not, in its mysterious figure of Arawn and in the Welsh folklore connected with him, a clue to the midwinter associations of Bercilak and his connection with Morgan le Fay.[40] In *Pwyll* the still half-mythic Arawn hunts with fairy hounds, wears grey wool, and engages in annual combats with Havgan (Summer-White)—an apparent reminiscence of the strife of summer and winter. In Welsh folklore Arawn was also identified with that Wild Huntsman who, in Welsh as in European folklore, rode with his dogs on the winter winds. As late as 1276 it was remembered by Adam de la Halle that Morgan le Fay had once had for lover Hellekin, chief of the "chasse furieuse" [furious hunt], "le gringneur prinche qui soit en faerie" [the greatest prince that was in fairyland]. Before this date, then, the wanton Morgan was associated with a wild huntsman of whom, perhaps, some faint traditional trace remains in the wintery world of Bercilak, in the fury of his three hunts, in the occasional wildness of his manner (1087). But in any case Bercilak as regal host and midwinter huntsman, as tester, through his own wife, of a hero, as a shape-shifter, finds an ancient prototype in the Welsh Arawn.

The Challenge and the Temptation, then, originated as entirely distinct stories. Who was responsible for their fusion into one of the best plots in medieval fiction?[41] We have seen that both elements appear combined in *Lanzelet,* and that this form of the Temptation, if read in the Anglo-Norman source of *Lanzelet,* may even have provided some suggestions for the *Gawain*-poet. But in other respects *Lanzelet* differs so widely from the English poem (and from *Bricriu's Feast,* with its

---

[40] R. S. Loomis, "More Celtic Elements in *Gawain and the Green Knight*," *JEGP,* XLII, 181–183; Wales, pp. 81–85.

[41] See A. C. Baugh, *A Literary History of England* (New York, 1948), pp. 236–238; G. Kane, *Middle English Literature, A Critical Study of the Romances, the Religious Lyrics, Piers Plowman* (London, 1951), pp. 73–76; *Sire Gauvain,* ed. Pons, p. 15.

early versions of the Challenge) that it cannot be regarded as the model for the combination in *GGK*. It is, therefore, still an open question whether the English author derived the Challenge and the Temptation from separate lost French texts (as well as the *Caradoc* version of the Challenge and the *Perlesvaus* version of the Temptation) and fitted the two stories together; or whether he found this highly artistic combination ready made by some French poet of unusual talent. Even if the latter alternative could be proved correct, one can hardly doubt that the English poet found large scope for his own genius in the adaptation of the plot to his special purposes and ideals.

He may well, indeed, have provided the one plot element which is completely non-Celtic in origin. The mutual promise of Bercilak and Gawain, to give each other what each has won at the end of each day, motivates a whole series of consequences. The motif of an Exchange of Winnings, as Hulbert demonstrated,[42] appeared in a medieval Latin poem known as the *Miles Gloriosus*. A poor knight becomes the partner of a rich citizen; they agree to exchange their winnings. The citizen's faithless wife becomes the knight's mistress and gives him of her husband's treasure. The husband, suspicious, tries thrice to trap the knight, but is ultimately driven forth from his own home. This *fabliau,* now thought to have been written about 1175 in the Loire valley,[43] could have contributed nothing but the exchange idea to *GGK*. No other Arthurian narrative makes any use of the motif, and the deftness with which it is integrated into *GGK* bespeaks the English poet's skill in design and his sensitive perception of character. Gawain, facing the deadly head-cutting test, keeps the protective girdle given him by Bercilak's wife. He breaks his promise and presently suffers deep

---

[42] *MP*, XIII, 699 f. The text of the *Miles* is published by Gustave Cohen, *La "Comedie" Latine en France au XIIe Siécle* (Paris, 1931), I, 181–210.
[43] E. Faral, *Les Arts Poetiques du XIIe et du XIIIe Siécle* (Paris, 1924), pp. 3–6; F. J. Raby, *A History of Secular Latin Poetry in the Middle Ages* (Oxford, 1934), II, 65 ff.

shame and remorse. The poet, aware of weakness even in the noblest, thus saves his hero from a "schematic perfection" and humanizes him by his fault and his pain. This treatment of the Exchange motif can hardly be due to anyone but the Englishman who so deliberately fashioned his whole story to a "fine issue" and a finer end.

II. LITERARY ART

The artistry which is revealed in the construction and style of *GGK* is exceptional. Kittredge noted (p. 4) passages which must be considered, because of their individuality, the poet's own. They include the traditional yet original passage on the seasons; the elaborate account of Gawain's arming, so precise and so contemporaneous in detail; the spirited hunting scenes equally exact and expert; the courtly dialogues between Gawain and his temptress, which reveal such delicacy of characterization. This sophisticated familiarity with varied aspects of aristocratic life and thinking prompts the question whether it was due to observation only or came from the intimate awareness of one who had been born to high estate and "gentilesse."[44]

The poem bears witness not only to the author's acquaintance with earlier romances in French and English,[45] but also to his awareness of literary types. He speaks of his creation as a "laye" (30). The decapitation of the Green Knight is compared to the playing of an interlude (472), a short dramatic performance introduced between the courses of a ban-

[44] Gervase Mathew, "Ideals of Knighthood in Late-Fourteenth Century England," *Studies in Medieval History Presented to Frederick Maurice Powicke,* ed. Hunt, Pantin, and Southern (Oxford, 1948), pp. 354–362, notes similarities between the Chandos Herald's characterization of the Black Prince and that of Gawain in *GGK.*

[45] Hulbert noted in *Manly Anniversay Studies,* pp. 16–19, that with two exceptions all the names in *GGK* occur in the French *Vulgate* romances. See also C. O. Chapman, *An Index of Names in "Pearl," "Purity," "Patience," and "Sir Gawain"* (Ithaca, 1951).

quet.[46] Indeed, *GGK* seems to interfuse the well-knit, romantic matter of the former type with the dramatic manner of the latter. It keeps the unified structure of the Breton lais, and, like them, concerns itself with marvels and an exclusively aristocratic world.[47] But in preserving their pattern, the *Gawain*-poet transformed their fragile charm. Almost alone among poets before 1400, he told of winter with all its harsh rigors, its freezing rain and snows, its howling winds. He conjured up the sense of cold with an intensity hardly matched till Keats wrote the *Eve of St. Agnes.* He laid his scene realistically in the English north country, on heath and crag and in tangled forests of hoar oaks, hazel, and hawthorn. He swept through this wilderness three great hunts that seem transcripts from life. He breathed into courtliness the naturalness of fine, happy people, rejoicing, even joking together. Here, in truth, and at its best, is "merry England," splendid, stalwart, joyous, with its great Christmas and New Year feasts and frolics, inspirited by wine and mirth.

The *Gawain*-poet not only made of his romance a lai but also, in its dramatic effectiveness, something of an interlude, with which, as his own reference shows, he was familiar. Scenes are sharply set; speeches reveal character; gestures and bearing are indicated with lively verisimilitude. The Green Knight, enacting the role of the Challenger, does so with all the gusto of an accomplished mummer. He rolls his red eyes, wags his great beard, boasts and taunts derisively, and makes, after his decapitation, a tremendous, noisy exit.[48] Though at first he seems almost gigantic ("half etayn," 140), actually he towers only by a head or so over other men (332). Apart from his green hue

---

[46] L. B. Wright, "Notes on *Fulgens and Lucrece*: New Light on the Interlude," *MLN*, xli (1926), 97–100, and below, n. 49, on interludes at banquets.

[47] Robert M. Garrett, "The Lay of Sir Gawayne and the Green Knight," *JEGP*, xxiv (1925), 125–134.

[48] Elizabeth Wright, "Sir Gawain and the Green Knight," *JEGP*, xxxiv (1935), 157–163.

and separable head, he is represented as a fine, handsome, human figure. Later, at the Green Chapel, when he has finished his final testing of Gawain, he drops on the instant his role of magic horror and becomes again the gallant, benevolent Bercilak, full of warm goodwill. Though no moment in medieval romance surpasses in eerie terror that in which he held up his severed head and its eyes opened on Arthur's stricken court (446), he is primarily described, not as a supernatural being, but as a man acting a part. The gruesome incident of his decapitation is dismissed by Arthur himself as no more than a play, the device of an interlude (472). Like Chaucer in the *Franklin's Tale* (1140),[49] similarly indulging in a bit of rationalizing over the dramatic illusions of skillful magicians, the *Gawain*-poet was inclined to minimize marvels. He jokes a little about those Gawain encountered on his terrible journey; it would be too "tore" (hard, 719) to tell a tenth of them; anyway the fighting with giants and trolls was not so bad as the winter weather! He derisively pictured Morgan le Fay, though he called her a goddess, only as an ugly, squat, old lady.

As an artist the *Gawain*-poet had the habit of close visual observation and an exceptional sense of form, proportion, and design. As a connoisseur familiar with costly things and courtly taste and custom, he pauses to describe exquisite trifles of embroidery or jewelry, rich fabrics, fine armor. He dwells on the architectural details of the great castle that Gawain first sees shimmering through the distant trees, then in all the glory of its chalk-white, many-towered magnificence. The poet accents social sophistication; manners are polished, talk is an art. The conversations between Gawain and the lady suggest the advances, the retreats, of a courtly dance. Within the set pattern

[49] For illustration of an *entremets* presented at the French court in 1378 see L. H. Loomis in "Secular Dramatics in the Royal Palace . . .," *Spec*, XXXIII (1958), 242–255. The illumination accords with Chaucer's description (*Franklin's Tale*, ll. 1140–51) of the arts of "subtile trege-tours."

of perfect courtesy, wit meets wit; a gracious comedy of manners is enacted. Temptation is offered to Gawain and refused largely in the tone of light social badinage. One has but to read other society romances in Middle English to recognize the difference between them and the greater elegance, the more assured touch, of the *Gawain*-poet.[50] Moreover, in this romance, unlike many others, there is no inchoate rambling, no waste. The episodes move directly from cause to consequence and individual act and character are finely linked. Situations are repeated, but with skillful, deliberate variety and contrast. Court scenes at royal Camelot are different from those at Bercilak's castle; the three temptations of Gawain have subtle differences of tone and temper; the three hunts, whether they have allegorical significance or not, are as different from each other as are the hunted beasts; each hunt implies expert familiar knowledge.[51] The rich indoor revels, whether at Arthur's court or Bercilak's castle, are effectively alternated with cruel winter realities without, and so is the gay fellowship˙indoors with Gawain's stark loneliness as he goes by desolate crags to seek his death.

The romance has superlative art in its fashioning; it is mature, deliberate, richly seasoned by an author who never suggests minstrel servility or even compliment to those who hear him.[52]

[50] S. F. Barrow, *The Medieval Society Romances* (New York, 1924), Appendix. The English *William of Palerne,* though commissioned by Humphrey de Bohun, Earl of Hereford, has in comparison with its French original a homely tone. L. A. Hibbard, *Mediaeval Romance in England* (2nd ed., New York, 1960), pp. 214–223. Even Chaucer's *Troilus* is less consistently courtly than *GGK.*

[51] Savage in *JEGP,* xxvii (1928), 1–15; Savage, *The Gawain-Poet,* pp. 13, 32–48, 224.

[52] There are references to a listening audience in ll. 30, 624, 1996. For Chaucer's use of such minstrel tags as "I yow telle" and "be stille," see *Sources and Analogues of the Canterbury Tales,* ed. William F. Bryan and Germaine Dempster (Chicago, 1941), pp. 496–503. Like Chaucer, the *Gawain*-poet may well have expected his work to be read aloud. Such expressions may echo a minstrel convention, but they do not prove minstrel authorship.

He wrote in his own way and apparently for his own delight in a provincial dialect and in the alliterative verse which belonged to that same north country which he pictured with such startling vigor.

But above all else the romance has a quality of spiritual distinction comparable to that in the *Pearl.* Piety, devotion, purity of thought, are natural to it. Gentle meditations occur on Troy's vanished glory, on the swift passing seasons with all their yesterdays, on the pentangle as symbol of the endless interlocking of the knot of truth.[53] Richly informed about the lovely things of life, the poem is without asceticism or intolerance. It has no mysticism; Gawain is called the Virgin's knight (1769), but he sees no vision, goes on no holy quest. Its deep concern is not with evil, but with good. In this Gawain, the blithe young embodiment of chivalry at its best,[54] goodness is made manifest and radiant, but not, as in Galahad of the Grail romances, a supernatural virtue touched by a mysterious divinity. The "fine issue" of his story is not that he fell into vulgar sin, but that he failed to keep goodness perfect. Moral earnestness could hardly go farther.[55] Gawain's confession of his fault in breaking his word to save his life reveals a deep sense of man's responsibility for his every act, no matter how deadly the betraying circumstance. For the author, as for William of Wykeham, "Manners [in the sense of morals] maketh Man." Integrity knows no compromise. Wholeheartedly Gawain recognizes this rigorous truth and contrition overwhelms him. Unlike other Arthurian heroes, he returns to Arthur's court, not in conventional glory, but in self-confessed shame. Yet, as noted above,

[53] On the pentangle see Hulbert in *MP,* xiii, 721–730; R. S. Loomis in *JEGP,* XLII, 167–169; Savage, *The Gawain-Poet,* pp. 158–168; Ackerman, "Gawain's Shield: Penitential Doctrine in *Gawain and the Green Knight," Anglia,* LXXVI (1958), 254–265.

[54] Cf. B. J. Whiting, *MedStud,* IX (1947), 189–254.

[55] Mabel Day in *GGK,* p. xxxv, thought the story "the vehicle of a great moral lesson." A. C. Baugh strangely remarked (p. 236) that it was "in no sense a story told to enforce a moral."

that shame gave him new grace, and the Round Table achieved a new nobility by its act of compassionate fellowship. Henceforth all the knights will wear as a baldric the green girdle that was, to Gawain, the mark of his shame.[56] No other medieval poet, save Wolfram von Eschenbach, has so transformed traditional romantic materials by the grace of his own spiritual insight, or given them more enduring significance.

[56] Kittredge, pp. 139 f., rejected the girdle as a feature of Celtic origin, but see R. S. Loomis in *JEGP*, XLII, 149–155.

2

SIR GAWAIN AND THE GREEN KNIGHT: AN APPRAISAL

Morton W. Bloomfield

> The bridge
> Lunged over the river into the green chapel.
> But the ignis fatuus of a happy ending thawed
> The icicle that kept his heart together,
> The marrow of despair hissed out of his bones
> Patricia Beer, "Sir Gawain"

IN SPITE OF its language which is admittedly difficult and in spite of certain problems of literary history which beset it, *Sir Gawain and the Green Knight* has never been considered hard to interpret as a work of art.[1] The apparent obviousness of its genre and its combination of apparently straightforward narrative and notable passages of description do not lead one to suspect that complicated problems of intention or meaning are lurking beneath its vivid and attractive poetry. *Piers Plowman,* everyone agrees, is a difficult poem and has, at least since the sixteenth century, been recognized as such. Those who are attracted to it are stimulated to probe its significance and to elucidate its

Reprinted, by permission of author and the Modern Language Association, from *PMLA,* LXXVI (1961), 7–19.

[1] This paper is a longer version of a speech delivered before English Section I at the MLA convention in Chicago, December, 1959. I am much indebted to Professors John Conley, A. L. Kellogg, F. L. Utley, and R. M. Estrich for various suggestions and criticism. I also owe a great debt to the members of a seminar in the romance held in the fall of 1959 at Ohio State University: Sarah Appleton, Louis Sheets, and Robert Hall.

mysteries. No such stimulus comes to the much larger group who enjoy and study *Sir Gawain,* for, although much has been written on it, it has always been considered a relatively uncomplicated, beautifully organized, and masterfully presented obvious poem. Yet the more one studies *Sir Gawain* and ponders on its charms and organization the more one begins to wonder and speculate. Of course in one sense all literary or artistic masterpieces are miracles and occasion for wonder, but above and beyond the pleasure and surprise which come from great achievement and the feeling of perfection, some works create a peculiar sense of intellectual puzzlement as to the author's intention and tone and even on a more prosaic level as to the tie between a work and its milieu: intellectual, artistic, and social.

While I do not wish to suggest that *Sir Gawain* is as much of a problem as is *Piers,* I do contend that it contains many more complexities and puzzles than have hitherto been recognized. One gets the impression that criticism has not yet really come to grips with the romance. The purpose of this paper is to point to some of these difficulties, not all previously unrecognized, to relate them to current and past scholarship and criticism on the poem, and to suggest some possible solutions. Although I may do so later, I do not intend now to develop at any length the suggestions here put forth. At worst we may get some idea as to where we stand at present in *Gawain* studies, and at best some suggestions for fruitful future work. Needless to say, my choice of subjects and contributions is selective and is not meant to deny the importance of those which I do not mention here.

Although not considered complicated, *Sir Gawain* has not been neglected by interpreters and scholars in the hundred and twenty years since Sir Frederic Madden rescued it, in his edition of the poem, from the oblivion into which it had fallen for many centuries. On the contrary, since 1839 it has been the subject of much interest to both literary historians and the literate English-speaking public, as the size of a fairly complete

Gawain bibliography—some two hundred and fifty items not counting numerous incidental references—shows. In recent years, we find, as is general at present, a heavy shift of interest towards criticism of the poem and towards a stress on its meaning and structure.

We are all so busy appreciating poems today that we tend to neglect philology, upon the basis of which everything which may be drawn from literary documents rests. Philology must remain the basis of all sound literary work or we shall end in a morass of subjectivism. It was just this subjectivism and impressionism which led in the late nineteenth century to the application of positivism to literary study. To avoid the swing of the pendulum between a soulless objectivity and a pure subjectivity, we must at present stress the value of philological study, especially of the older literature. However, philology has never been, and especially today, cannot be, a purely mechanical task, although certain mechanical studies are of great help to it. Philology must be guided, especially in translation work, by a feeling for literary values and a sense of rhetorical probability.

The three main philological activities in older literature are the establishment of a text, the identification of the dialect, and the determination of the meaning of the words of a document. As to the former, in the case of *Sir Gawain* we are pretty much limited to what a close reading and interpretation of the one manuscript which contains the romance—B. M., Cotton Nero A.x—can tell us. In general we may say that unless a new manuscript of the poem turns up little remains to be done. A few reinterpretations of minims and letters, a few emendations can still be expected, but as far as an accurate reading of the only manuscript can take us, we have a satisfactory text. In the case of this manuscript, infrared photography may help us a little, especially to get under blots which disfigure part of the text. It is surprising what a very careful rereading of an original manuscript can do; and a keen eye and keen wit may yet turn up a few new readings. But Cotton Nero A.x has not been neglected in the past and to expect too much from this line of endeavor would surely be a mistake.

On the other hand, I think we may hope for a number of pleasant surprises from future work on the meaning and identification of the language of the poem. *Sir Gawain* is written in a difficult dialect which is not preserved in many documents. The whole state of Middle English dialect study is in an unsatisfactory position, partly because of factors beyond our control, like the paucity of documents, and partly because of factors under our control, like the absence of adequate tools. The latter is now being remedied, but it will still be some time before the *Middle English Dictionary* is completed, the study of English place names finished, and a linguistic atlas of England begun. We still need a fairly complete dialect dictionary of English. These difficulties beset all Middle English studies, but, because of the rarity of raw material and its innate difficulties, North West Midland is particularly affected. But, in spite of this, help is on the way, and the *MED* offers the most immediate prospect of relief. We have hardly yet exploited what has been printed there and what lies still unprinted in its files, in elucidating *Sir Gawain*. The wealth of material present and yet to come in the *MED* offers the most promising path for a solution of the number of *cruces* in which the poem abounds.

Even with the material we already have, we have not completely exploited the possibilities. In spite of Mrs. Wright's plea, we still have not made enough use of the *English Dialect Dictionary*[2] for the light it may cast on the vocabulary of the poem. Place-name study and the linguistic atlas are further promised aids. Place-name study, of course, will be primarily important for the contribution it can bring to clarifying Middle English dialects, not for the elucidation of place-names in the poem.[3]

[2] "Sir Gawain and the Green Knight," *JEGP*, xxxiv (1935), 161.
[3] We now possess a useful index of names in the four Cotton Nero poems in C. O. Chapman's *An Index of Names in "Pearl," "Purity," "Patience," and "Gawain"* (Ithaca, 1951).

The linguistic atlas should enable us to localize more exactly the dialect of the poem and explain some of the difficult words.

However, the problem is not merely to know the meaning of a large number of unusual words but also to understand properly their connotations. To translate *Sir Gawain* involves, of course, not merely a knowledge of Old and Middle English, Old Norse, Old French, and modern English and Scottish dialects, but an interpretation of the poem and a feeling for rhetorical fitness. The context determines the exact meaning of a word or the choice of alternatives; and this means a knowledge of the semantic environment of that word. The determining of context and texture demand a literary sensitivity and a common sense which have not always been applied to the interpretation of the basic meaning of *Sir Gawain* in modern English.

A good example of this matter may be seen in the question of how to translate "wonder" in line 16 of the poem. There is no problem here as to the basic meaning as the word is well-known. The general sense here is probably, as *NED* puts it, "an astonishing occurrence, event, or fact," but philological scholarship has wavered between taking the astonishment as due to a good or bad cause. In other words, should we translate the word as "marvel" or as "crime," both of which are "astonishing occurrences." Both meanings have support in Middle English lexicography.

Following Joseph Hall, Mrs. Wright suggested for the first time in an article in 1935[4] that it should be translated as "sorrow," "distress," or "crime," instead of as in its modern sense, making the lines read in modern English, "Britain . . . where war, vengeance, and crime at times have dwelled therein." Earlier editors read "where war, vengeance, and marvels, . . ." She established without difficulty other similar uses of the word and appealed to the whole line to support the rationality of her

[4] *JEGP,* xxxiv, 349.

translation. But Adrien Bonjour in 1951[5] carried the appeal to context even further and pointed out that the whole stanza contrasts good and bad things and that line 18 has even the same contrast in "and oft both bliss and blunder." Bonjour enables us to see a basic setting up of oppositions in the first stanza and indeed perhaps in the whole poem. Here philology and literary sensitivity are beautifully united to the enrichment of both.

Thus literary criticism must frequently be combined with philology and even, though I am here offering no examples, with literary history. As each grows or deepens, the other two approaches are bound to be affected. It must be admitted, however, that each study must be considered as independent in its own right and should only come together on certain levels and on certain problems.

I do not wish to give the impression that we shall perhaps some day understand to everyone's satisfaction what the poem means and intends or all the facts of its literary history. Some questions will always remain in doubt. Some lexicographical solutions, in particular, will doubtless never be universally accepted. Some will depend on what interpretation one assumes for the poem or parts of it. Some lexicographical ambiguities will never be removed. Real progress can, however, be made even if only the proper alternatives are understood or if impossibilities are revealed as such. In this sense, with the help of the new tools and a deeper insight into the external history and internal meaning of the poem, we shall make philological advances in our study of *Gawain*.

Literary historical problems in plenty remain to be solved in the study of *Gawain*. The more puzzling of these may be enumerated as follows: Who was the author of the poem? Is he also the author of the other English poems in the Cotton Nero MS.? When was the poem written? What is the relation of the poem to the times and to the geography of England?

[5] " 'werre, and wrake, and wonder' (Sir Gawain, l. 16)," *English Studies,* XXXII, 70–72.

What were the poet's sources? Some of these questions are closely dependent on each other as may be clearly seen. Yet for purposes of analysis we may separate them.

In recent years scholars have been chary of suggesting an author for our romance. There has, on the other hand, been less hesitancy in suggesting possible historical prototypes, especially for the Green Knight. Since the virtual disappearance of that universal genius Huchown of the Awle Ryle and Ralph Strode as claimants for the honor of writing *Sir Gawain,* only three or four possible names have been suggested—John Donne, John Prat,[6] John Erghome,[7] and very recently Hugh Mascy.[8] Modern scholars are rightly wary of such suggestions, although of course speculation does no harm. Most of the evidence put forth is very slight and often rests upon the unproved assumption that the four Cotton Nero poems are by the same author leading to hypothetical arguments based on a hypothetical assumption. Internal evidence or unproved external evidence forms a very weak basis for any substantial case. I think we may say that, unless new evidence turns up, the problem of the author will remain unsettled.

There were various green knights and green squires running around Europe in the last half of the fourteenth century, and the temptation to identify one of them with Bercilak has been great. Braddy has suggested Ralph Holmes for this role[9] and

---

[6] For these two, see Oscar Cargill and Margaret Schlauch, *"The Pearl* and Its Jeweler," *PMLA,* XLIII (1928), 105–123.

[7] Put forward by C. O. Chapman in "The Authorship of the *Pearl,"* *PMLA,* XLVII (1932), 346–353. Henry L. Savage in *The Gawain-Poet, Studies in His Personality and Background* (Chapel Hill, 1956), Appendix K, argues the poet may have had some Chancery experience.

[8] See *Sir Gawain and the Green Knight,* trans. Brian Stone, The Penguin Classics L 92 (London and Baltimore, 1959), pp. 128–129.

[9] "Sir Gawain and Ralph Holmes the Green Knight," *MLN,* LXVII (1952), 240–242. See also P. A. Becker, "Der grüne Ritter," *Archiv,* CLIX (1931), 275–276, and S. R. T. O. d'Ardenne, " 'The Green Count' and *Sir Gawain and the Green Knight,"* *RES,* N.S., x (1959), 113–126.

Highfield has chosen Simon Newton.[10] In none of these cases is there any probability that, even on the basis of internal, let alone external evidence, there could be any good reason for the poet to allude to these men under the mask of Bercilak. The *roman à clef* theory has recently been urged by Henry Savage, a notable scholar of the poem, who sees in the story of Gawain a covert allusion to the fortunes of Enguerrand de Coucy who married a daughter of Edward III.[11] This too does not seem very probable, and the evidence is of such a hypothetical character that one is rightly suspicious of the claim.

In spite of the widespread acceptance of the theory of a common authorship for *Gawain,* the *Pearl, Patience,* and *Purity,* I still consider the case not proved. John W. Clark has in the past twenty years been pointing to various weaknesses in the theory, and at the least he has shown how difficult it is to prove.[12] It is not easy to separate dialect from personal linguistic characteristics. I am especially suspicious of arguments for dating and authorship which rely on cross arguments from the other poems. The mathematical probability of an hypothesis based on an hypothesis is very slight.

Attempts to fix *Sir Gawain* in time and space and to relate it to its milieu have largely been concerned with possible historical allusions, with the identity of the scene of the action at the castle and Green Chapel, with the geography of Gawain's journey, and with the relation of the poem to the Order of the Garter. All this, while not unimportant, is certainly rather limited and limiting. There are other problems of milieu to which attention should be given and which have more immediate

---

[10] "The Green Squire," *M Æ,* xxii (1953), 18–23.

[11] Cf. his *"Sir Gawain* and the Order of the Garter," *ELH,* v (1938), 146–149. Dr. Savage does, however, argue his case circumspectly.

[12] See, e.g., "Observations on Certain Differences Between *Cleanness* and *Sir Gawain and the Green Knight,*" *PQ,* xxviii (1949), 261–273; " 'The *Gawain*-Poet' and the Substantival Adjective," *JEGP,* xlix (1950), 60–66; and "On Certain 'Alliterative' and 'Poetic' Words in the Poems Attributed to the *Gawain*-Poet," *MLQ,* xii (1951), 387–398.

bearing on *Sir Gawain* as a work of art meaningful to us in our milieu. Before I turn to these new problems, however, I should like to say a few words about the older ones.

For some strange reason, the problem of the dialect of the poem has in general been connected with the location of Bercilak's castle and Green Chapel. Although everyone who has dealt with the philological problem of the dialect puts the poem in Lancashire, Western Yorkshire, Cheshire, or Derbyshire, the exact location within this area is difficult. The present tendency is to favor southern Lancashire.[13] In the minds of some investigators, the location of the dialect seems to be reliable evidence for locating the castle where the *Gawain*-poet wrote his poem or where Bercilak held court. This does not seem to me to be very soundly based. Why a poet should have to put the scene of his poem and be himself located in the area of the dialect he uses in writing is not at all evident. Yet we find this unsound and dubious assumption made in almost every case when these questions arise. The dialect of a poem certainly tells us something about the place of origin of the writer, if we can be sure that the scribe has not transformed it into his own dialect, but it is not necessarily that of the scene of the poem. A Scotsman could write about Yorkshire, a northern Lancashireman could write about southern Lancashire. In all these matters caution is surely necessary.

The attempt to find historical allusions in *Gawain* has also been bedevilled by a paucity of evidence and an enthusiasm for hobbyhorses. I suppose as Kittredge has said "thought is free," but one at least should distinguish between facts and hypotheses. Our knowledge of fourteenth-century England is still surprisingly incomplete and we may yet make some discoveries which will cast light on the historical circumstances behind our romance. We would all benefit in various ways by

---

[13] See J. P. Oakden, *Alliterative Poetry in Middle English*, I (Manchester, 1930), pp. 72–87 and p. 257, and Savage, *The Gawain-Poet*, passim.

the publication of various medieval documents and treatises, mainly in Latin and French, still unpublished, and we may even actually turn up something on our poem. As regards documents, however, it must be recognized that official records rarely help us to decide a literary question, for we do not find in the Middle Ages that all-encompassing interest in literary creation which is a mark of a later period. As we all know, the Geoffrey Chaucer of the contemporary records is not once identified as the poet near our hearts.

However, there are several fields of inquiry in the milieu which have hardly yet been studied with our poem in mind. Perhaps we may best indicate them by raising again some questions. What is the meaning of the "alliterative revival" in fourteenth-century England? What is the significance of the later flowering of Arthurian romance in England? To what extent is *Sir Gawain* a poem written in high style? What evidence is there of a baronial opposition to London in this period? What did chivalry mean to the aristocracy of fourteenth-century England? What audience was *Sir Gawain* written for? Was it written to give fourteenth-century noblemen a thrill?

All these questions have a bearing on the relation of *Gawain* to its milieu. Except perhaps for some remarks of Émile Pons,[14] very little attention has been paid to these matters. Hulbert has, of course, looked into the meaning of the alliterative revival in general. Earlier Ten Brink had associated Edwardian nationalism with this movement.[15] But in the past thirty years little,

[14] In his edition *Sire Gauvain et le Chevalier Vert* (Paris, 1946), pp. 46 ff. Cf. the few but suggestive remarks of Gollancz in "Chivalry in Medieval English Poetry," Chapter VII of *Chivalry, A Series of Studies to Illustrate Its Historical Significance and Civilizing Influence,* by Members of King's College, London, ed. Edgar Prestage, The History of Civilization, ed. C. K. Ogden (New York, 1928), pp. 175–178.

[15] See J. R. Hulbert, "A Hypothesis Concerning the Alliterative Revival," *MP*, XXVIII (1931), 405–422, and B. Ten Brink, *Early English Literature (to Wiclif),* trans. H. M. Kennedy, Bohn's Standard Library (London, 1883), pp. 329 ff.

if anything, has been done relating *Sir Gawain* to the wider issues of the century. In short, what exactly is the meaning of *Sir Gawain* in terms of fourteenth-century culture? This question sums them all up.

They all lead too into the whole fascinating subject of the lateness of the medieval English literary flowering. While France and Germany had lost interest in Arthurian legend or at least only treated it in debased fashion by 1350 or earlier, England suddenly at that time began, if we ignore a few earlier works mainly in Anglo-Norman, to create an Arthurian literature. Why? Perhaps the answer lies merely in language. It was not until the fourteenth century that English finally vanquished Anglo-Norman. This may not be the entire explanation. Compared to France, English culture and literature were *retardataire* in the fourteenth century. England was able to make use of the Italian renaissance before France perhaps because of this very fact. Unlike his French contemporaries, Chaucer was not weighed down by a glorious literary tradition. Just as today Spain, for instance, is in some particular ways more modern and up-to-date than England and France because it was so terribly behind when it came into our century and thus was able to adapt foreign ideas more freely, so perhaps Chaucer and Gower could pick up the new developments in Italy without the burden of a past. The older English literary achievement had been forgotten by the fourteenth century, and English writers perhaps felt that they could create as they liked without a load of great masterpieces on their shoulders.

The rise of English nationalism under Edward III must have been an important factor in this matter. There is evidence that Edward deliberately strove to rehabilitate chivalry and knighthood. The Arthurian legend provided England with a ready-made aristocratic myth of its past glories. Unlike France which could look back to Charlemagne, England could only offer the misty and ambiguous figure of Arthur.

Indeed there were rich ambiguities in the whole Arthurian

corpus. Arthur, Gawain, Lancelot, and the others were both worthy and ridiculous figures. They were to be taken seriously and admired and at the same time to be laughed at for their childishness. And besides, much of it was in conflict with an aroused and serious Christianity which was a strong feature of late medieval life. For all this the romances provide much evidence. Courtesy and courtly love were both necessary to elevate human nature and at the same time silly in their pretensions.

The problem of milieu is much more than finding the exact location of the Green Chapel or discovering who the poet had in mind when he created the Green Knight. The intellectual and ideological feel of late medieval life needs to be related to the poem. The decline of feudalism and the reaction to that decline will help to explain the poem. Of course even in the twelfth century we find laments over the decline of chivalry, and like most ideals it never was on land or sea; but there is objective evidence for a decline in the later Middle Ages, no matter how stylized some of the complaints were.[16] The relation of this movement and counter movement to the English nobility and conditions of life in late fourteenth-century England have yet to be investigated.

Fourteenth-century poetic theory and rhetoric also stimulate

---

[16] On this whole subject, see Raymond Lincoln Kilgour, *The Decline of Chivalry as Shown in the French Literature of the Late Middle Ages* (Cambridge, Eng., 1937). This book, of course, concentrates on France. For England, see Gervase Mathew, "Ideals of Knighthood in Late-Fourteenth-Century England," *Studies in Medieval History Presented to Frederick Maurice Powicke,* ed. Hunt, Pantin, and Southern (Oxford, 1948), 354–362 (who uses, inter alia, *Sir Gawain* for evidence). Cf. also Kurt Lippmann, *Das Ritterliche Persönlichkeitsideal in der mittelenglischen Literatur des 13. und 14. Jahrhunderts,* Inaugural-Dissertation . . . der Universität Leipzig (Meerane, 1933); and Dietrich Sandberger, *Studien über das Rittertum in England vornehmlich während des 14. Jahrhunderts,* Historische Studien 310 (Berlin, 1937). Sandberger brings much evidence to show how late chivalry flourished in England. "Im 14. Jahrhundert ist dann England so 'ritterlich' wie nur irgendein Land" (p. 241).

difficult questions. What, for instance, was the attitude of the fourteenth-century writer toward his material? To what extent was he dominated by rhetorical theory, especially the theory of styles? That he took them seriously there can be no doubt, but what exactly did high style in English mean at that time? Was high style even possible in the mother language? Could comedy and high style be wedded in any way? What is the significance of the narrator in medieval literature? To what extent were ironies possible? The love of decorative detail in *Gawain* and much of the poetry of the period is probably a reflex of the idea of courtesy and chivalric manners. One does not hasten into action but dwells on the form. Furthermore, the poet of *Gawain* stresses the aspect of wonder and suspense in his romance. James V. Cunningham has studied in interesting fashion the relation of wonder to literature in a fascinating chapter in his book *Woe or Wonder, The Emotional Effect of Shakespearean Tragedy*.[17] He is primarily concerned with the role of wonder in tragedy, but it also has its place in comedy. Cicero, he tells us, connected wonder with ornate or figurative diction and a charming style (p. 76). This is a notable feature of our poem. Wonder has various meanings, and that which arises from the unforeseen (*agonia*) seems to fit the mode of its employment in our romance. It is possible that such wonder, as opposed to other types, is appropriate to comedy. In all this our poet may be following a little known rhetorical precept. The whole rhetorical tradition has hardly yet been explored for this and other matters.[18] Much of the material for this work

[17] (Denver, 1951), pp. 62–105. See also Benjamin P. Kurtz, *Studies in the Marvellous,* Univ. of Calif. Pubs. (London & Berkeley, 1910), especially Chapter I.

[18] See, however, Derek A. Pearsall's interesting "Rhetorical 'Descriptio' in *Sir Gawain and the Green Knight,*" *MLR,* L (1955), 129–134, which has some very good things to say about the *Gawain*-poet's use of rhetorical devices in descriptions which have long been praised for their naturalism. On this last point, see G. Plessow in *Gotische Tektonik* . . . (Munich, 1931), pp. 144 ff.

lies in manuscripts unprinted and in Latin, but not all of it is unavailable.

Finally as part of literary history, let us turn to the sources of *Gawain*. This section will also serve as a bridge to problems of literary criticism as such. In recent years both the mythic and religious elements in *Gawain* have received much attention, not merely as source material or background but as alive in the poem as part of the poet's deliberate intent. John Speirs raised the myth issue in an important article some ten years ago,[19] and several scholars and critics have recently made much of the religious element in the poem. On the latter point, Miss Willcock has said, "the poem grows more moral, religious and even mystical with every succeeding editor or commentator."[20]

Until the thirties scholars engaged in source study were for the most part primarily interested in the literary and to some extent the folklore elements in *Sir Gawain*. Miss Weston, in her early treatment of the Gawain figure,[21] suggested that Gawain was originally a sun hero and was related to the Irish hero Cuchulinn. But even she was primarily interested in the literary sources of *Sir Gawain* when she confined her attention to our romance. Sir E. K. Chambers was the first to suggest in 1903[22] that the green man of the peasantry reappears as the

---

[19] "Sir Gawain and the Green Knight," *Scrutiny*, XVI (1949), 274–300 (reprinted with some minor changes in *Medieval English Poetry, The Non-Chaucerian Tradition*, [London, 1957], pp. 215–251).

[20] "Middle English . . . Before and After Chaucer," *YWES*, XXVIII (1947), p. 90.

[21] *The Legend of Sir Gawain, Studies upon its Original Scope and Significance*, Grimm Library 7 (London, 1897). Gaston Paris also recognized a mythic quality in Gawain. For a literary history of Sir Gawain in the Middle Ages and later, see B. J. Whiting, "Gawain: His Reputation, His Courtesy and His Appearance in Chaucer's *Squire's Tale*," *MedStud*, IX (1947), 189–234.

[22] *The Medieval Stage* (Oxford), I, 185–186. It may be noted that there is a slight confusion in myth and source study as to whether the dying-rising god is Bercilak or Gawain. Perhaps they should be considered doublets.

challenger in *Sir Gawain.* Cook a few years later[23] saw the Indo-European tree or vegetation god in Bercilak. In 1912 Henderson repeated Cook's idea that the Green Knight was a tree-god.[24] In 1916 Kittredge wrote a brilliant book on the Irish and Old French sources or analogues of *Sir Gawain,* dividing the narrative into two main themes—the Beheading or Challenge and the Temptation.[25] The immediate source, however, was, he believed, a lost French romance. One has only to read Welsh and Irish sagas to recognize that, although some of the matter of *Gawain* may be Celtic, its literary form approximates that of the great French romances. *Sir Gawain's* immediate source may not be French, it may indeed be English, but it is a poem in the French literary tradition. Kittredge had the literary sensitivity to see that. But Kittredge would have no truck with vegetation or other myths. He did not deny their total relevance to the study of the sources of the romances but dismissed them as too speculative to be worthy of much thought.

The problem of the main themes of *Sir Gawain* has been taken as settled once and for all by Kittredge. I am not, however, completely satisfied that this is the case. This is a matter of more than antiquarian importance in source study, for the themes are what determine where one is to look for sources. It is possible, for instance, that the temptation theme might be considered part of the benevolent (or imperious) host theme and best studied as such. Further and other divisions of the story could be made. "The exchange of winnings" theme, for instance, has been suggested. I must admit, however, that the

---

[23] "The European Sky-God VI, The Celts (contin.)," *Folklore,* XVII (1906), 308–348; 427–453, esp. 338 ff.

[24] *Miscellany Presented to Kuno Meyer* (Halle, 1912), pp. 18–33.

[25] *A Study of Gawain and the Green Knight* (Cambridge, Mass.). Kittredge believed that the two themes were united for the first time by the unknown French romancer who wrote the lost source of the poem, but as Buchanan (see note 29 below) and perhaps Hulbert (see next note) have urged, there is evidence even in the Irish material that the two themes were at least related.

criteria for determining the themes are difficult to establish and partly depend on an interpretation of the poem. We are back to literary criticism again.

At about the same time as Kittredge, Hulbert suggested a mythic theme for the poem[26]—that it or its lost original, like the *Fled Bricrend,* was concerned with a test for winning a fairy mistress. Morgan le Fay initiated the whole business of the story because of her love for Gawain. Her motives enunciated in the poem by Bercilak—to frighten Guenevere and to test the pride of Arthur's Court—are dismissed as a later addition. Like many commentators wedded to the historical method, Hulbert did not claim that *Sir Gawain,* as at present constituted, presents this theme directly—he could hardly do that—but that the fairy mistress story accounts for the general organization of the tale for some of its apparently inexplicable details. He, like most source scholars, was concerned with the evolution of the story, not the final product. Often in this approach and in its more modern version—myth analysis—the actual work of art which presumably calls forth the whole investigation is a minor episode in the history of a story or myth which has a disembodied viability of its own. I am not claiming this neglect of the work may not at times be justified as a method, but its limitations should be recognized. Hulbert's particular interpretation of the source of this Gawain tale has only been taken up with any thoroughness by Otto Löhmann in 1938.[27] Much more popular has been the vegetation myth theory, adumbrated in Chambers, Cook, and Henderson.

Professor Loomis a few years later in his general explorations of Celtic sources and parallels to Arthurian legend began a

---

[26] In "Syr Gawayn and the Grene Knyȝt," *MP,* XIII (1915–1916), 433–462; 689–730.

[27] *Die Sage von Gawain und dem grünen Ritter,* Schriften des Albertus-Universität . . . 17 (Königsberg and Berlin).

series of articles and books which did not neglect *Sir Gawain*.[28] Although he does not deny mythic elements in the background of the main characters and perhaps even the story of *Sir Gawain,* Professor Loomis is primarily concerned with written and hypothetically reconstructed sources.[29]

The whole subject took, however, a new turn in the thirties and forties when, with the rise of myth criticism or, as Jean Paul Sartre puts it, the new mythology of myth, interest shifted to the mythic meaning of the elements in the sources in *Gawain,* as well as in other works. Some of this work was scholarly and some not, depending on whether the main purpose was to stress the ultimate mythic sources of *Sir Gawain* or to stress the vitality of these sources in the finished work of art. In the history of the interpretation of our poem in this light five names may be mentioned—Nitze, Krappe, Coomaraswamy, Zimmer, and Speirs.[30] The first two—Nitze and Krappe—are

[28] See *Celtic Myth and Arthurian Romance* (New York, 1927), pp. 39–123; "Gawain, Gwri, and Cuchulinn," *PMLA,* XLIII (1928), 384–396 (a theory somewhat modified later); "The Visit to the Perilous Castle," *PMLA,* XLVIII (1933), 1000–35; *JEGP,* XLII (1943), 149–184 (revised as "Welsh Elements in *Gawain and the Green Knight,*" *Wales and the Arthurian Legend* [Cardiff, 1956], pp. 77–90): "Morgain La Fee and the Celtic Goddesses," *Spec,* XX (1945), 183–203; and *Arthurian Tradition and Chrétien de Troyes* (New York, 1949), pp. 41 ff.; 146 ff., 278 ff. et passim.

[29] Following Loomis' method, the contributions of Alice Buchanan in "The Irish Framework of *Gawain and the Green Knight,*" *PMLA,* XLVII (1932), 315–338, and Roland Smith in "Guinganbresil and the Green Knight," *JEGP,* XLV (1946), 1–25, should be noted. Smith shows some important parallels to the poem in the Finn cycle. Before his article, only the Ulster cycle had been used in source work on the poem. An important recent discussion of the sources of the poem may be found in Albert B. Friedman, "Morgan le Fay in *Sir Gawain and the Green Knight,*" *Spec,* XXXV (1960), 260–274. Friedman makes some very telling points against the theories of both Buchanan and Loomis.

[30] William A. Nitze, "Is the Green Knight a Vegetation Myth?" in *MP,* XXXIII (1935–1936), 351–366; A. H. Krappe, "Who *Was* the Green Knight?" in *Spec,* XIII (1938), 206–215; Ananda Coomaraswamy, "Sir Gawain and the Green Knight: Indra and Namuci," *Spec,* XIX (1944), 104–125; Zimmer in *The King and The Corpse,* ed. J. Campbell, Bol-

strictly scholars in their approach. Nitze argues that the root of the *Sir Gawain* story is a vegetation myth best preserved in the *Perlesvaus* analogue. Krappe finds the root in a journey to the realm of the dead for the purpose of defeating death. Zimmer and Speirs, on the other hand, are not so much concerned with the nature of the myth at the basis of the romance, although Speirs finds it to be a vegetation story and Zimmer seems to favor a conquest of death interpretation, as with the presence of mythic and ritual elements alive in the poem as we have it now; and Coomaraswamy falls somewhere in between. The latter gives us new analogues to the beheading episode but stresses the powerful psychic appeal of the myth as present in the poem. He fits it into his great synthesizing view of life and story wherein myth gives perpetual meaning to both. Speirs's work, however, has been the central event of modern scholarship for our poem. His position is argued with such vigor and dogmatism that he has given new life to *Gawain* scholarship. In a sense he has set the terms for most work on the poem since 1948. Even those who write on the poem from a different point of view feel constrained to place their contribution in relation to his. He has certainly made the mythological theory the dominant frame of reference for subsequent critical work, most of which does not, however, accept his theories.

Charles Moorman recently has criticized both Speirs and Zimmer[31] for neglecting *Sir Gawain* as a poem and argues that as literary critics we may accept the myth element as in the poem, but we must emphasize what the *Gawain*-poet did with the myth in the particular work of art he created. A myth critic must not merely identify the genus of the myth the poet chooses but also the differentia as developed in the poem.

lingen Ser. xi (New York, 1943), pp. 67–95; and John Speirs, "Sir Gawain and the Green Knight," *Scrutiny*, xvi (1949), 274–300, and some further material in subsequent issues.

[31] "Myth and Mediaeval Literature: *Sir Gawain and the Green Knight*," *MedStud*, xviii (1956), 158–172.

How is the source or pattern used in the poem? Moorman himself argues that the genus is a variety of the *rites de passage* ritual and myth and tries to show how it lives in the poet's hands. He also stresses the Christian element in the finished poem. Gawain's *rite de passage* serves to test the whole Arthurian court and to teach them the value of chastity and loyalty. Guenevere, who incidentally is a very minor character in the poem, in particular is being shown up. "What the critic can say . . . is that the myth of the hero's journey from innocence to knowledge underlies the poem and to a large extent determines its specific structure and theme."

This whole question of myth is a complicated one. Part of the problem is a difficulty in knowing what these critics and scholars claim. If a scholar is arguing that the original story behind *Sir Gawain* is a myth or partly a myth, one surely cannot object. If a scholar or reader is claiming that in order to understand the poem in its deepest sense today one should interpret it in mythic terms or relate it to subconscious archetypes, one again surely cannot object if he prefers to think that way or if he can be happy only in the subconscious or on the pre-Christian mythic level of meaning. If, however, the claim is being made that the author of *Sir Gawain* is deliberately conscious of the mythic or ritual element in his poem and is using it for deliberate effect to an audience which would understand it, then one has a right to raise questions. The whole problem is concerned with historical actuality. Is our task to discover what the *Gawain*-poet was trying to do? If so, then whether myth is consciously alive in *Sir Gawain* is a problem which can be tackled by the historical method—at least theoretically.

The proponents of the mythic interpretation of *Sir Gawain* in this sense find very little in the poem itself to support their hypotheses. Speirs, to take one example, gives us the phallic towers of Bercilak's castle; the word "ver" (1. 866) which may or may not mean "spring" as Speirs would like to have it; the holly branch and big beard of the Green Knight; the pentangle;

the importance of the Christmas-New Year season in the poem; the old woman (Morgan) and the young woman;[32] the presence of a chapel "in the earth"; by some curious argumentation the hunts; and I suppose the beheading game itself. This is not a very impressive list, especially if we remember that all castles have phallic features, that New Year is the usual time for the beginning of Arthurian adventures, that comparing a beard to a bush is a well-known metaphor, that old and young women are pretty common in life and so forth.

There is no doubt that pagan rituals were still alive in the fourteenth century, as they are today, but there is much doubt that the participants had any notion of their meanings. And besides, these ritual relics were to be found among the folk. *Sir Gawain* is one of the few undoubtedly aristocratic poems of the English Middle Ages extant. It would be surprising if in this courtly and Christian atmosphere of a poem perhaps written entirely or partly in high style, we could find alive mythic and ritualistic elements. Of Moorman's attempt to save both the poem and the myth we may say that, however satisfactory his theory may be, it is hard to find in practice any specific evidences of a "rite de passage" ritual in *Sir Gawain* unless all testing is to be regarded as a type of *rite de passage*. Gawain is perhaps humbler at the end of his adventure than at the beginning, but just what has he been initiated into? He has perhaps learned that all human beings including the best are weak, but this lesson is not the purpose of the usual *rite de passage,* even a Christianized one. If he had been a good Christian, he should have realized this from the beginning; it is not secret knowledge. Then too the Court, as Moorman himself indicated, for which the whole affair was managed, is no better or wiser; and besides *rites de passage* are for individuals, not institutions. To me at least Moorman has fallen into the trap he has so

---

[32] Mrs. Laura Hibbard Loomis in *"Gawain and the Green Knight,"* see above, p. 14, suggests that Bercilak's wife is a double of Morgan as an analogue in the *Vulgate Lancelot* seems to show.

carefully delineated and whose dangers he has so vividly portrayed. Without being specific as to what a *rite de passage* means, without, in other words, establishing his genus, he makes the differentia he discusses lose the characteristics of differentia. Not only this; he has to force the plain meaning of the text to fit it into his theory. The shade of the golden bough[33] obscures the poem for one reader at least.

The Christian and moral elements in the poem on the other hand are obvious from beginning to end. The ethical and religious interpretation of the poem is not new. W. P. Ker in 1912 made this point clear in his excellent little book in the Home University Library on Medieval English literature. I am sure that he was not the first to do so,[34] and he was certainly not the last. In recent years the Christian element and aim of the poem have received increased emphasis. There have been strong differences of opinion on various topics, as for instance whether the purpose of the temptation by the lady is to test Gawain's loyalty or chastity, or whether the poet emphasizes Gawain's failure as a Christian or his nobility of character while admitting he is not perfect, or whether the sources of the temptation scene are secular romances or saints' lives.[35] Yet there has been a continuing interest in this approach.

[33] See M. J. C. Hodgart, "In the Shade of the Golden Bough," *Twentieth Century*, CLVII (1955), 111–119, esp. 116–117. Hans Schnyder in "Aspects of Kingship in *Sir Gawain and the Green Knight*," *ES*, XL (1959), 289–294, considers the romance to be, at least in part, a rebuke of Arthur as a bad king.

[34] Cf. ". . . all this art [of the *Gawain*-poet] is in the service of moral ideas." B. Ten Brink, *Early English Literature*, p. 347.

[35] Else von Schaubert, "Der englische Ursprung von Syr Gawayn and the Grene Knyȝt," *ES*, LVII (1923), 330–446, is the foremost exponent of the latter in her attempts to posit an English rather than a French lost original for the poem. It may be of some interest here to point out that the temptation of a good man by a woman would probably suggest to medieval man, certainly before some of the tales in the Golden Legend, the story of Joseph and Potiphar's wife, a connection not hitherto made as far as I am aware. On this Biblical story and legend in the Middle

The poem is fairly and squarely Christian. Pride is the great sin, the Virgin Mary helps humanity, the characters are continually going to Mass and confessing. Recently Ackerman has discussed the Christian significance of the pentangle and the association of the various quintuplets mentioned in the poem at this point with the sacrament of penance.[36] As he writes, "the stress in the sixteen-line interpretation of Gawain's pentangle falls on the hero's deeply religious devotion, even when one takes into account the five chivalric virtues. Moreover, the poet chose, for the most part, to express this fundamental aspect of Gawain's character in language made familiar to his audience by the confessional" (p. 265). A sermon by Thomas Bradwardine delivered just after the victory at Crécy has very recently been published[37] in which he claims that victory in battle comes from God alone and refers to seven erroneous theories which claim to explain military prowess. One of these is that sexual virility accounts for military success. Bradwardine takes some pains to refute this explanation. This part of the sermon shows us that some men in the fourteenth century believed that there was a connection between lechery and courage. Perhaps like Bradwardine, the author of *Sir Gawain* is also trying to combat this idea by showing us a hero chaste as well as courageous.

Ages, see F. E. Faverty, "The Story of Joseph and Potiphar's Wife in Mediaeval Literature," *Havard Studies and Notes in Philology and Literature,* xiii (1931), 81–127.

[36] "Gawain's Shield: Penitential Doctrine in Gawain and the Green Knight," *Anglia,* lxxvi (1958), 254–265. I am not convinced that Ackerman has completely proved his case. The five wits are associated with sin, true; but they are also associated with the origin of all knowledge, good or bad. A recent discussion of the penance theme in the later part of the poem may be found in John Burrow, "The Two Confession Scenes in *Sir Gawain and the Green Knight,*" *MP,* lvii (1959–1960), 73–79.

[37] Heiko A. Oberman and James A. Weisheipl, "The *Sermo epinicius* ascribed to Thomas Bradwardine (1346)," *Archives d'histoire doctrinale et littéraire au moyen âge,* xxv (1958), 295–329. The passage referred to occurs on pp. 323–329.

I think in the coming years we will find further and deeper religious aspects and significances in the poem.[38] Yet I am inclined to agree with George Kane when he writes that the success of our poem does not fundamentally arise "from the concepts of conduct upon which the characters act. These are, to be sure, noble and gracious enough, and reflect a good knowledge of human behaviour. . . . The exceptional success of this romance comes from other sources than the principles of behaviour upon which its action is based." Kane, however, finds its success in the acute visualization of the action and setting.[39]

This religious and ethical dimension, as well as the mythic dimension, still seems to me to leave unanswered the question of the poet's primary intention. Here we pass over completely into the problem of literary criticism, although we have already been deep in it, a circumstance which shows how difficult it is to separate background from foreground in literary analysis.

A third possibility which has been much ignored, although suggested by a few,[40] is a comic or humorous intention. John

[38] George J. Engelhardt's "The Predicament of Gawain," *MLQ*, XVI (1955), 218–225, also makes an important point about the religious element in the poem. It emphasizes the weakness of Gawain and his moral predicament, the significance of which is revealed only because of Gawain's apparent integrity. His strength is his weakness. "Actually it [*Sir Gawain*] is a humane and sympathetic presentation designed to reveal how human and imperfect is even a supposedly perfect knight such as the pentagonal Gawain" (pp. 224–225, note).

[39] *Middle English Literature, A Critical Study of the Romances, the Religious Lyrics, Piers Plowman* (London, 1951), pp. 73–76. The quotation above is from p. 76. Professor Baugh makes the same point: "Though it [*GGK*] exemplifies the knightly virtues of courage and truth, it is in no sense a story told to enforce a moral." *A Literary History of England* (New York, 1948), p. 236. On the *Gawain*-poet's descriptive and visual powers, see the recent article by Alain Renoir, "Descriptive Techniques in Sir Gawain and the Green Knight," *Orbis litterarum*, XIII (1958), 126–132.

[40] See Elizabeth M. Wright, "Sir Gawain and the Green Knight," *JEGP*, XXXIV (1935), 157–158 and G. H. Gerould in "The Gawain Poet and Dante: A Conjecture," *PMLA*, LI (1936), 31. Mrs. Wright in the above article (pp. 158–161) also suggests that in the beheading theme

Conley in an unpublished paper on the romance, which he has been kind enough to show me, argues that *Sir Gawain* is fundamentally humorous, although by no means unserious. The beginning tells us that the subject of the poem is marvels and the treatment throughout is touched, often strongly touched, by humor. Laughter and smiles are frequently referred to in the text. The vividness of the language, the subtleties of the lines, the extraordinary lightness of tone, all bespeak a sophistication, an irony, a sense of humor which illuminates the whole thing from beginning to end. Not only, however, do we find within the poem the humor which arises from the author's attitude towards his characters and their involvements but another kind of humor in his attitude towards his audience and readers. The author is playing a game with us just as Morgan is playing a game with Arthur's court. He is keeping us in a state of suspense, holding back information, and fooling us.

Humorous romances are not unknown in the Middle Ages, and this genre can contain such tensions and oppositions. None of them of course treats these matters in exactly the same way as our poem does, and few if any equal our author's literary virtuosity. But not all romances are straightforward tales of adventure, or rich pageantries of chivalry, or even religious quests, but some indeed are at one and the same time witty, ironical, and religious. Such a one is, I believe, *Sir Gawain*.

we have a description of a feast day dramatic entertainment. She stresses the dramatic and theatrical elements in the two meetings between Gawain and the Green Knight. Joseph Eagan, S.J., in "The Import of Color Symbolism in *Sir Gawain and the Green Knight*," St. Louis Univ. Studies, Ser. A, Hum. I, 2 (St. Louis, 1949), 11–86, sees the romance, at least on one level, as a satire against the average contemporary romance with its glorificaion of adultery and a decadent chivalry. "The *Gawain*-poet wishes to write a genuinely Christian poem to glorify true Christian chivalry in which the virtue of chastity held the foremost place" (p. 62). One gets the impression that Father Eagan falls back on satire to extricate him from the difficulties that this highly Christian interpretation of the romance gets him into.

Two writers, Francis Berry and William Goldhurst,[41] have recently stressed the tension in the poem between the civilized and courtly element and the primitive and vitalistic element. Berry writes of the many contrasts in the poem which may be classified under these two headings—getting and spending, begetting and dying, humanity and nature, and so forth. These contrasts are beautifully seen in the person of the Green Knight who is both civilized and amoral at the same time. "He testifies to an assumption that moral behaviour, though of vast importance, is subservient to and dependent on something even more primary—creative energy. In the poem Gawain and his 'society' humbly come to terms with the Green Knight. They had been in danger of forgetting their own *sine qua non*. . . . The poem involves the divine and the human, the natural and the magical and presents a pattern of these categories in which potential antagonisms between them are conciliated, and this in a partly comic temper."

Goldhurst makes the same point, perhaps less subtly, but stresses this paradox and tension as it appears in the style of the poem "which combines the qualities of straightforward vigor with a suggestiveness and a subtle, almost elegant, lightness of touch." Each of the characters is a combination of antitheses. The Green Knight is a beheader and a civilized courtier. Gawain is a rugged warrior and capable of delicate and refined reactions, Bercilak's wife possesses both refinement and sex appeal. Elements in the poem betray a similar ambivalence—the mound is a chapel, the girdle is an ornament and a sexual symbol. "The poem suggests that at best life is but a truce

[41] Berry, "The Sublime Ballet: An Essay on Sir Gawain and the Green Knight," *Wind and Rain* (Winter 1949–1950), 165–174, (which I have not been able to consult), and "Sir Gawayne and the Grene Knight," in *The Age of Chaucer,* A Guide to English Literature I, ed. Boris Ford, Pelican Book A290 (London, 1954), pp. 148-158 and Goldhurst, "The Green and the Gold: The Major Theme of *Gawain and the Green Knight,*" CE, xx (1958–1959), 61–65.

between natural impulses, and allegiances to the virtues which civilized creatures are pledged to uphold."

That these antithetical forces are present in *Gawain* cannot be doubted, but it is a large question whether any poet could be a kind of Bergson in the fourteenth century. This opposition between the untamed forces of nature and human civilization which precariously opposes it seems extraordinarily unmedieval to me. It sounds too much like nineteenth and twentieth century romantic thought to be a satisfying interpretation of the poem.

Nor is there much in the poem itself to bear out this interpretation. The same throbbing meter which Berry and Goldhurst find in *Sir Gawain* is also to be found in *Purity* and *Patience* and *Piers Plowman* where it hardly indicates any life force. I do not sense any continual struggle between civilization and barbarism in the poem, although both elements are certainly present. The Green Knight, who is subdued by Gawain's courtesy and loyalty,[42] is hardly the amoral life force blindly striving ever onward. He was given a task and the gift of re-heading himself by Morgan le Fay, but other than this gift and other than an ability to act like a scornful bogeyman when necessary, he possesses a perfectly moral and civilized human character. As for contradictions in the characters, we may say that all characters are contradictory. Lear is a child and a hero; Hamlet acts and does not act; Becky Sharp has her moments of remorse; Leopold Bloom is both lecherous and civilized. We may say of almost any work of art that it combines opposites of this sort. The problem is whether the point of the work is to set these antitheses into sharp relief and whether it is basically built around them. I cannot see that *Sir Gawain* is constructed along these lines.

---

[42] Note that the problem of who subdues whom in the encounter between Gawain and Bercilak is not easily answered. Berry argues that Gawain comes to terms with Bercilak.

In more sober wise, Markman recently has argued from genre—that our poem falls into the category of romance, a narrative which concentrates on testing a hero.[43] The primary purpose of the poem "is to show what a splendid man Gawain is" (p. 575). Gawain is pitted "against a marvelous, unnatural man" with the intent of discovering "what a perfect knight can do when he is forced to face the unknown" (p. 575). Magic, not mythology, directs the marvelous occurrences within the romance. Gawain is, however, a man and has his weaknesses, but the poet is on his side. Gawain's courtesy and loyalty are fundamental to the meaning of the poem and are part of the poet's vision of life which stresses decorum.

Markman has emphasized the genre of the poem with its hero, its testing, and its atmosphere of the marvelous. All this is to the good. I would suggest, however, that romance is not a simple genre but a highly complex one and that there are many varieties of romance. The important point is to specify more precisely to what subtypes or types *Sir Gawain* belongs. There are comic as well as serious, religious as well as amorous, psychological as well as objective, episodic as well as tightly organized, romances. The romance genre is by no means a unified monolithic type. Much more needs to be done on this matter.

Miss Dorothy Everett has also in recent years stressed the testing element in the poem.[44] Like Markman and many other earlier critics, she underlines its ethical content. She writes "the first concern of the poem is thus with conduct; that is, it is moral in the true sense of the word" (p. 77). As I have mentioned above, this view is gaining much ground today and is more or less widely accepted. With perhaps the exception of Kane who specifically denies that the conduct of the hero is the

---

[43] "The Meaning of *Sir Gawain and the Green Knight*," PMLA, LXXII (1957), 574–586.

[44] *Essays on Middle English Literature*, ed. P. Kean (Oxford, 1955), pp. 68 ff.

main concern of the poet, most scholars and critics, even those who are strongly addicted to the mythological interpretation, seem to agree on the importance of this element. I think it cannot be denied, but the question is how central is this matter? What is the poet's first intention? Although I do not agree with Kane that it is the decorative and visual which the poet wishes to elevate, I think he is making an important point—that the ethical side can be overvalued. I do not believe the poem was written fundamentally to present us with a good man who emerges somewhat stained or humbled from his encounter with the world of evil or of the supernatural. The humor, suspense, and tone of the poem belie the centrality of this interpretation.

If we look closely at the narrative structure of our romance, we find that the poet uses suspense as his organizing principle. We pass from ignorance to knowledge after the suspense has been built up to an agonizing climax. If we examine the formal divisions of the poem, those in the manuscript, to which Mrs. Hill has called our attention,[45] we may, I think, see this. Madden in his edition ignored, in dividing the poem into its major parts, all but four of the nine large intitials with which the text is adorned. All editions since have followed his predilections in the matter; but there is a good case for dividing the work into nine divisions of which only the first corresponds to our present system. It is surprising that this suggestion has not been taken up by literary critics of the poem. In fact, the whole subject of formal divisions in medieval poems, including those of Chaucer, has frequently been ignored. The ninefold division corresponds to points of new suspense. The descriptive technique of the poem is also guided by this principle. I cannot go into this subject here in the detail it requires, but if the romance is analyzed in terms of suspense and wonder the formal and stylistic principle of the romance becomes clearer.

[45] "Madden's Divisions of *Sir Gawain* and the 'Large Initial Capitals' of Cotton Nero A.x," *Spec,* XXI (1946), 67–71. I am indebted in the details of my interpretation here to the investigations of Miss Sarah Appleton.

This ignoring of the manuscript divisions in *Sir Gawain* seems to me to be characteristic of the refusal of much scholarship and criticism to come to grips with our poem. As I implied earlier, *Gawain* seems to cast a spell on its commentators. There have been few if any close investigations of the structure and diction of the poem, if we except the positivistic studies of earlier days when such investigations were undertaken in a very mechanical fashion. The poem has to be looked at closely.

I regard the poem as an aristocratic romance reflecting a many-faceted solidity which is both comic and serious. It is meant to entertain and to some extent teach a sophisticated audience. Its style is probably mixed and part of its humor lies in the juxtaposition of high and medium style. It is a combination of secularism and religion, of the marvelous and the real, of the subjective and the objective, of the decorative and the direct, of the vague and the clear, of courtesy and horror, of the elevated and the plain. There is a solidity about *Sir Gawain* which encompasses a variegated world.

The treatment of time in the poem is most interesting. We have a beginning and an end in the distant past. The story itself is laid in the closer past. The poet as narrator-character suggests that he is in our presence telling us of what happened long ago in Arthur's days. These events are, moreover, the outcome of a much longer history going back to the Trojan War and the earliest ancestors of the race. Even Aeneas, we are told, was found wanting.[46] Moreover we get the building of the poem on the passage of a year. Cyclic time or the time of nature is superimposed on linear time or the time of history, in order to contrast the two and to point up Gawain's dilemma. The winter

---

[46] I cannot accept the suggestion of Gollancz and Day in their EETS, O.S. 210, edition of the poem (London, 1940) that "þe tulk" who was tried (or distinguished) for his treachery was Antenor, who would hardly be called "the trewest on erthe." The introduction to this edition by Mabel Day contains an excellent summary of the problem of *Sir Gawain*'s sources.

to come is not merely the same as last winter but different. Further, when the author writes of the temptation scenes, he tells us of the hunting activities going on at the same time.[47] Against the very nature of narration, we are plunged into two events happening simultaneously. The *Gawain*-poet is one of the first poets in English to handle the difficult problem of simultaneity in narration.

Besides all this, we have an inner or psychological time represented on occasion, when the narrator speaks of events occurring inside Gawain's head.[48] Events are sometimes seen as subjective duration.

All this seems to be reflected in the poet's curious use of tenses which should be studied—especially his shifting between past and present and occasional use of the subjunctive. *Sir Gawain* is soaked in time in all its aspects, and this rich chronological perspectivism is one of the strongest elements in the sense of solidity we get from reading the poem. It, along with the rhetorical descriptions, is part of the richness against which these strange, tense, and comic events of the plot play themselves out. These many dimensions of time are part of the bulwarks of life; they give security and strength. They are the framework of the human universe into which fantastic and puzzling irrationality penetrates and which it seems to wish to destroy. Here we have a cosmic humor in which the fragility of life and honor are threatened against a solid and rich background akin to the density of reality itself.

[47] Bercilak may have some features of the "wild huntsman"; see R. S. Loomis in *JEGP,* XLII (1943), 170–181, where similarities of *GGK* to the Welsh Mabinogi of Pwyll are pointed to.

[48] See Everett, pp. 78–79 et passim. The alternation throughout the poem of inside and outside is a most significant feature and helps to create the sense of solidity I find in the poem. I am indebted to Mr. Robert Hall for an awareness of this feature of organization. Mrs. Loomis suggests somewhat this point, see above, p. 21. The romance is at its densest during the temptation scenes, when action goes on in the castle and out of it, in Gawain's bedroom and elsewhere, and within Gawain's soul and without, all at the same time.

Except when he deliberately violates the illusion, the poet endeavors to maintain a distance between his poem and the reader which is necessary to true comedy. Time is functional to this purpose. It helps to create the impression of another world both similar to and different from our own which keeps the reader away from the events taking place. They are far enough to preserve their integrity and strangeness and near enough to interest us. If the reader were to get too closely involved, he might find a tragic horror too great to be borne. The wonder would turn to fear and the delight and curiosity which are always a product of objectivity would be lost. Occasionally, however, especially in the temptation and journey scenes, we are deliberately brought into the poem by being told what the hero is thinking. These passages are, I believe, deliberate and are justified by the circumstances. We get close to tragedy for the heart of Gawain's predicament. But on the whole, life in *Sir Gawain* is "apprehended in the form of spectacle rather than in the form of [inner] experience."[49]

The pastness of the whole poem makes a major contribution to its ideal and aristocratic as well as its comic nature. Things, however, are not quite what they seem. Gawain, the perfect knight, is also a human being, and the Green Knight is really only a mask. His wife only seems to be unfaithful. The old harmless lady is really a witch. The court is silly and yet capable of honor. Nature is both horrid and benign. Life is a tissue of contradictions, even in its most aristocratic and idealized form.

---

[49] Maynard Mack, in the introduction to his edition of Henry Fielding's *Joseph Andrews,* Rinehart Editions 15 (New York and Toronto, 1948), p. xv.

On the mixture of jest and earnest in medieval literature, see Appendix IV to Ernst Robert Curtius, *European Literature and the Latin Middle Ages,* trans. W. R. Trask (London, 1953), pp. 417–437. There is a long tradition connecting the realm of the erotic with comedy which suggests a comic side to the temptation scenes. See Walter Pabst, *Novellentheorie und Novellendichtung, Zur Geschichte ihrer Antinomie in den romanischen Literaturen,* Universität Hamburg, Abhandlungen aus dem Gebiet der Auslandskunde, Band 58, Reihe B, Band 32 (Hamburg, 1953), p. 25.

Time also serves to bind and order the poem just as its stanzaic form does. The timeless but clearly segmented present as revealed in the cycle of the year is firmly embedded in the vaguely known past. Time functions as a part of the decorum and restraint of the poem which are dominant features of its background. This decorous, calm, and aristocratic world is menaced by the indecorous, wondrous, and mysterious, but only for a while. Order and decorum reestablish themselves with a laugh after we have been both held in thrall and amused. The rich irony and humor of the whole situation are suddenly revealed, but then we return to the stability that time perspective can give. The jewel has been seen in a strange light but then it is put back into place—somewhat different but still recognizable.

As I have suggested above, the ambiguities of the Arthurian legend in the fourteenth century perhaps give us a clue to all this. In an age and a country which deliberately tried to keep the fading aristocratic ideals alive by tournaments and the founding of chivalric orders, we find a poet striving to present both the serious and the comic side of this aspect of his times. *Sir Gawain* both praises and belittles the past and the ideal. It tries to come to terms with the political and ideological tensions of its age by the dissolving force of humor and clarity, and it definitely assumes the importance of loyalty and Christianity. Life is perhaps at bottom such a suspenseful and wondrous game. By means of an art so vivid and so rich that many have been tempted to regard it as life itself, the *Gawain*-poet has created a new world which both beckons to and laughs at our own. The great charm of the poem perhaps is due to this curious mystery which both amuses and sobers, delights and frightens us at the same time, as it teeters on the edge of tragedy and defeat but at last safely brings us back to the solid ground of a happy ending. It all happened long ago and the past is after all both unreal and solid, and certainly far from us, and even slightly comic just because it is the past.

PART TWO:

CRITICAL ISSUES

3

THE ANTHROPOLOGICAL APPROACH

C. S. Lewis

IT IS NOT to be disputed that literary texts can sometimes be of great use to the anthropologist. It does not immediately follow from this that anthropological study can make in return any valuable contribution to literary criticism. The attention now paid by medievalists to the mythical and ritual origins (real or supposed) of the romances suggests a widespread belief that it can. I want to consider how far this is so.

It is clear that an anthropological statement (supposing it to be a true one) can often explain some detail in a text. Thus Gawain's property[1] of growing stronger as the sun ascends can be explained as the last vestige of a myth about the sun-god. But let us be quite clear in what sense we are using the word "explain." We mean "to account for causally" (as in "we can easily explain his behavior by the fact that he was drunk"). The word has a different meaning when we say that someone first "explained" to us the Deduction of the Categories or the beauties of the Virgilian hexameter. To "explain" in this second sense is to open our eyes; to give us the power of receiving, or

Reprinted, by permission of the executors of the C. S. Lewis estate, from *English and Medieval Studies Presented to J. R. R. Tolkien on the Occasion of His Seventieth Birthday,* ed. Norman Davis and C. L. Wrenn (London, 1962), pp. 219–230.
[1] *The Works of Malory,* ed. E. Vinaver (Oxford, 1947), I, 161 (Bk. IV, 18); III, 1216–20 (Bk. XX, 21–22).

receiving more fully, what Kant or Virgil intended to give us. The causal explanation of Gawain's peculiarity "explains," in this other sense, nothing whatever. That peculiarity remains, in Malory's book, a complete irrelevance. Nothing leads up to it; nothing of any importance depends on it. Apart from it there is nothing divine and nothing solar about Gawain. All that he does, suffers, or says elsewhere would have exactly the same value if this odd detail had been omitted. The anthropological explanation may be true and it may have an interest of its own; but it cannot increase our understanding or enjoyment of one single sentence in the *Morte*.

I proceed to a more complicated instance. R. S. Loomis stresses the "astonishing disharmony," the offenses against "common sense and ordinary morality," the "absurdities," and the "irrational freakish features," in the literature of the Grail. He concludes that "no procedure could be more reasonable than to seek the cause of the sanctification of the Grail legends in a series of misunderstandings."[2] Now since the Grail, as distinct from various analogues to it in pagan stories, is fully sanctified in all the Grail stories we have, the "cause of the sanctification" means the cause of its character in those stories— Chrétien's, Wolfram's, and the rest. We need not examine the theory that this is due to misunderstandings, for we are here concerned not with its truth or falsehood but with its literary relevance.

There are two ways in which we could interpret Professor Loomis' procedure. One is that he is leaving the literary quality of these romances severely alone and is exclusively interested in the pagan myths from which he believes them to be derived. If that is so, then he is doing something which however legitimate in its own field makes no contribution to literary criticism. Alternatively, if we give full force to the charges of absurdity and

[2] "The Origin of the Grail Legends," *Arthurian Literature in the Middle Ages* (Oxford, 1959), pp. 274–294, esp. p. 287.

freakishness which he brings, we could take him to be saying in effect, "Here is a great deal of shockingly bad fiction. I will explain how Chrétien and his fellows come to be guilty of it. They were led astray by blunders—mistaking *cors* (a horn) for *cors* (a body) or *sang real* for *saint graal.*" I am myself very disinclined to believe that this is the correct account of Professor Loomis' activity. Indeed, if he gave this account of it himself, I should venture to believe that he was misrepresenting his own experience and doing himself a grave injustice. The spectacle of a great scholar spending a lifetime of learning to discover why some bad literature was bad would be a portent that clamored for explanation no less than the Grail itself. And if this were what he was doing, this also would have hardly any critical interest. It is, though far more complex, essentially the same sort of thing that a textual critic is doing when he explains a meaningless passage by dittography. If the Grail romances are nonsensical this fault is neither lessened nor aggravated by the discovery of its causes. Meanwhile the specifically literary problem remains untouched. What we want to know as critics is how and why these romances, with all their elusiveness and mystery, delighted so many medieval readers and delight so many today. Is it in spite of this character or because of it?

We must now make a distinction. The Celtic cornucopia, supposing it to be a source of the Grail, is irrelevant for literature because the inward side of the horn stories, their spirit and quality, is hardly at all present in the romances. How could it be, if the romances so misunderstood their sources that they mistook a horn for a body? Where the parallel between the Grail romance and the Celtic analogue is most striking, the abyss between them in atmosphere and significance may be most emphatic. The question "To whom shall this cup be given?" in *The Prophetic Ecstasy*[3] is certainly in one way very like the question "whom does one serve with the Grail?" But

[3] Loomis, p. 282.

the first question is answered. Its literary function is to introduce a list of the kings of Tara. It has much the same purpose as the vision of future heroes in *Aeneid* VI or the figures on the shield in *Aeneid* VIII or the phantoms in *Macbeth* (iv. i). The second question is not even asked. Perceval's failure to ask it—which is the ganglion of the whole episode—leads to mysterious and almost illimitable disaster. If the medieval poet knew the Celtic story at all (which I need not deny), it has been to him merely a starting point from which he went on to invent something radically new, indeed incommensurable. That new invention, not its trivial and external similarity to some earlier thing, is the proper object of literary criticism.

But this is only one possible relation between a literary text and an anthropological background. There is another.

In the sagas, or *Hamlet,* the ethos of a society where revenge was not, as with us, a passion, but an obligation, is operative throughout. A certain attitude toward the dead is similarly operative throughout the *Antigone.* To appreciate these works we certainly need to grasp these ancient outlooks. But that is because they have more than a merely causal connection with the works. They are not antecedents but presuppositions, still immanent and alive in the completed product. The authors reckon on our understanding them. Not merely on our knowing them externally as historical curiosities, but on our entering into them with imaginative sympathy. And this fact usually enables us to dispense with anthropological study. The authors themselves, speaking from within the archaic ethos, recreate it in our minds. Anthropology might have told us that such and such customs existed. But the authors do not need to tell; they show, they infect, they constrain. It is they who bring the anthropology to life, not vice versa.

And surely this must always be so. It has been maintained that Bercilak in *Gawain and the Green Knight* "is"—that is, was influenced by—an *eniautos daimon*.[4] Let us suppose, for purposes of argument, that this is so. The question is which of the two, *eniautos daimon* or Bercilak, throws light on the other.

Bercilak is as vivid and concrete as any image I have met in literature. He is a living *coincidentia oppositorum*; half giant, yet wholly a "lovely knight"; as full of demoniac energy as old Karamazov, yet, in his own house, as jolly as a Dickensian Christmas host; now exhibiting a ferocity so gleeful that it is almost genial, and now a geniality so outrageous that it borders on the ferocious; half boy or buffoon in his shouts and laughter and jumpings; yet at the end judging Gawain with the tranquil superiority of an angelic being. There has been nothing really like him in fiction before or since. No one who has once read the poem forgets him. No one while reading it disbelieves in him.

But what is the *eniautos daimon?* It is a concept; something constructed from the actual practices of the ancient world and the conjectured practices of our own ancestors. I have never seen Jack in the Green. None of us have, as believers, taken part in a pagan ritual. We cannot experience such things from inside. We may sometimes know, and sometimes guess, that certain myths were told and certain rites enacted. We do not know what it felt like. That world-old religion, with its baffling mixture of agriculture, tragedy, obscenity, revelry, and clowning, eludes us in all but its externals.

To expect that the *eniautos daimon* should help us to understand Bercilak is to expect that the unknown should illuminate the known; as if we hoped that a man would learn more about the taste of oranges on being told that it is like the taste of some other fruit which he has never eaten.

The opposite process is the only rational one. Tell me that

---

[4] John Speirs, *Medieval English Poetry. The Non-Chaucerian Tradition* (London, 1957), pp. 218 ff. [*eniautos daimon* = annual seasonal spirit. Ed.]

the unknown fruit is like an orange, and I have learned something. I learn nothing about the quality of Bercilak from being told he is derived from the daimon; I may learn something about the daimon. Perhaps this rumbustious, irresistible figure has preserved for me just what anthropology can never penetrate; has given me knowledge-by-acquaintance (*connaître*) where anthropology could give me at best knowledge-about (*savoir*). If this is so, then our poetic experience has helped us as anthropologists, but our anthropology has not helped us to read the poetry. When savage beliefs or practices inform a work of art, that work is not a puzzle to which those beliefs and practices are the clue. The savage origins are the puzzle; the surviving work of art is the only clue by which we can hope to penetrate the inwardness of the origins. It is either in art, or nowhere, that the dry bones are made to live again.

Mr. Speirs maintains the literary relevance of such origins on two grounds. One is that they affect the poet; the other, that a knowledge of them affects the reader.

After quoting the place about the perilous fountain from *Ywain and Gawain* (325–342),[5] he connects it conjecturally with a rainmaking ritual. He then very properly asks what difference this makes to the poetry; especially since the poets may have known nothing about the ritual origin. Part of his answer is that, whether they knew the origin or not, "they surely inherited with such episodes something of the traditional reverence towards them, a sense of their mystery, a sense too of the mystery of all life."

Now our only evidence for how the poet felt is what he wrote. This passage apparently makes Mr. Speirs feel reverence and a sense of mystery; he infers that the poet had felt it too. Mr. Speirs, whatever else he may be, is a very honest critic; if he says that the passage makes him feel like that, we may be sure it does. But I am not equally sure that the conclusions he

[5] *Medieval English Poetry*, p. 117.

wants us to draw will follow. For one thing, as I shall suggest presently, Mr. Speirs's sensation may not result from the quality of the poetry in the direct fashion he supposes; I can imagine a somewhat different process. But suppose it is the actual writing that has done the trick. And suppose, further, that the feelings an author arouses in a sensitive reader are always the same as he had himself. We could then say: "The author of this passage felt reverence and a sense of mystery." But where is the evidence that ritual origins are the only or commonest source of such feelings or that such feelings always result from (even a forgotten) ritual origin? Might not the poet equally well be awed and mystified by a mere unexplained magic fountain such as this purports to be? Might he not have believed in such things? Is it not more probable he believed in them than that he cared about rain-rituals? Or, even without belief, might not the idea of perilous adventures in enchanted forests have moved him deeply? It moved Milton.

This type of criticism which always takes us away from the actual poem and the individual poet to seek the sources of their power in something earlier and less known—which, in fact, finds the secret of poetic pleasure anywhere rather than in talent and art—has lately received a dolorous stroke from Professor Vinaver.[6] He has cured us, if we can be cured, of the bad habit which regards the finished romances as mere rubble left over from some far statelier, nonexistent building. This is the reverse of the truth. The romance is the cathedral; the anthropological material is the rubble that was used by the builders. He has shown as regards one particular story that every step away from the dark origins is an advance in coherence, in suggestion, in imaginative power.

But I must now turn to the second part of Mr. Speirs's theory —or rather to his second theory, for the two are independent. Besides doing something to the poets, the ritual origins, or the

---

[6] "The Dolorous Stroke," *M Æ,* xxv (1957), 175–180.

knowledge of them, or the conjecture of them, does something to the reader.

The mere conjecture that the perilous fountain has something to do with rainmaking means for Mr. Speirs "that the episode is more serious than simply a sport of fancy." It means "that we might have to correct our way of taking these episodes as if they belonged to something of the order of a boy's adventure story—taking them, that is, too easily."[7] Elsewhere he says that "anthropological facts or even guesses" may make the reader of medieval literature "alert to things which he might not otherwise have noticed."[8]

This is where Mr. Speirs's honesty is invaluable. He lets us see what is really going on in the minds of some anthropologizing critics. But for anthropology "we" should have taken the ferlies in medieval romance like trivial excitements in a boy's blood. "We" should have taken them "too easily." Without anthropological preparation "we" may leave some things unnoticed altogether.

I have no doubt whatever that this is true to the experience of Mr. Speirs and of many of his generation. For them the garden of marvelous romance is—as it was not either for medieval or for nineteenth-century man—a walled and locked-up garden to which anthropology is the only key. They become free of it only if they carry the golden bough. This awakens in them a sensibility they otherwise lack. This being so, one understands for the first time why they value—why in a sense they are right to value—anthropology so highly. For if to them the only choice lies between taking the Grail as if it were a mere surprise-packet out of Boiardo or Munchausen and achieving an awed and solemn response with the aid of some Celtic cauldron, it is certainly well that they should embrace the second alternative.

[7] *Medieval English Poetry*, p. 117.
[8] Ibid., pp. 23–24.

With this, it may be said, I have conceded the whole position. Anthropology increases the sensibility, and even the attention, of certain readers. Therefore it does throw light for them on literature. I admit it. But let us be sure exactly what we mean.

Anything that helps anyone to read more sensitively and attentively is welcome. But there are helps of different kinds. On the one hand they may consist of knowledges or sympathies which enable the reader to enter more fully into the author's intentions. History is often such a help. So is scholarship. So is experience; *ceteris paribus* we read love poetry and religious poetry more perceptively if we have had some experience of love and of religion. But there are other helps that have no intrinsic connection with the art or matter of the book but merely dispose us psychologically to be pleased. They are accidental in the sense that their necessity varies from one reader to another, and for the same reader from time to time, and the best readers need them least. Health, quiet, an easy chair, a full, but not too full, stomach, can all help in this way. Some approach a book receptively because it is recommended, others because it is forbidden. Children are attracted by colored pictures, adults by fine paper and printing. One is attracted and another repelled by the knowledge that "everyone is reading this."

To discover, exhibit, and supply helps of the first kind is critically relevant and useful in the highest degree. But helps of the second kind are more properly mentioned in an autobiography. They are facts about this or that reader rather than about literature. There seem to me grounds for assigning to the second, or merely subjective, class the help which Mr. Speirs and his contemporaries derive from anthropology.

In the first place it is not universally necessary. At a great price (in the way of anthropological study) Mr. Speirs obtains his freedom to respond deeply and solemnly to the romances; but earlier generations, including my own, were free born. We never thought of responding—never had power to respond

—in any other way. The ferlies, simply for what they are shown to be in the texts, conquered us at once and have never released us. We stand amazed when our juniors think to interest us in the Grail by connecting it with a cauldron of plenty or a prehistoric burning glass,[9] for the Grail as Chrétien or Malory presents it seems to us twenty times more interesting than the cauldron or the glass. Apparently there has grown up a generation in whom, for reasons I will not discuss here, the direct response has been inhibited. They find that anthropology releases the inhibition. I congratulate them. But it merely restores to them powers which humanity often has without any such preliminary ascesis. The insight into romance which it gives them is new to them, not to men in general. The fact that they needed such therapy is a fact about them, not about the literary quality of the romances. To regard their anthropological approach as a discovery in literary criticism is like regarding insulin as a discovery in gastronomy. I am very glad diabetics now have insulin. But it is a medical, not a gastronomic, discovery.

In the second place, it is clear that the therapeutic value of the anthropological ascesis does not depend on the *fact* of ritual origins. The fact, if it is one, and if it produces literary results, must have been doing so before anyone knew about it, just as poison will kill or alcohol intoxicate us whether we know we have taken them or not. If a ritual origin worked that way, readers of the romances would receive its exciting effect without knowing its existence. If that were so, why should we need to learn of it before we can fully enjoy the romances? And indeed Mr. Speirs does not think we need exactly "learn" in the sense of "coming to know." The connection between the perilous fountain and a rainmaking ritual is, on his own showing, a "conjecture."[10] In *Maiden in the mor lay* the reference

<hr>

[9] Lady Flavia Anderson, *The Ancient Secret* (London, 1953).
[10] *Medieval English Poetry,* p. 117.

to a well-spring merely "suggests the possibility"[11] that the poem is connected with well-worship. Obviously what does the therapeutic work is not the fact but the mere idea of ritual origins; the idea as an idea, not known to be true, not affirmed, but simply entertained. The case is not like that of a man who gets sick from eating poison or drunk from taking spirits. It is as if a suggestible person felt sick or felt drunk simply at the idea of having done so. If he believes (however erroneously) that he has, or even if without belief he dwells on the idea, the vomit or the euphoria will follow. It makes no difference to the utility Mr. Speirs finds in his anthropological ideas whether they are true or false.

Thirdly, the anthropological "softening" is not the only one available. Others find their inhibitions similarly released by the idea that ferlies are Jungian outcroppings from the collective unconscious. Others, though not in academic circles, can enjoy them by thinking they are the hieroglyphs of an ancient, but still living, esoteric wisdom. Since all three exercises serve the same purpose, it is natural to ask what they have in common. The answer does not seem to me to be very difficult.

All are alike in suggesting that the ferly actually presented to us in the old poem or romance is the far-borne echo, the last surviving trace, the tantalizing glimpse, the veiled presence, of something else. And the something else is always located in a remote region, "dim-discovered," hard of access. On this its value depends, I think, in all three exercises; almost certainly, in the anthropological one. Are ancient rituals in themselves—rituals that lie in broad, historical daylight and need not be groped after—so moving? I should be surprised if all those who are moved by the idea that the Grail story "is really" a ritual respond with equal excitement to the full-length descriptions of ritual in the *Aeneid* or Leviticus. The whole pleasure comes from feeling, as they read of the ferly, that "more is meant than

[11] Ibid., p. 63.

meets the ear," that they have surprised a long-kept secret, that there are depths below the surface, that something which the uninitiate might pass over as a triviality is big with meaning. They must have the sense of descending to "the Mothers." Who would bother to pluck the golden bough unless it led you to *res alta terra et caligine mersas* ["things sunken deep in the earth immersed in darkness," *Aeneid* VI, 267]?

Now all these sensations are in my opinion considerably like those the authors meant to give you. The romancers create a world where everything may, and most things do, have a deeper meaning and a longer history than the errant knight would have expected; a world of endless forest, quest, hint, prophecy. Almost every male stranger wears armor; not only that there may be jousts but because visors hide faces. Any lady may prove a fay or devil; every castle may conceal a holy or unholy mystery. The hero is a sort of intruder or trespasser; always, unawares, stumbling on to forbidden ground. Hermits and voices explain just enough to let us know how completely he is out of his depth, but not enough to dissipate the overall mystery. The hard, gay colors make this world very unlike that of Kafka, but it has some of the same qualities. You might call it inverted (or converted) Kafka; a Kafka who enjoyed the labyrinth.

Until our own age readers accepted this world as the romancers' "noble and joyous" invention. It was not, to be sure, wholly unrelated to the real world. It was invented by and for men who felt the real world, in its rather different way, to be also cryptic, significant, full of voices and "the mystery of all life." There has now arisen a type of reader who cannot thus accept it. The tale in itself does not seem to him to provide adequate grounds for the feelings to which he is dimly aware that he is being prompted. He therefore invents new grounds for them in his own life as a reader. And he does this by building up round himself a second romance which he mistakes for reality. This second romance is a distorted version of the first one. It also is a quest story, but it is he, not Perceval or Gawain, that is on the quest. The forests are not those of Broceliande but those of anthropological theory. It is he himself who quivers at the surmise that everything he meets may be more important, and other, than it seemed. It is to him that such hermits as Frazer and Miss Weston, dwelling in the heart of the forest, explain the *significacio* of the ferlies. Prompted by them, he does not, like Perceval, omit to ask the all-important question.

And he has his reward. He gets in the end an experience qualitatively not unlike the experience the romancers meant to give. The process is very roundabout. He rejects the fiction as it was actually written. He can respond to it only indirectly, only when it is mirrored in a second fiction, which he mistakes for a reality. This is better than nothing. But it might do a good deal of harm to real literary and cultural history and even to anthropology itself if it were taken as a serious contribution to any of these disciplines. And to criticism it has already done some. Already there are students who describe as "enjoyment of medieval literature" what is really the enjoyment of brooding upon things (mostly hypothetical) in the dark past with which that literature is, often so doubtfully, connected in their minds. Mr. Speirs himself would reassure us by the proposition that in a poem "one cannot find what is not there."[12] But the instances of thinking you have found what is not there are generally allowed to be pretty numerous. Is Mr. Speirs himself quite sure that the allegory Fulgentius found in Virgil, or the philosophy Chapman found in Homer, were really there? Is he absolutely convinced that the *Song of Solomon* was really and truly about "The mutual love of Christ and his Church"? The forest is after all enchanted: mares have built nests in every tree.

[12] *Medieval English Poetry,* p. 24.

4

GAWAIN AND THE GREEN KNIGHT AS ENTERTAINMENT

R. H. Bowers

THE WEST MIDLAND vocabulary of *Gawain and the Green Knight* is difficult, so difficult that reading the poem may prove more of a discipline than a delight. So it is fully understandable that the discipline required may put a critic in a solemn, earnest frame of mind when he interprets the poem as a whole. Yet the narrative itself has usually been regarded as clear, straightforward, and fully realized; its characters, for the most part, acting from clear, explicit motives. In this respect it differs sharply from another great poem of fourteenth-century England, Chaucer's *Troilus,* where the motives of Criseyde and her uncle Pandarus are often puzzling and baffling. Nevertheless, *GGK,* like all great literature, is too complex to submit to any final, monistic interpretation which critics might advance. In this paper I shall review three such interpretations in order to restore an important aspect of the text, the aspect of delight and entertainment which is in danger of being submerged by too much solemn, somber criticism.

The first essay (by Alan Markman) suffers from a failure to see *GGK* as a member in good standing of a literary genre, sharing features and motifs with other Middle English romances; the second essay (by Charles Moorman) suffers from extrap-

Reprinted, by permission of author and editor, from *Modern Language Quarterly,* xxiv (1963), 333–341.

olation, from reading into the poem things which the poem does not realize and make the reader feel; the third essay (by John Burrow) suffers from a *pars pro toto* procedure, of stressing one important theme in the poem to the exclusion of the whole. For the most part, my method shall be the old one of comparison and contrast with other ME romances, the method which Coleridge once urged be employed in seeing Shakespeare in relation to his fellow dramatists in order to try to see him whole.[1] Of course all methods are but analytical tools which must be used with the caution and humility due all great art which, in its superb self-sufficiency, resists and resents all final commentary.

Needless to say I am not concerned with commentaries which are not primarily concerned with literary criticism, such as the effort of Henry Savage to establish John of Gaunt's French brother-in-law Enguerrand de Coucy, a French knight of dazzling renown who sojourned in England from c. 1363 to c. 1377, as the model for Gawain; or the speculations about Gawain's genealogy and general literary reputation indulged in by Celtic traditionalists; or the efforts of John Speirs to make us desert the text of the poem and ruminate about sun-gods, vegetation myths, pollarding, and what not.[2]

Everybody agrees that *GGK* is a courtly romance with the happy ending usually found in other members of the same

---

[1] For convenient reference all citations from Middle English metrical romances (unless otherwise stated) are taken from Walter H. French and Charles B. Hale, *Middle English Metrical Romances* (New York, 1930). These citations are purely illustrative and do not pretend to be exhaustive. All citations from *Sir Gawain and the Green Knight* are taken from the Tolkien and Gordon corrected text (Oxford, 1930).

[2] See Henry L. Savage, *The Gawain-Poet, Studies in His Personality and Background* (Chapel Hill, 1956); B. J. Whiting, "Gawain: His Reputation, His Courtesy and His Appearance in Chaucer's *Squire's Tale*," *MedStud.*, IX (1947), 189–254; John Speirs, *Medieval English Poetry. The Non-Chaucerian Tradition* (London, 1957), pp. 215–251.

genre.[3] Everybody agrees, I suppose, that the function of the marvelous action (adventure, plot) of a romance is to test and hence "develop" the static character of the protagonist to its full chivalric potentiality. Everybody agrees that the hero is presented as an idealized aristocrat, not as a grubbing bourgeois or an inarticulate peasant, and that his adventure has no political or economic significance whatsoever. But Markman, if I read him fairly, insists that "human conduct" is the heart of the poem, that the hero is a "real man" with no "superhuman quality," and that for the modern reader to sympathize with the humiliation of Gawain after he receives a nick in his neck is to realize what it means "to be alive in the world."[4] To be sure, Markman constantly insists that *GGK* is a romance, but he does not adequately consider the features of romance as a literary genre with the attendant advantages and limitations which any genre necessarily contains. One obvious limitation is that it can represent only a small segment of human experience, since it can deal successfully only with the yearning for the "good old days" when knighthood was in flower (*GGK,* lines 2521–23).[5]

[3] The concept of genre is a clumsy critical tool since it can do scant justice to the uniqueness of any first-class work of art. Furthermore, there are different kinds of romance in ME literature: for example, some romances deal with wars between Saracens and Christians. Yet the concept of genre is indispensable in the writing of literary history and in problems of classification. See the sensible views on the concept of ME romance in George Kane, *Middle English Literature, A Critical Study of the Romances, the Religious Lyrics, Piers Plowman* (London, 1951), pp. 1–103.

[4] See Alan M. Markman, "The Meaning of Sir Gawain and the Green Knight," *PMLA,* LXXII (1957), 574–586.

[5] The sentimental and primitivistic contrast between alleged contemporary degeneration and supposed former virtue was commonplace in Middle English literature: e.g., *Winner and Waster* (ed. Gollancz), lines 5–30; *Ywain and Gawain,* lines 33–40; Lydgate, *Reson and Sensuallyte* (EETS, E.S., No. 84), lines 3141–3214. For discussion, see George Boas, *Essays on Primitivism and Related Ideas in the Middle Ages* (Baltimore, 1948).

Of course, the poem is concerned with "human conduct," but so are other poems and so is most literature—such a highly generalized comment is of little critical use. And Gawain is not a real man, although he is fully realized as a character in fiction —which is an entirely different matter. Rather he is an idealized knight seen and depicted wholly from the outside by an affectionate narrator whose presence is always felt. Gawain had no genuine inner life; the term "conscience" occurs but once in the poem (1196) and that in a perfunctory way. There is nothing problematical in the poem, not the slightest questioning or probing of the social values of the aristocratic caste. And this aristocratic attitude is normally found in ME romance, which represents life as spectacle or pageant. Gawain may have no "superhuman quality," but like other heroes of ME romance, he has little difficulty in disposing of bears, serpents, and giants (720–722) while on his perilous initiation into full knighthood. True, the poet considers these feats of little moment, far less serious than the freezing cold which almost incapacitates the hero. For the world into which Gawain sallies forth is a special kind of world especially designed to prove a knight errant. Don Quixote, his mind distorted by the romances which he had read, sallied forth into a natural world which had not been designed to prove a knight errant—hence the irony or comedy or realism which that juxtaposition fomented. For it must be conceded that the art of Cervantes is more penetrating, and ultimately more realistic, than the art of *GGK,* in the proving of human ideals or preconceptions by testing them in the workaday world. Yet the romantic art of *GGK* is completely successful in rendering a nonrealistic world very real: it works, of course, through verisimilitude. It creates an impervious world of belief through its brilliant polychromatic rendition of scenes of rich banquets, of venery, of the wild terrain of northern Wales. It fills the apprehension of reader or auditor[6] with thermal, echoic, kinetic, and tactile images in abundance. It presents not so much "imaginary gardens with real toads in them," as imaginary gardens with fully realized toads. The verisimilitude of *GGK* has, it would appear, made Markman read *GGK* more as history than as fiction. And when we read fiction as history, awareness of art is apt to be overlooked.

One way of pointing up the art of ME romance is to consider the abundance or *copia* of the rendition and to remember that *GGK* is a relatively long poem of 2,530 lines, some 1,000 lines longer than the average ME metrical romance. Abundance of concrete detail is essential to the creation of another world of belief; fiction has to get in front of the reader and blot out his actual world in order to substitute its own self-sufficient world. The superiority of the *GGK* poet in this respect to his confreres may be easily established. An example will suffice. In the ME *Sir Perceval of Galles,* the redness of the antagonist, the Red Knight, who is a malevolent enchanter, is sketched in exactly two lines: "Prekande on a rede stede; / Blode-rede was his wede" (605–606). In this instance the poet has not done his proper work; he is demanding that the reader imagine and visualize a red knight. Unlike a good impressionistic painter, he has not supplied those necessary details or ingredients which would facilitate the construction of a mental picture by the reader. The contrast of this abrupt description with the fifty-line representation of the Green Knight in *GGK,* or catalogue of his external attributes, when he first enters the stage, speaks for itself (151–206). Of course, differences in the literary art of the ME romances are differences of degree, not kind, or differences of the individual skill of poets working with

---

[6] There are references to a listening audience in *GGK,* lines 30, 624, and 1996; hence the poet may well have planned his work to be read aloud. But *GGK* exhibits none of the clumsy devices of a minstrel's oral literature; see Bertram H. Bronson, "Chaucer's Art in Relation to His Audience," in *Five Studies in Literature,* Univ. of Calif. Pubs. in Eng. (Berkeley, 1940).

similar materials and sensibilities. The ME metrical romances abound in catalogues of knightly magnificence. Most of them, however, as in the description of the antagonist Graysteele in the ME *Eger and Grime* (953–977), consist of simple enumeration rather than a skillful plaiting of details, as is accomplished by the *GGK* poet. The catalogue, one of the oldest and most ubiquitous of literary devices, has been evaluated in a variety of ways: as a feature of an older tradition that regarded the poet as a polymath and the long narrative poem as an encyclopedia; as an ostentatious parade of book learning; as sheer aristocratic magnificence, as in the different types of wood used in the funeral pyre of Chaucer's Arcite; or as rhetorical *copia*. Like anything which demands to be taken seriously, it is easy to parody—witness *Sir Thopas*. But surely one of its most important functions can be to help create the world of fiction and facilitate the willing suspension of disbelief.

A strenuous, and I think unsuccessful, effort to read *GGK* as a "semiallegorical presentation of the whole history and meaning of the Round Table" has recently been made by Charles Moorman.[7] In order to prove his argument, Moorman tries to demonstrate that the poet depicts Arthur's young court as already showing clear signs of incipient corruption in matters of sex and faithfulness. In contrast, says Moorman, the court of Bercilak is depicted as morally superior. His argument runs somewhat as follows: Gawain is tempted and tries to conceal the gift of the girdle; ergo, since this is a corrupt deed and since Gawain was a member of Arthur's court, the entire court is corrupt. It would be tedious to analyze Moorman's entire argument; a few points will suffice to show how farfetched it is. For the poet never makes us feel any corruption in Camelot as Shakespeare makes us feel that there is something rotten in Denmark.

---

[7] "Myth and Medieval Literature: *Sir Gawain and the Green Knight*," *MedStud.*, xviii (1956), 158–172.

(1) For example, as "evidence" of the alleged corruption of Arthur's court, Moorman argues that Arthur first greets the Green Knight, who is bearing a holly twig as token of peace, rudely (276–278) as contrasted to the friendly greeting given to the fully armed Gawain by Bercilak (1035–36). Actually, the first thing Arthur says is: "Wyȝe, welcum iwys to þis place . . ." (252). To be sure, Arthur is rude later; but in response to the Green Knight's rudeness.

(2) Moorman invokes Bercilak's explanation to Gawain of the decapitation trick, that Morgan had sent him to assay the Round Table, and interprets the substantive *surquidre* (2457) as meaning pride in the dyslogistic sense of arrogance. Moorman then takes this interpretation literally, rather than as a narrative or dramatic statement, as evidence of the alleged degradation of the Round Table. But if we read the word in context, it seems much more likely that the poet is using the term *surquidre* in a eulogistic sense of self-respect or loyalty to the ideals of knighthood:

> Ho wayned me vpon þis wyse to your wynne halle
> For to assay þe surquidré, ȝif hit soth were
> Þat rennes of þe grete renoun of þe Rounde Table . . . .
> (2456–58)

The question was: Is the great reputation for integrity (*trauþe*) which the Round Table enjoys really warranted? Furthermore, Moorman forgets that Bercilak had previously accused Arthur's court of lacking *sourquydrye* (311) in the sense of self-respect. Of course, both statements are appropriate to their own narrative contexts; nothing that a poem states cancels out another statement; the apparent contradictions merge and exist as different perspectives; and a narrative poem—especially one composed for oral delivery—has to make its points clear as it progresses. Actually, Bercilak's explanation to Gawain comes as an afterthought and is not really organic to the main body of the poem.

(3) Moorman quotes line 945, which states that Bercilak's wife is "wener þen Wenore," as evidence that she is morally superior to Guenevere. The line merely states that she is prettier. Her conduct in the narrative, if we take it literally rather than as a necessary role in the comedy of testing the hero's loyalty to his host, is highly immoral. There is no substantial evidence that the Guenevere of *GGK* is in any way immoral. We are merely told by Bercilak at the end of the poem that Morgan disliked her and wanted to frighten her to death by the decapitation trick (2460–62).[8]

Possibly Moorman could have made a more persuasive case for his argument about the degradation of Arthur's court by using the ME romance *Sir Launfal*. In this poem Arthur appears as a cranky cuckold, and Guenevere as a nymphomaniac, who, like Potiphar's wife, bears false witness against the titular hero and is blinded for this act of falsehood by Dame Tryamour, the fairy protectress of Sir Launfal (1006–1008). Here the reader can feel the degradation because it has been fully realized and is organic to the poem.

The *GGK* poet was retelling an old tale of Arthur's day which he had heard "in toun" (31) or read in a book (2521). Thus he was faced with the problem of "modernizing," of adding human and dramatic motivations as well as pictorial verisimilitude to the magic tales of decapitation and temptation which he intertwined for his plot. Hence some discrepancies were bound to arise between the improbable causes of the magical tales and the motivations appropriate to the fourteenth century. Yet audiences not accustomed to naturalistic expectation may not have demanded that a poetic action be both possible and probable. The decapitation and temptation tales in *GGK* are

---

[8] Albert B. Friedman, in "Morgan le Fay in *Sir Gawain and the Green Knight*," *Speculum*, xxxv (1960), 260–274, says about all that needs to be said on the much debated subject of that elusive witch; he argues that Morgan "functions solely as a foil to enhance the beauty of Gawain's temptress."

essentially practical jokes which the antagonist, Bercilak, enjoys to the hilt, as his continual loud laughter shows. And the victim, in the glare of exposure and publicity, responds like any victim of a practical joke—in shame and anger.

GGK is a predominantly secular poem, although, of course, it makes proper genuflection to Christianity, as does most medieval literature. Gawain is a Christian knight who attends Mass and makes his moan to Mary in time of duress (1769); the poem, like many ME metrical romances, such as *The Earl of Toulouse,* concludes with an apostrophe to Our Lord. Chivalry always paid formal respect to Christianity: in the biography (it is really a secular hagiography) of the Black Prince, who died in 1376, the Chandos Herald, in glorification of his subject, stated that: "Car il pria a Dieu mercy / Et pardon de touz ses mesfaits" [He prayed for mercy from God / And pardon for all his misdeeds] (4192–93).[9] Actually some ME romances contain such heavy Christian coloring that A. C. Baugh has argued that possibly the surviving fifteenth-century texts of these poems may be redactions made by clerics.[10] Nevertheless, *GGK* is essentially a secular poem, providing a secular context for the religious and moral theme of penance represented in the two confession scenes involving Gawain which have been analyzed as follows by John Burrow, with a wealth of illustration drawn from medieval penitential literature.[11]

After the first two temptation scenes in Bercilak's castle, Gawain merely attends Mass, as do other knights in other ME romances, such as *The Avowing of Arthur* (689). But after the third tempting by his host's wife, Gawain seeks out the priest of the castle, seeks absolution, and is shriven prior to his perilous

[9] *Le Prince Noir: Poème du Héraut D'Armes Chandos,* ed. Francisque-Michel (London and Paris, 1883).

[10] See A. C. Baugh, "The Authorship of the Middle English Romances," *Annual Bulletin of the Modern Humanities Research Association,* XXII (1950), 13–28.

[11] See John Burrow, "The Two Confession Scenes in *Gawain and the Green Knight*," *MP,* LVII (1959–1960), 73–79.

encounter at the Green Chapel. At this point he conceals the gift of the girdle and the consequent violation of hospitality in the "swapping game" which he had entered into with his host. In the second confession scene at the Green Chapel (2360–94), Bercilak enacts the role of priest and "absolves" the hero after the affair of the girdle is revealed and after the hero's abject admission. Finally, according to Burrow, the poem ends on a mixed note of penance and laughter: Gawain and the knights of Arthur's court agree to wear a penitential green baldric as token of the adventure of the Green Chapel, and the knights laugh loudly at the excessive reaction of Gawain to his humiliation. Burrow's essay is an important contribution to the understanding of *GGK*; it is well considered and carefully documented. I wonder, though, if the two confession scenes are not being taken too seriously and too literally since they occur within the over-all context of practical joking.

In the first confession scene, the poem states that Bercilak's priest assoils Gawain "surely" (1883–84). But this is really impossible since Gawain has deliberately concealed the affair of the girdle from the priest with timidity aforethought. Possibly the poet is nodding, possibly he considers the matter of the girdle insignificant at the moment. But it is more likely that he is caught between the demands of the plot and the demands of verisimilitude and is unable to harmonize them. For the plot demands that Bercilak later play his practical joke on the unsuspecting victim who assumed that he could conceal the matter of the girdle: "For hit is my wede þat þou wereȝ" (2358).

In the second confession scene, a tone of irony is heard in the merry laughter of Bercilak before the action takes place (2336, 2345). Later, Bercilak, the practical joker, uses the metaphorical language of a priest in "absolving" the dismayed hero: "I halde þe polysed of þat plyȝt, and pured as clene / As þou hadeȝ neuer forfeted syþen þou watȝ fyrst borne" (2393–94). Bercilak cannot be speaking literally since he is not a priest; also, he is a magician and the ironic perpetuator of the practical jokes from start to finish. So the two confession scenes exist within an ironic and comic context. But they do afford sufficient human motivation and feeling to help satisfy the demands of verisimilitude on magic tales that never were on land or sea.

The high comedy of *GGK* is accentuated by the constant laughter that occurs throughout the poem. I do not believe that the laughter and gay spirit of the poem has been sufficiently emphasized. The Green Knight and his playful wife are constantly laughing, he in the loud merriment of a practical joker, she in sophisticated amusement. After the decapitation scene, Arthur and Gawain burst into laughter as if they had just witnessed a merry interlude: "At þat grene þay laʒe and grenne" (464). And Arthur and his court laugh loud when Gawain, covered with shame and confusion, relates his chastening adventure at the Green Chapel (2514).

No doubt laughter in a ME romance is sometimes difficult for a modern reader to interpret—unless the poet is at pains to be specific. Just what kind of laughter was it? What were the poet's intentions? In the ME *Avowing of Arthur,* Gawain rescues a damsel in distress from the toils of the wicked Sir Meneleafe of the Mountain. She then laughs—either in nervous, agonized relief or in sophisticated amusement because she had never taken the abduction seriously (510). I read the laughter in *GGK* as good-natured and gay. Certainly it contrasts sharply with the small amount of laughter in other ME romances, most of which are utterly devoid of humor. There is some laughter —but it is usually scornful laughter: the scorn of knights for cowards, of nobles for peasants, or rough Homeric laughter at the physical discomfort of others. In the ME *Ipomadon,* when the hero feigns indifference to participation in a tournament and hence appears a craven recreant, the Queen's female attendants "hym to scorne louʒghe / Thereoffe had þey ioye inowghe" (2997–98). When the protagonist of the ME *Sir Cleges* breaks the porter's arm in brutal retaliation for a prior slight, "The lordes lowe, both old and yenge / And all that wern with þe kynge" (517–518). In the raucous ME *Sultan of Babylon,* the lusty Christian Princess Floripas laughs uproariously whenever a Saracen is slaughtered (2258, 2602). In the ME *Sir Launfal,* the villainous Lombard knight Sir Valentine, in a tourney that proves ultimately fatal to him, laughs loudly and prematurely when he humiliates the hero by knocking him off his horse (577).

So I would argue that the laughter in *GGK* should be granted its proper place in setting the tone and hence the meaning of the poem. The poet sees the idea of chivalry whole, with affection and good-natured understanding, not with the humorless and uncritical adulation of a Froissart or the bitter scorn of a Commines. He depicts good-natured aristocrats, free from bourgeois envy and wrangling. He depicts Gawain not as perfect in any absolute sense—that kind of perfection is possible only in Our Savior—but as perfect as a son of Adam, blemished by venial sin, can be in this transitory world.[12] The concepts of romance and chivalry retain their virtues, as do the glamorized tapestries of courtly life, static, isolated from the actualities of the worlds of politics and economics. Chaucer loved them at their best, as witness the inception of *The Squire's Tale* or the full, glowing pageant of *The Knight's Tale,* while he ridiculed their abuse at the hands of poetasters in *Sir Thopas.*

As I stated at the beginning of this paper, the West Midland language of *GGK* makes the reading of the poem a discipline when it should be a delight. But that hypothetical person, the general reader, introduced to the poem for the first time in a

---

[12] The testing of a "perfect" knight has concerned many critics. George J. Engelhardt, in "The Predicament of Gawain," *MLQ,* XVI (1955), 218–225, first pointed out the parallel between the pentagonal virtues of Gawain and the five testings: the first three by Bercilak's wife, the fourth by the guide (2091–2159), and the fifth by Bercilak himself at the Green Chapel.

decent modern paraphrase, can feel the delight and entertainment that many fourteenth-century readers must have felt, especially the delight and comedy of the first three temptation scenes, which cannot be too highly praised. For after all, the fundamental purpose of ME romance is entertainment, not didactic instruction, although it properly adds enough moralizing or sentiment to give a poem ballast and protect it against a puritan charge that it lacks *utilitas*. The job of didactic instruction belongs to the Middle English sermon. The job of the court poet or minstrel is entertainment at a festive occasion; the preacher's job is moral edification on a solemn occasion. There is a time and place for both, in fourteenth-century England as well as in the England of today.

5

CHRISTIAN SIGNIFICANCE AND ROMANCE TRADITION IN *SIR GAWAIN AND THE GREEN KNIGHT*

M. Mills

RECENT YEARS HAVE seen some interesting new developments in the study of medieval literature, but none more remarkable than the increasing popularity of the "exegetical" approach, by which the events of a fictitious narrative are held to stand for points in the Christian faith, or map the progress of the human soul. Whatever case can be made for such an approach in broad terms (by claiming, for example, that the reader of the time expected to have to crack the nut of fable in order to extract the kernel of real significance), its application to specific texts produces some very unexpected results. Hans Schnyder's recent monograph on *Sir Gawain and the Green Knight (GGK)*[1] provides a number of examples of these, for instance: "In . . . *GGK* all the hunted animals convey connotations of evil, and this is doubtless the reason why the author of the poem seems so involved in the outcome of the hunts and never tires of triumphantly describing the final slaying of the pursued animals"

First published in *Modern Language Review,* LX (1965), 483–493, and here reprinted by permission of the Modern Humanities Research Association and of the author. [The editors are grateful to Prof. Sam J. Borg for his aid in translating passages of Old French in this article.]
[1] Bern, 1961. All references to *GGK* in this article are to Sir Israel Gollancz's edition, EETS, O.S. no. 210 (London, 1940).

(p. 63). But it would be ungracious as well as ultimately sterile to attempt to catalogue all the points at which his interpretation seems over-ingenious. However eccentric parts of his study may be, it cannot simply be ignored, and it seems particularly worthwhile to take up his implied comparison between *GGK* and the thirteenth-century *Queste del Saint Graal* (*QSG*):[2] "a considerable time before the composition of *GGK* Arthurian romance was used as a convenient vehicle for purely allegorical purposes, for a representation of the journey inwards" (p. 36), and see what light the Old French text throws upon the texture and narrative method of the Middle English romance. Fortunately for us, such a comparison is made easier by the fact that the two works have in common a large number of romance patterns and motifs.[3]

It is worth noting at the outset that even the most purely "secular" romances are in some respects well adapted to support a Christian meaning. Their habit of multiplying unforeseen adventures between the hero's departure from Arthur's court and his arrival at his objective is a case in point; such incidents rarely have much obvious relevance to this objective, but may yet combine to suggest that an untried knight (like Perceval) or one with a reputation to retrieve (like Erec) is worthy of the order to which he belongs. In *QSG* such suggestions are made quite explicit. The good (Christian) knight regards his adventures not as an occupational hazard, but as proof positive that he is fit to undertake the search for the Grail. For this

[2] Ed. A. Pauphilet, Classiques Français du Moyen Age, 33 (Paris, 1949).

[3] Since this article was submitted for publication, Professor Smithers has dealt in depth with a number of other aspects of the relevance of *QSG* to the study of *GGK;* see "What Sir Gawain and the Green Knight is About," *M Æ,* XXXII (1963), 171–189. In particular, he notes a number of points at which the Green Knight resembles the hermits of the Old French romance, suggests that the *Gawain*-poet may actually have known *QSG,* and regards a contrast between "spiritual" and "secular" knighthood as of fundamental importance to *GGK.*

reason Galahad meets with more adventures than can ever be related by the author (p. 195),[4] while the spiritually dessicated Gawain and Hector loudly complain of the uneventful time they are having (p. 147). That this is no accident is pointed out to them by one of the hermits who so thickly populate the forests of the *Queste*: "Les aventures qui ore avienent sont les senefiances et les demostrances dou Saint Graal, ne li signe dou Saint Graal n'aparront ja a pecheor ne a home envelopé de pechié" [The adventures which are about to take place are the signs and manifestations of the Holy Grail. And the signs of the Holy Grail will never appear to a sinner or to a man steeped in sin] (p. 160 f.). Furthermore, the very unpredictability of so many of the incidents in the secular romances might imply that the hero, far from being master of his fate, was at all times subject to Fortune, and from this it is only a step to the view that the Christian knight is essentially a passive agent, fighting only when he must and totally dependent on the will of God. Such dependence is fostered by the vagueness with which the Grail Quest is defined in space and time; deprived of the human or talismanic guides usual in the secular romances, the hero must wander at hazard until God wills that he should attain to his goal: "Sire, fet li hermites, nus ne vos puet enseignier la voie, se la volentez Dieu ne vos i mainne" [Sir, says the hermit, no one can show you the way if the Divine Will does not bring you to it].[5] The basic pattern of events in *GGK* offers similar opportunities to an author with a taste for Christian allegory. It is true that since the number of incidents is very restricted, there will be less possibility of variety or subtlety in the delinea-

---

[4] Compare *GGK* 718 f.:

> So mony meruayl bi mount þer þe mon fyndeȝ,
> Hit were to tore to telle of þe tenþe dole.

[5] *Perlesvaus, Le Haut Livre du Graal*, ed. Nitze and Jenkins (Chicago, 1932–1937), I, 948 f. In this romance there is much less formal allegory than in *QSG*, but there is an important scene of exegesis in lines 2153–2252.

tion of spiritual progress, but this narrower range of action has the negative virtue of avoiding the bloodshed inseparable from the endless bouts of fighting in the romances. In *QSG* such combats are retained in something very like their original form, and it is clear that the author's ingenuity is exercised in assimilating them into their new context. At one point, he excuses the manslaughter on the grounds of the diabolical nature of the enemy (p. 231), but this entails a rather suspicious amount of verbal juggling, and Galahad is not easily convinced that the bloodshed was unavoidable. A solution probably more to his taste was to shift the responsibility for such actions to knights like Gawain, who were never meant as patterns of perfection, and so could be condemned without reservation: "Et certes, se vos ne fussiez si pechierres come vos estes, ja li set frere ne fussent ocis par vos ne par vostre aide, ainz feissent encore lor penitance . . . et s'acordassent a Dieu" [And certainly, if you were not the sinner that you are, the seven brothers would never have been slain by you nor with your help, but would yet do penance and put themselves right with God] (p. 54).

In *GGK* this problem never really arises. On the rare occasions on which the hero's incidental adventures are mentioned, it is in so laconic a fashion as quite to gloss over the possibility of bloodshed:

> At vche warþe oþer water þer þe wyȝe passed,
> He fonde a foo hym byfore, bot ferly hit were,
> & þat so foule & so felle þat feȝt hym by-hode.
> (715–717)

(It should also be noted that the other opponents mentioned in this stanza are no more than beasts or monstrous human beings.) The general impression does nothing to disturb the picture of Gawain as a passive, suffering agent, that emerges so clearly from the description of the hardships of winter in lines 726–732.

We may conclude, therefore, that the broad outlines of *GGK* are perfectly well suited to a romance in which the hero was a devout Christian; we may also concede that the very economy of its structure would be well adapted to support a reasonably self-consistent allegory of the Christian life. The point at issue is, of course, whether the *Gawain*-poet produced the second of these at the same time as writing the first, and to attempt an answer we shall—with the the help of *QSG*—investigate the following points: (1) Does the author make use of romance motifs that by their own nature suggest a spiritual meaning? (2) Where his material is not of this kind, does he attempt to rectify the balance by directing our attention towards the new (or true) significance of it? (3) Do any full-scale passages of exegesis suggest that the author of *GGK*, like that of *QSG*, would always bring out the moral or theological *significatio* in full, or that he might leave the reader to work out some points for himself?[6]

(1) *QSG* is particularly useful in pointing out the differences between those adventures which adapt themselves naturally to a Christian significance and those which need a certain amount of reworking before they can do so. As might be expected, incidents of the first type are those which had some aura of the supernatural about them in their primitive form. A striking example is found in the author's borrowing from Chrétien's *Charrete*[7] of the encounter with the apparently ferocious but actually harmless lions at the entrance to the Perilous Castle. The incident in Chrétien already has a significance that goes beyond its surface meaning in that—like some other moments in the same romance—it communicates the idea that the more resolutely dangers are faced, the more quickly they evaporate. In other words, it implies some degree of faith, although of an

---

[6] Mr. Schnyder makes much of this second possibility: "the modern student of medieval literature has to bear in mind that allegorical writers, working for scholarly and courtly circles, knew exactly that their audience was . . . looking forward to having its ingenuity taxed." (p. 29)

[7] Ed. M. Roques, CFMA, 86 (1958), ll. 3032 ff.

unspecified kind, and it is therefore quite logical for the author of *QSG* to have taken matters a stage further by making the issue one of trust in God. Lancelot, faced with the two lions guarding the Grail Castle, draws his sword only to have it knocked from his grasp by a hand from heaven. A voice reproaches him for trusting more in his weapons than in the power of his creator (p. 253).

The severely restricted action of *GGK* makes it unlikely that it could offer many examples of the use of such supernatural motifs, and the only part of the story that is really affected is the Beheading Game itself, most notably its conclusion at the Green Chapel. At this point we can detect more than one layer of evocative material. At the most fundamental level, the first of the beheading stories in *Bricriu's Feast* (the so-called Terror version) contributes the sinister effect of setting the scene in wild country: on the other hand, some of the most impressive of the individual details recall material associated with the Grail theme of the Perilous Chapel ("þe place . . . ful perelous is halden," the guide warns the hero in line 2097). Particularly important are the visits to such a chapel described in the Second and Third Continuations of *Perceval*.[8] In both of these, a corpse is said to lie on the chapel altar, and the candle or taper that is the only source of light in the building is suddenly extinguished by a black hand. On the second visit Perceval is obliged to fight, in the dark, with this hand, and at one point sees a face that can only be the devil's appearing at a window.[9] This is perhaps the most sensational version of the scene, but it is also worth mentioning two episodes which stand near the beginning of *Perlesvaus*. The first concerns *la chapele Saint Augustin;* the second, *li chastiax du Noir hermite* [the castle of the Black hermit]. Both of these buildings are situated at the bottom of a

[8] See especially lines 34434 ff. and 39787 ff. of *Perceval le Gallois,* ed. C. Potvin (Brussels, 1866–1871).

[9] Compare *GGK* 2193: "Now I fele hit is þe fende, in my fyue wytteȝ."

gorge (ll. 283, 747; compare *GGK* 2144 f.), while the second is also described as "hideus" (compare the "ugly" of *GGK* 2190) and stands near a mountain stream: "qui . . . aloit si ledement bruiant que ce sanbloit estre esfodres de tonnoire" [which . . . rushed with such noise that it seemed to be a clap of thunder] (752 f.).[10] There is nothing inherently evil about the chapel (although it proves fatal to anyone but the person destined to visit it), but the castle is later identified with hell, and the hermit who keeps it with the devil (2180–83).

Whatever else the author of *GGK* made of the scene at the Green Chapel, he did not take very far the suggestion that the Christian hero was on the point of encountering the powers of darkness, nor indeed could he have done so in view of his source material. For in spite of some ambiguous traits in his pedigree, the composite figure of the Host and the Green Knight is imagined throughout in so benevolent a light that he cannot really assume the diabolical aspect of the monster of the *Second Continuation*.[11] And yet we are made to feel the imminence of an evil as malevolent as that which actually materializes in the earlier text. Both Gawain and the reader are convinced that the devil is on the point of appearing, and while the Chapel contains neither corpse nor tomb it has in itself enough resemblance to a burial mound to suggest that the meeting will be fatal to the hero. It is also noteworthy that, in belying by its primitive appearance the expectations aroused by the word "chapel," it doubles the hero's misgivings; that the

[10] Compare the description of the noise of the grinding in *GGK* 2199–2204, of which the context ("biȝonde þe broke," 2200) and some of the phrasing ("hit wharred and whette as water at a mulle," 2203) suggest and earlier account which had nothing to do with the beheading story, and in which the noise was produced by the stream alone.

[11] Nor indeed does the author's tendency to rationalize his effects suggest that he would ever have allowed the *deablerie* to be as concretely embodied (or to go as far) as in this text.

term could be used of so obviously unhallowed a spot seems deeply perverse to him:

> "Þis is a chapel of meschaunce,—þat chekke hit by-tyde!
> Hit is þe corsedest kyrk þat euer I com inne."
>
> (2195 f.)

In this respect *GGK* carries to extremes a detail in *QSG* that conveys the true nature of the "chapel" to which Bohort is led by the false hermit: "Boorz quiert amont et aval, mes il ne voit ne eve beneoite ne croiz ne nule veraie enseigne de Jhesucrist" [Bohort looks up and down (the chapel), but sees neither holy water, cross, nor any true sign of Jesus Christ] (p. 178). Here too, the shortcomings of the fabric are clearly significant. But the differences in tone between these two passages are more important than any similarities of detail. In *QSG* our apprehension of the real nature of the "chapel" guides our response to the people who inhabit it, and the justness of this response is confirmed by later events. In *GGK,* however, the Green Knight and Chapel can only stand for the devil and one of his works in a very temporary sense, and the real point of the identification is to augment the already powerful sense of doom that informs the whole of this section. Gawain's reaction is emotional and instinctive, and it would be overliteral to tease any spiritual significance out of the fact that the five senses so highly praised in 640 let him down so badly in 2193.

No other of the romance motifs used in *GGK* possesses the spiritual and imaginative potentialities of the Green Chapel, but it could be argued that since some form of the Perilous Castle must lie behind Bercilak's dwelling, this last had possessed certain Otherworld features which the poet could easily have exploited if he had wished it to suggest the Heavenly City—which is what Mr. Schnyder maintains it does suggest.[12] But far from enlarging on this aspect of the castle, the poet seems largely

---

[12] "The poet employs overtones that can scarcely fail to create an atmosphere of otherworldliness" (p. 55).

to have suppressed the kind of detail conventionally used in medieval poetry of Otherworld palaces and cities:

> Cristal la piere resanbloit
> Dont li palais estoit tos fais
> Et a conpas trestos portrais;
> A vaute fu covers d'argent
> Et par desus a pavement.
> Une escarboucle sus luissoit,
> Plus que solaus resplendissoit
> Et par nuit rent se grant clarté
> Con se ce fust en tans d'esté.[13]

[The palace was built wholly of a stone which looked like crystal and was all painted with consummate art. The vault was covered with silver and the walls above were tiled. A carbuncle shone up high and glowed brighter than the sun. And at night it gave off as much light as if it were summertime.]

Only *GGK* 772, "As hit schemered & schon þurʒ þe schyre okeʒ," belongs to this tradition.[14] In the same way, we might at first suppose that the Temptation scenes by presenting a situation charged with moral and spiritual danger could easily be made to figure a wider conflict between the powers of good and evil. This kind of enlargement of the spiritual horizons is actually achieved in *QSG*, in the scene of Perceval's temptation. Like Gawain, Perceval comes to his senses before he has actually committed sin with the lady, crosses himself—and so causes the whole enchantment to vanish—and attempts to make reparation for his weakness by wounding himself in the thigh (pp. 108–110). The hermit he encounters a little later spends most of his time in outlining the wider spiritual issues that were in-

[13] Renaut de Beaujeu, *Li Biaus Descouneus,* ed. G. Perrie Williams, CFMA, 38 (1929), ll. 1908–16.

[14] Contrast the very full use of such imagery in the description of the Heavenly Jerusalem in *Pearl* 989 ff. Even the *escarboucle* survives in modified form:

> Of sunne ne mone had þay no nede;
> Þe self God watʒ her lombe-lyʒt. (1045 f.)

volved. The lady, he says, was not just the occasion of a single mortal sin but the devil incarnate, and as such there are no limits to her ambitions as a temptress; her round tent symbolizes the world, her concern that Perceval should not remain outside in the sun, the fear that the sinner might feel the beneficent influence of the sun of Christ (p. 114).

By contrast, the scenes in *GGK* have a rather parochial air about them. The author's own comments never once suggest that the lady is anything more than she appears to be; their function is simply to remind the reader of the dangerous tendencies of the elegant and cheerful exchanges:

> Þus hym frayned þat fre & fondet hym ofte,
> Forto haf wonnen hym to woȝe, what-so scho þoȝt elleȝ. (1549 f.)
> Gret perile bi-twene hem stod,
> Nif Mar[y]e of hir knyȝt [con] mynne. (1768 f.)

Moreover, the generally lighthearted tone makes it difficult to give full literal (let alone allegorical) weight to any Christian imagery that appears. Even the sign of the cross, that is attended with such devastating results in *QSG*, "Et lors fist le signe de la croiz en mi son front, et maintenant vit le paveillon verser, et une fumee et une nublece fu entor lui, si grant que il ne pot veoir goute; et il senti si grant puor de totes parz qu'il li fu avis que il fust en enfer" [And then he made the sign of the cross on his forehead, and thereupon saw the tent collapse, and a cloud of smoke enveloped him, so thick that he could not see a thing; and he smelled such a foul stench all around him that he thought he was in Hell] (p. 110), becomes part of a half-humorous pretense on Gawain's part that he has only just realized that the lady is standing beside his bed:

> Þen he wakenede & wroth & to-hir-warde torned
> & vn-louked his yȝe-lyddeȝ & let as hym wondered,
> & sayned hym, as bi his saȝe þe sauer to worthe with hande.
> (1200–02)

Here as elsewhere, the texture of the poem discourages any attempt to extract a coherent spiritual significance from the action.

(2) We must now turn to the use of "secular" motifs in a way that contradicts rather than exploits their original tendency; a use that makes it necessary to provide careful pointers to the new meaning, to prevent the traditional implications from dominating the scene. Perhaps the best example of this in *QSG* is an incident that forms part of a complex episode in which Bohort is the principal actor:

> il encontra . . . deus chevaliers qui menoient Lyonel son frere tout nu en braies sus un roncin grant et fort, les mains liees devant le piz, et tenoit chascuns plein son poign d'espines poignanz, dont il l'aloient batant si durement que li sans li sailloit de plus de cent parz contreval le dos, si qu'il en ert sanglanz devant et derrieres. Et il ne disoit onques mot, come cil qui estoit de grant cuer, ainz soffroit tout ce qu'il li fesoient si com s'il n'en sentist riens. (p. 175)
>
> [He came upon . . . two knights who were leading away his brother Lyonel, clad only in his breeches, on a huge and stout pack horse, his hands bound in front of his chest. And each knight held a handful of sharp thorns with which they kept hitting him so hard that his blood flowed down his back from more than a hundred places, and he was covered with it in front and behind. And never did he say a word, brave man that he was, but suffered all they were doing to him as if he felt nothing of it.]

This recalls such scenes as the maltreatment of the nephews of Gawain by Harpin in Chrétien's *Yvain*,[15] and the natural reaction of the reader, as of Bohort, is to feel pity for Lyonel and a certain impatience with a maiden who, by choosing just that moment to be threatened with rape, makes her own claim on Bohort's chivalrous instincts, and so prevents him from going immediately to his brother's rescue. These reactions seem confirmed by what follows: Bohort meets with a hermit who shows him the corpse of Lyonel and reproaches him with having a false sense of priorities. In other words, the natural effect of the scene is reinforced by testimony that—in the context of *QSG*—has almost the authority of Holy Writ. And yet these reactions are mistaken. Lyonel is not really dead at all and is

[15] Ed. M. Roques, CFMA, 89 (1960) ll. 4084–96.

proved by his subsequent conduct to be a scoundrel; the hermit is in fact diabolical and subsequently leads Bohort into a place where he is subjected to sensual temptation. With such deliberate denial of expectation, it is essential that the author should provide clear hints of the true nature of both Lyonel and the hermit; the first of these (which suggests that Bohort was quite right to abandon Lyonel's cause in favor of the maiden's) occurs in a dream in which the hero sees a rotten trunk close to two beautiful lilies and is warned: "se tu voiz tele aventure avenir, que tu ne lesses pas ces flors perir por le fust porri secorre. Car se trop grant ardor les sorprent, eles porront tost perir" [Should such an adventure befall you, take care not to let these flowers perish just to save the rotten trunk. For if too great a heat catches them, they may soon perish] (p. 171). This is far from specific,[16] but at least warns us that Bohort will soon be faced with a situation in which he has to choose between two possible courses of action, while the course recommended uses terms (*ces flors, se trop grant ardor les sorprent*) much more likely to apply to the maiden and the misguided young man who attempts to force her, than to Lyonel and his two tormentors. As for the false hermit, hints of his true nature are given from his first appearance ([*il*] *chevauchoit un cheval plus noir que meure* [(he) was riding a horse blacker than a berry])[17] and become progressively stronger. The formula *ce li est avis* [so it seems to him] casts doubts on whether the dead body that he shows to Bohort is in fact that of Lyonel, and the suspect nature of the chapel to which he leads the hero is obvious from its lack of cross and holy water.[18] Most dubious of all are the terms in which this "hermit" expresses the opinion that Bohort should have helped Lyonel in preference to the maiden: "Certes mielz fust que toutes les puceles dou monde fussent

[16] It is not explained in detail until p. 187.

[17] As a general rule the hermits of *QSG* are much less mobile than this, of greater age, and (sometimes) robed in white.

[18] See the quotation on p. 92.

despucelees qui il fust ocis" [Better, certainly, that all the maidens in the world were deflowered than that he should be slain] (p. 179). No more unlikely verdict could have been expected, in view of the otherwise constant exaltation of chastity in *QSG*.

When we turn to *GGK* we find the author much less concerned to provide pointers to the real meaning of deceptive events. Even on the purely literal plane, he says nothing that allows us to grasp the schemes and true motives of the host and the two ladies of the castle; instead, the revelation of these is put off until the very end of the romance, where it comes as a considerable shock.[19] On the other hand it could be argued that he does suggest that the information provided by Gawain's guide to the Green Chapel is misleading. Some hint of this is certainly necessary, since the place is not really "perelous," the knight who keeps it not "þe worst vpon erþe," nor one who fights with a club (as 2105 implies). What pointers there are appear in 2121 ff., where the guide is made to propose something as obviously out of key with the general moral tone, as the hermit's low rating of chastity had been in *QSG:*

> & [I] hete yow fyrre
> Þat I shal swere bi God & alle his gode halȝeȝ,
> As help me God & þe halydam & oþeȝ in-noghe,
> Þat I shal lelly yow layne & lauce neuer tale
> Þat euer ȝe fondet to fle for freke þat I wyst.

His willingness to perjure himself might be held to brand him as a renegade Christian from whom no good counsel can ever be expected, and, by extension, make it likely that he will also misrepresent facts when it serves his purpose to do so. But it is one thing to abstract this, retrospectively, from the text, and quite another to feel that it really cancels out the powerful sense of menace evoked by the untrustworthy companion,

---

[19] To Dr. von Schaubert this tendency to mislead the reader was one of the author's chief artistic sins, and one unthinkable in an Old French writer of romance (*Englische Studien*, LVII (1923), 396 f.).

especially when we remember that the author has already alluded to the meeting at the Green Chapel in very much the same terms as the guide:

> þat tene place
> Þer þe ruful race he shulde re-sayue.
> (2075 f.)

It all comes rather too late; even if we draw the inferences about the guide's character, we are still expecting the worst for the hero.

(3) It remains to consider the large-scale passages of exegesis that are to be found in *GGK*. In *QSG* passages of this kind occur throughout the text, are developed at considerable length, and are by far the most important means by which the author communicates the allegorical meaning to the reader. For it is noteworthy that, in spite of all the hints with which they are supplied, the heroes of the quest are rarely inclined to work out this meaning for themselves. Even when the "significant" adventure or vision involves traditional Christian symbols (such as the bird that feeds its offspring on its own blood on p. 167 f.), the knights will do no more than assert that there must indeed be *mout grant senefiance* [a deep significance] there, and then go off in search of the nearest hermit to get the whole story. This could spring from the conviction that exegesis was a skilled trade, at which amateurs ought not to try their hand; it could on the other hand suggest that the author wished to insure that his meaning was grasped by the less as well as the more alert of his readers—could betray, in fact, a very natural desire to insure against the possibility of being misunderstood.[20]

In *GGK* there are really only two passages of this kind; the description of the pentangle and the explanation which the Green Knight gives of the events of the story in 2345 ff. The

---

[20] Neither possibility much supports Mr. Schnyder's view of author-reader relationships in the Middle Ages.

first of these is relatively straightforward and neatly self-contained. But it should be noted that although the pentangle is a happy choice as an emblem of Gawain's virtues (since it combines the perfection and unity of the circle[21] with a degree of inner variety that offers greater opportunities to the allegorist), the actual filling out of the "fyue and sere fyue syþeȝ" has placed a certain strain upon his powers (the introduction of the hero's "fyue fyngres" as one of the five groups has all the appearance of being a makeweight). More successful is the way in which these virtues are related to some fixed points of the Christian faith, and the interdependence of the two suggested by juxtaposing Gawain's personal emblem with an image of the Virgin, on his shield. The untypical self-consistency of the whole passage recalls the method of *QSG* more firmly than anything else in *GGK;* recalls, indeed, the description of Galahad's shield in the former, since at one point in its career this had carried a Christian icon as valuable in battle as the one that so heartened Gawain (*GGK,* 650); "Et quant il se vit en tel peril que il cuidoit veraiement morir, il descovri son escu et vit ou mileu un home crucefié qui toz estoit sanglenz. Si dist les paroles que Josephes li ot enseigniees, dont il ot victoire et honor et fu gitez des mains a ses anemis" [And when he saw himself in such mortal peril, he bared his shield and saw in the middle of it a man on a cross all covered with blood. And he uttered the words which Joseph had taught him. This brought him victory and honor, and he was delivered from the hands of his enemies] (p. 32 f.). But both before and after this time it was marked with a simple red cross, and so, in its own way, relates an emblem to a Christian image.

The second passage—the hundred or so lines that follow the encounter at the Green Chapel—is more fully characteristic of the poet, and in spite of some confusing elements (notably

---

[21] Since it "ne samned neuer in no syde, ne sundred nouþer" (659); compare the description of the Pearl of Great Price as "endeleȝ rounde" in *Pearl* 738.

the diffuse presentation and an alternation of tone from indulgence on the part of Bercilak to frantic self-accusation on that of Gawain), its most significant features are undeniably Christian.[22] But it is equally important to recognize that there is no attempt to interpret any of the incidents of the tale in the rather *recherché* manner of *QSG*. None of these is made to stand for wider Christian issues (as Bohort's defense of the oppressed chatelaine is seen as the defence of Holy Church against its enemies on p. 185 of *QSG*), nor does Bercilak regard the animals of the hunting scenes as emblems of diverse spiritual conditions (as *li torel vairié* [the spotted bulls] represent the sinful knights of the Round Table on p. 156). The tone is at all times realistic and practical; Bercilak contents himself, either with pointing a fairly obvious moral ("Bot here yow lakked a lyttel, sir, & lewte yow wonted," 2366), or with establishing a simple causal relationship between Gawain's varying performance in the test of loyalty and the different nature of the three blows struck at him. In short, in this passage as in the rest of *GGK* there is little to suggest that the author intended the reader to extract any *senefiance* more abstruse than a recognition of the value of Christian morality. Moreover, the tardy appearance of this passage (like that in which the guide's true nature is revealed) seems part of a broader tendency to build up a most powerfully imaginative effect and then largely dispel it by rationalization.[23] It is, I think, significant that Mr. Schnyder should hardly ever take this side of *GGK* into consideration at all.

And yet it must be said that however little this passage encourages a fully allegorical reading of *GGK,* it does—in an

[22] Mr. John Burrow, indeed, has demonstrated that the scene is in many respects an informal "confession" that in sincerity exceeds that which Gawain makes to a priest in 1876–84. See "The Two Confession Scenes in Gawain and the Green Knight," *MP,* LVII (1959), 73–79.

[23] The startling effect of the *first* appearance of the Green Knight is partly negated by Arthur's reassuring "explanation" of the scene to Guenevere (467–473).

oblique fashion—support Mr. Schnyder's rather critical attitude towards Gawain.[24] For Gawain, by three times accusing himself of the sin of *couetyse* as well as of *cowardyse* (2374, 2380, and 2508) as well as by some untypically bitter and cynical statements about women (2414–28), seems here to evoke a side of his character that the author of *GGK* normally took pains either to suppress or make respectable—his evil reputation as a seducer, who is bound to fail in the supreme test: "Gauvain n'a jamais été un héros du Graal: chevaleresque, intrépide, courtois, il est toujours sensual, brutal avec les femmes avec quelque chose de désabusé qui lui interdit le gain et la conquête des Objets Merveilleux" [Gawain was never a Grail hero: chivalrous, intrepid, courteous, he is always sensual, brutal with women, and has a touch of disillusionment which prevents him from winning and conquering the Marvelous Objects].[25] Particularly interesting to the study of *GGK* are certain romances in which his character is generally admirable, but tarnished to a greater or lesser degree by past weaknesses. In Wirnt von Gravenberc's *Wigalois,* for example, he is prevented from complete success in a test of virtue by the fact that:

> als ichz ofte hân vernomen:
> eine maget wol getân
> die greif er über ir willen an,
> sô daz si weinde under schrê.
> deheiner slahte untugent mê
> er von sîner kintheit nie
> unz an sînen tôt begie.[26]

[As I have often heard it said: He seized a maid of wondrous beauty against her will, so that she wept and cried. No other kind of breach of virtue did he commit from his childhood to his death.]

[24] Which receives exuberant expression on pp. 50 and 72 of his study.
[25] J. Marx, *La Légende Arthurienne et le Graal* (Paris, 1952), p. 387.
[26] Ed. J. M. N. Kapteyn (Bonn, 1926), ll. 1510–16. Wirnt's efforts on Gawain's behalf are in their way as unremitting as those of the author of *GGK*; see the apologetic tone of lines 562–577.

Perlesvaus places a stronger emphasis on his previous short-comings of this kind. In an episode long recognized as cognate with one of the Temptation scenes in *GGK*,[27] his past reputation as a philanderer is evoked by the ladies who are attempting to seduce him (although in fact lines 1259–61 make it plain that he has been a reformed character ever since entering upon the Quest for the Grail): "Par Dieu, fet l'une a l'autre, se ce fust cil Gavains qui niés est le roi Artu, il parlast a nos autrement, e trovissions en lui plus de deduit que en cestui; mes cist est uns Gavains contrefez" [Certainly, says one lady to another, if this were Gawain, King Arthur's nephew, he would speak to us in another fashion, and we should find in his company more diversion than we do in this one's. This is a fake Gawain, if you ask me]. Against this passage Miss Thomas set *GGK* 1297 ff.:

> "So god as Gawayn gaynly is halden,
> And cortaysye is closed so clene in hym-seluen,
> Couth not ly3tly haf lenged so long wyth a lady,
> Bot he had craued a cosse bi his courtaysye,
> Bi sum towch of summe tryfle at sum tale3 ende."[28]

The interest of the comparison to the present discussion is that it shows to what extent the author of *GGK* contrived to adapt some of the less admirable sides of his hero to agree with his new, almost completely noble characterization of him. He does not—like the authors of *Wigalois* and *Perlesvaus*—choose to view Gawain's carnal frailty as something that was once a fact, but is now over and done with, but instead throws a veil of ambiguity over both his past reputation and his present conduct. This is to some extent a matter of terminology. His traditional skill as a lover becomes a familiarity with good breeding ("hendelayk," "cortaysye") in all its forms, and as such is the outward sign of an inner moral purity. Of course, both aspects of Gawain have been so thoroughly stressed in the rest of the

---

[27] By Miss M. C. Thomas: see p. xxxiii of Gollancz's edition.
[28] Note also Gawain's "Þa3 I be not now he þat 3e of speken" (1242).

work that we are conscious, not of any discrepancy between
his past and present behavior, but (helped by the author's com-
ments) of one between the lady's brand of "courtesy"—which
in reality is simply lechery—and that of Gawain. From Gawain's
own point of view, however, this solution has its disadvantages,
since it makes his defense against the lady's advances very much
more difficult. His namesake in *Perlesvaus* can simply refuse to
take any notice of his temptresses, and Bohort in *QSG* will even
allow the ladies of the tower to commit suicide rather than
imperil his own soul (p. 181 f.), but Gawain, trapped by the
two-edged quality of "cortaysye," cannot defend his purity by
simple rudeness, since to do this would impair the very quality
that the lady is menacing in a more obvious way:

> He cared for his cortaysye, lest craþayn he were,
> And more for his meschef, ȝif he schulde make synne.
> (1773 f.)

Moreover, the clear-cut reactions of the heroes in *QSG* and
Perlesvaus are made easier by the fundamental kinship that
exists between the character of the spiritually good knight and
that of the Grail Quest he has undertaken. In *GGK* there is
no such equivalence; Gawain has almost all the qualities of a
knight of the Grail, but what he is *explicitly* seeking relates only
to the more mundane of those qualities—loyalty and endur-
ance—not to chastity or spiritual intensity.

In the scene with Bercilak, the "Old Gawain" of tradition
emerges still more obviously; the knight who failed at the Grail
Castle because of his pride and inability to keep his mind off
the opposite sex: "Apres regarda la pucele[29] qui tant estoit bele
et gente et plaisans si sesmerueille moult de la grant biaute
dont elle est si plaine . quil ne set riens del uaissel" [Then he
looked at the maiden who was so fair, elegant, and comely that
he is filled with wonder at her great beauty; so much so that

[29] The Grail bearer.

he is oblivious of the vessel].[30] Certainly the moral that closes his outburst against women in *GGK* could have come from this Gawain at his most cynical:

> hit were a wynne huge
> To luf hom wel and leue hem not, a leude þat couþe.
>
> (2420 f.)

which is not precisely a counsel to chastity. For a very brief space, this "Old Gawain" tends to stand between us and the author's carefully groomed hero. Here, as in the Temptation scenes, the two characters are not related in terms of past and present, but simply coexist (though more awkwardly than before). The process may have been assisted by Gawain's self-accusation of "couetyse," to which attention has already been drawn. This troublesome word, taken by Mr. D. F. Hills to mean "inordinate love of self, of one's life,"[31] but seen by Mr. J. Burrow as little more than a token of Gawain's extravagant and badly-focused remorse,[32] may possibly have been meant here in the sense of "lustful desire," and so belong to the kind of characterization of Gawain that is implied by his explosion against women. Of course, even if this interpretation is correct, "couetyse" must refer less to an actual sin than to the imagining of such a sin by a hypersensitive conscience. But it can hardly be an accident that the picture which this passage gives of a Gawain who is convinced that he has failed in the supreme testing adventure because of his lecherous tendencies should so exactly correspond with the traditional Gawain who really did fail in the Quest, and who actually *used* women in the manner of the Old Testament examples of *GGK* 2416–19. As in the Temptation scenes, there has been some accommodation of the old tradition to the new context and "sen"—largely by the

---

[30] H. O. Sommer, *The Vulgate Version of the Arthurian Romances* (Washington, 1908–1913), IV, 344.

[31] "Gawain's Fault in *Sir Gawain and the Green Knight*," *RES.*, N.S., XIV (1963), 124–131.

[32] J. Burrow, *MP*, LVII (1959), p. 77 f.

heavy underlining of the venial nature of the fault by the Green Knight—but some features have proved intractable and stand out rather noticeably. Even in the most careful hands the Arthurian motifs possessed a will of their own, and in asserting it, produced results confusing to later critics in search of a single master key to their text.

PART THREE:

STYLE AND TECHNIQUE

6

THE STYLE OF *SIR GAWAIN*

Larry D. Benson

I. THE ANALYTIC FUNCTION OF THE SYNTAX

THE POTENTIAL DISADVANTAGES of the alliterative syntax of *Sir Gawain and the Green Knight*—its tendencies toward mere repetition of form and content—are far outweighed by its advantages. Like the varied synonyms, this syntax is less an ornament than a tool of analysis, a method of defining concepts at the same time it presents them, and it leads to a style that depends upon particulars and implies rather than states the generalizations. This is apparent even in the traditional formulas, for most of them are analytical, formulized enumerations and progressions that provide a ready means of defining a concept by the parallel juxtaposition of its parts. The solid texture of *Sir Gawain* is largely due to the poet's development of this analytical syntax. For example, the common full-line formula for expressing the general idea that a city has been destroyed is that which appears in the *Destruction of Troy:* "Betyn and brent doun vnto bare askes" (line 5007). The formula is naturally analytical; it defines the destruction by the events—first

Reprinted from *Art and Tradition in Sir Gawain and the Green Knight* by Larry D. Benson, pp. 151–166, by permission of Rutgers University Press. © 1965 by Rutgers, The State University. The abbreviations *WA* and *MA* stand for *The Wars of Alexander* and *Morte Arthure*. All quotations from *Sir Gawain* are taken from Tolkien and Gordon's edition (Oxford, 1930).

the city broken down (by siege engines) and then the burning
—and by their result—"vnto bare askes." The *Gawain*-poet
extends the analysis even further when he writes "þe borʒ brit-
tened and brent to brondeʒ and askeʒ" (2). The substitution
of "brondeʒ" for a modifier of "askeʒ" extends the analysis
to the result, and by coupling this with the preceding line, which
is based on the formula used to report an attack on a town—
"Siþen þe sege and þe assaut watʒ sesed at Troye"—the
analysis is extended to a brief narrative: first there was the siege
(the necessary bombardment of the walls) and then, when a
breach was made, the assault itself, after which the city is first
reduced to rubble and then put to the torch, leaving flaming
brands and finally ashes.

The same technique, the same dependence on analysis and
specification rather than generalization, is used throughout the
poem, whether the events are as grand as the fall of Troy or
as relatively simple as the Green Knight's mounting his horse.
The usual full line formula for narrating this act is "Stridis into
stele-bowe, stertis vpon lofte" (*WA, 778*); "He sterte tille his
sterepe and stridez one lofte" (*MA, 916*). The *Gawain*-poet,
as usual, extends the analysis the formula provides. The Green
Knight turns,

> And syþen boʒeʒ to his blonk, þe brydel he cachcheʒ,
> Steppeʒ into stelbawe and strydeʒ alofte.
>
> (434–435)

The additional detail—"þe brydel he cachcheʒ"—is just enough
to fill out the vivid little scene provided by the formula, and we
see each stage of the action as the Green Knight seizes his bridle,
steps into the stirrup, and swings himself onto his mount.

That the three verbs are stages of a single action is apparent
from the "he" that governs them, for the poet introduces a
new subject only when a new action begins. The lines preced-
ing those quoted contain a different series of verbal variations
ending with "Boʒeʒ to his blonk," and they describe the one

smooth movement in which the challenger reaches out, snatches up the head, holds it aloft, and turns to his horse (432–435a). Mounting the horse is a new act and so it calls for a new subject, the "he" of the second half-line of the passage quoted above. In short, the introduction of a new subject rather than a new verb defines the major actions analytically presented by the variations.

This trait sometimes leads to apparently puzzling constructions:

> Þe burne blessed hym bilyue, and þe bredeʒ passed—
> Prayses þe porter bifore þe prynce kneled,
> Gef hym God and goud day, þat Gawayn he saue—
> And went on his way with his wyʒe one.
>
> (2071–74)

Gawain's act of departing is not completed until he "went on his way." The poet therefore introduces no new subject for "went" even though the actions of the porter intervene between that verb and its subject. Likewise, modern usage does not allow constructions like this:

> ʒet quyl Al-hal-day with Arþer he lenges;
> And he made a fare on þat fest for þe frekeʒ sake.
>
> (536–537)

The second "he" refers to Arthur, a faulty reference from our point of view. Yet the reference is clear within the context of the poet's style, for the new subject implies a new action rather than a continuation of "lenges."

As the pronouns show, alliterative verse has its own syntactic rules, quite different from ours, and because of this the analytical function of variation probably escapes many readers. It is a generally paratactic syntax, characterized by simple connectives such as "and" and by the frequent omission of connectives altogether. Within the sentence the relationships between the variations are thus implied by their position rather than by explicit statement, and ellipsis is as characteristic of the period as repetition.[1] The usual structure of variation begins with a first half-line that contains a complete clause followed by the other half-lines that vary only the significant element. In verbal variation the subjects are elided, so that the effect is of a series of compressed clauses rather than simply a compounding of verbs: "Mist muged on þe mor, malt on þe mounteȝ" (2080). In nominal variation the verbs are elided: "For hit is my wede þat þou wereȝ, þat ilke wouen girdel" (2358). The varied elements are simply juxtaposed and the meaning depends on the context of the variation and the structure of the period. Consequently, the elliptical phrases are sometimes puzzling. A phrase like "Ticius to Tuskan" (11), for example, is meaningless in itself, a fact that led Madden, the first editor of *Sir Gawain,* to emend it to "Ticius to Tuskan *turnes.*" As later editors recognized, "turnes" is unnecessary; in context the parallel "Romulus to Rome ricchis" clarifies its later variation in the elliptical "Ticius to Tuskan."

The meaning of whole sentences is also often a matter of position rather than explicit statement, and asyndeton is almost as common in the poem as ellipsis. When the poet analyzes Arthur's reaction to the Green Knight's taunt, he writes:

> Wyth þis he laȝes so loude þat þe lorde greued;
> Þe blod schot for scham into his schyre face
>   and lere;
> He wex as wroth as wynde.
>
>   (316–319)

It is clear that first Arthur was annoyed, then he blushed for shame, and finally he became enraged, and it is almost equally obvious that the annoyance caused the shame, which then led to the anger. Yet the poet states none of these relations. He places the clauses side by side and allows their meaning to

---

[1] Kemp Malone, *A Literary History of England,* ed. A. C. Baugh et al. (New York, 1948) p. 28, remarks that all variation involves ellipsis, even appositive constructions.

emerge from the juxtaposition. Nonalliterative writers occasionally used asyndeton in this way, and it was a standard rhetorical tool (*dissolutio*) for achieving brevity, but in *Sir Gawain* and most other alliterative poems it appears throughout the work. This is hard on modern editors, who have to punctuate this verse, and, as almost any printed alliterative poem will show, dashes and semicolons are about the only solutions they have found. The hearer, however, has no such problem, for the parallel structures themselves make the syntactic relations clear.

When a connective is used, it is most often the simple *and,* which may smooth the transition from one clause to another, but which, like asyndeton, leaves the relationship undefined. The varied clauses are merely placed side by side, in sharp contrast to the sometimes elaborate subordination characteristic of nonalliterative writers such as Chaucer. For example, when the lady slips into Gawain's room, the *Gawain*-poet writes:

> Hit watȝ þe ladi, loflyest to beholde,
> Þat droȝ þe dor after hir ful dernly and stylle,
> And boȝed towarde þe bed; and þe burne schamed,
> And layde hym doun lystyly, and let as he slepte;
> And ho stepped stilly and stel to his bedde,
> Kest vp þe cortyn and creped withinne,
> And set hir ful softly on þe bed-syde.
>
> (1187–93)

But when Pandarus slips into Troilus' room, Chaucer writes:

> But Pandarus, that wel koude ech a deel
> The olde daunce, and every point therinne,
> Whan that he sey that alle thyng was wel,
> He thought he wolde upon his werk bigynne,
> And gan the stuwe doore al softe unpynne,
> And stille as stoon, withouten lenger lette,
> By Troilus adown right he hym sette.
>
> (*Tr,* III, 694–700)

In the passage from *Sir Gawain* the position of the clauses rather than the repeated "and" establishes the syntactic relations; in the passage from *Troilus* each clause is explicitly related to the others, first by connectives such as "Whan that" and then by the adverbial phrases that cluster about the final clause and explain exactly the connection of "he hym sette" to the rest of the action.

Such a cluster of adverbial phrases is rare in *Sir Gawain,* where the compounding of clauses rather than modifiers prevails. Consequently, compared to Chaucer's nonalliterative style, even the *Gawain*-poet's grammatically complex sentences seem to depend more on juxtaposition than on subordination. For example, the well-known similarities between the Green Knight's entry into Camelot and the entry of the strange knight into Cambyuskan's court in *The Squire's Tale* extend even to the periodic grammatical structures that the poets use to emphasize the contrast between the abrupt entry and the music and jollity of the feast that it interrupts:

> And oþer noyse ful newe neʒed biliue,
> Þat þe lude myʒt haf leue liflode to cach;
> For vneþe watʒ þe noyce not a whyle sesed,
> And þe fyrst cource in þe court kyndely serued,
> Þer hales in at þe halle dor an aghlich mayster.
>
> (*GGK,* 132–136)

> And so bifel that after the thridde cours,
> Whil that this kyng sit thus in his nobleye,
> Herknynge his mynstralles hir thynges pleye
> Biforn hym at the bord deliciously,
> In at the halle dore al sodeynly
> Ther cam a knyght upon a steede of bras.
>
> (*SqT,* 76–82)

The *Gawain*-poet's clauses are set out one after another with a minimum of connectives, and each of his five lines contains a clause, even the fourth with its elided "watʒ." Chaucer's clauses, on the other hand, are carefully subordinated in a pattern of elaborate modification.

The Chaucerian ease and fluency that later narrative poets took as their ideal is dependent upon this careful and explicit establishment of syntactic relations. However, Chaucer's triumph should not obscure for us the merits of the alliterative style. Perhaps there is less danger of this today than there was forty or fifty years ago, since modern poets, especially the Imagists with their insistence on presenting details rather than generalizations, have made us more receptive to a style based on variation. The technique of Pound's little poem "In a Station of the Metro" (which I quote in its entirety) is not much different from, though more compressed than, the variation of alliterative poetry:

> The apparition of these faces in the crowd;
> Petals on a wet, black bough.

Like the modern writer, the alliterative poet defines his concepts by the juxtaposition of their parts, capitalizing on the clash of perspectives that this technique allows. Such a style, in which the parts of an action, object, or concept are juxtaposed with a minimum of explicit explanation, leads at once to a multiplication of specific detail and to a structure that renders the details meaningful.

II. VARIATION: THE NARRATIVE STRUCTURE

The major importance of variation to the critic of *Sir Gawain* is the key it provides to the structure and meaning of the narrative, for the style of this poem is organic, and its basic stylistic trait affects every part of the work. The structure of the sentence, with its varied parallel constructions, its ellipses, its dependence on juxtaposition and analysis, is the model for the narrative as a whole. Because the style of the individual line and sentence has been so imperfectly understood, the structure and meaning of the poem have never been clear. It is no accident that the "unity" of the best alliterative poems has been a central problem for their critics, for the reader who approaches them with the same concept of structure that he brings to Chaucer or Gower is apt to find them badly constructed and poorly unified—a judgment that has been passed at some time or other on every good alliterative poem from *Beowulf* to

Sir Gawain. Scenes and episodes in such works do not exist in the straightforward causal order of most narratives. Each forms part of a series of variations composed of other passages similar in form and content, and the meaning of each is modified and illuminated by its variations, even though, as in the sentence, their relation is implied rather than stated explicitly.

The Chaucerian style leads to a completely different kind of narrative. Chaucer designates his characters with a small, repetitive vocabulary. He elaborately insists upon the exact designation, and his apparent eagerness to avoid ambiguity even leads him to combine the demonstrative adjective with the proper noun—"Lo heere this Arcite and this Palamoun."[2] That construction never appears in the work of the *Gawain*-poet; he often designates his character by "the" plus a noun—"þe knyȝt"—a construction that Chaucer almost never uses. Chaucer's syntax is marked by the same insistence on clear and exact specification—"Bifil that in that seson on a day"—and his narrative technique as a whole is characterized by the same trait. In *The Knight's Tale,* for example, when the narrator shifts from one line of action to another, he emphatically signals the transition to his audience:[3]

> Now wol I stynte of Palamon a lite,
> And lete hym in his prisoun stille dwelle,
> And of Arcita forth I wol yow telle.
> *(KnT,* 1334–36)

When the *Gawain*-poet shifts from one line of action to another, he does so within a single sentence:

> Þe lede with þe ladyeȝ layked alle day,
> Bot þe lorde ouer þe londeȝ launced ful ofte,
> Sweȝ his vncely swyn . . .
> (1560–62)

---

[2] See Cornelius Novelle, "The Demonstrative Adjective *This:* Chaucer's Use of a Colloquial Narrative Device," *MS,* XIX (1957), 246–249.

[3] Ruth Crosby, "Chaucer and the Custom of Oral Delivery," *Spec,* XIII (1938), 413–422.

And ȝe he lad hem bi lagmon, þe lorde and his meyny,
On þis maner bi þe mountes quyle myd-ouer-vnder,
Whyle þe hende knyȝt at home holsumly slepeȝ,
Withinne þe comly cortynes . . .

(1729–32)

Chaucer avoids such abrupt transitions because as a narrator he is so eager to confide in us; he does not want us to miss his meaning. His *Knight's Tale* is built on parallels and contrasts as finely wrought as those in *Sir Gawain,* but he is not content to leave his tale without Theseus' explicit pointing of the moral. In the *Troilus* Chaucer himself draws the meaning out for us, standing apart from his story to address the "yonge fresshe folkes, he or she." In the *Gawain*-poet's narrative, as within the sentence, the variations are juxtaposed without comment and the meaning is allowed to emerge from the structure. Gawain and the Green Knight each have a last word, and the less personal voice of the narrator does not intrude to tell us which is right.

H. L. Savage's analysis of the relation between the hunting and temptation scenes is probably the best-known explanation of narrative variation in *Sir Gawain* (though Savage, of course, does not call it "variation").[4] Until his article appeared, few critics understood the structure of the poem; indeed, one scholar argued for an English source on the basis of the apparent lack of skill with which the parts are joined together.[5] The two sets of scenes that Savage studied seem completely different. One takes place in a bedroom, the other in the forest. One concerns the niceties of courtship, the other the vigorous excitement of the chase, and one is almost pure action, the other almost pure dialogue. Yet, much as these two sets of scenes

[4] "The Significance of the Hunting Scenes in *Sir Gawain and the Green Knight," JEGP,* xxvii (1928), 1–15. Now reprinted as Chapter ii in Savage's *The Gawain-Poet, Studies in His Personality and Background* (Chapel Hill, 1956).

[5] Else von Schaubert, "Der englische Ursprung von *Syr Gawayn and the Grene Knyȝt," Englische Studien,* lvii (1923), 330–346.

117

differ in content and emphasis, their form is the same. As Savage demonstrates, they are almost exactly parallel, providing different but parallel viewpoints on a situation whose meaning can be understood only in the light of both narratives. Taken alone, Bercilak's hunt is just an exciting account of the chase, the temptation scenes sophisticated bedroom comedy with a ludicrous reversal of roles. Together they are a set of variations that blend to point up the nature of Gawain's trial and the extent of Bercilak's involvement in it. The lady, we realize, is not merely attempting to enjoy her lord's absence. She is as intent upon her prey as Bercilak upon his. Bercilak's pursuit of his quarry becomes a commentary on the lady's pursuit of Gawain, and Gawain's skillful replies become meaningful as the desperate fox "trantes and tornayeeȝ" in parallel fashion, finally attempting to escape through trickery only to run upon Bercilak's waiting sword.

The parallel series of scenes themselves have other parallel variations throughout the poem; Bercilak's capture of the fox is related to his final capture of Gawain, and its form is related to each of the previous hunts and to the lady's final victory. The lady's scene of triumph is related both to the hunts and previous temptations and to the other scenes in which bargains are made and broken, from the challenge itself, to the guide's temptation of the hero, to the final confrontation between Gawain and the Green Knight. The same principles that Savage discovered in the temptation scenes appear wherever one looks in the poem, for the parallel juxtaposition of apparently unrelated episodes is the basic characteristic of the narrative,[6] appearing even in the combination of the parallel but contrasting temptation and beheading tales, which posed the major problem of unity for the early critics.

Within the narrative one also finds the same sort of periodic, bracketing frameworks that contain and control the variations

[6]See Sylvan Barnett, "A Note on the Structure of *Sir Gawain and the Green Knight*," *MLN*, LXXI (1956), 319.

within the sentence. In the first fit, for example, each major stage of the action has its parallel variation, and each set of variations is bracketed within a limiting framework. The scene opens and closes with the feast that brackets the episode, which is indeed, as Arthur tells Guenevere, an "interlude" occurring between its courses. Within that framework is the Green Knight's amazing entrance and equally astonishing departure. When he enters, the action of his entry is suspended for the description of him and his equipment, which, as we have seen, is actually two descriptions juxtaposed by means of variation. Then the entry resumes and, once in the hall, the Green Knight states his challenge; the conditions he states are repeated, with more sinister overtones, when he leaves. Then Arthur accepts the challenge, but Gawain interrupts the action as suddenly as the Green Knight had done, and he also makes a request of Arthur. The king grants his request, and he kneels to receive the axe, just as the Green Knight, after a restatement of the bargain, bows to receive Gawain's blow, which is parallel to the blow that Arthur begins to deliver. The beheading is the heart of the episode, surrounded by the parallel structures. And the whole episode, including the feast itself, is enclosed within yet another set of parallel passages, the catalogue of Arthur's ancestors and the narrator's characterization of the king at the beginning of the poem, followed by his new comments on the king at the end of the first fit and the catalogue of the seasons at the beginning of the next.

In its broad outlines the entire poem is constructed on the same principle. It begins with the Troy story and a scene of happy celebration. Then follow the challenge and the beheading, the arming and departure of Gawain, and his journey to Bercilak's castle. There, after more banqueting, he undergoes three days of temptation, each day parallel to the others and all three days paralleled by the hunting scenes. Then Gawain again arms and departs. There is another journey, the return-blow, and finally the journey back to Camelot, where there is yet another celebration at court and a final reference to the Troy legend at the poem's end. The beheading plot brackets the temptation within its parallel delivery and return-blows, and the temptation itself is composed on a complex of variations within that framework.

From the standpoint of Chaucerian verse, this seems a peculiar and subtle method of narration. However, it was common in the poet's own literary tradition. The best Old English poetry was also built on the principle of structural variation. Poems like *The Wanderer* and *Seafarer* depend for their effect on parallel, secular and religious, restatements of the speakers' situations; and *Beowulf*, like *Sir Gawain*, is concentrated on a relatively small number of episodes that resemble one another in structure and content (Beowulf's three battles with the monsters) and that form significant parallel contrasts (Beowulf's initial triumph and final tragic death). The structure of the narrative is concentrated and appositional, enclosed within the framework of the burials at the beginning and end.[7] Evidently some of the Old English narrative techniques survived even in Middle English alliterative poetry, since one finds the same concern with parallels, contrasts, and variations in the narrative structure of poems such as *Morte Arthure, Golagros and Gawane,* and the *Awntyrs of Arthur* (all, like *Sir Gawain,* Arthurian poems of the northern, heavily ornamented and formulaic tradition of alliterative verse).[8]

So ancient a technique could be used in the fourteenth century because the general aesthetic of the period was especially

[7] For a full discussion see Brodeur, *Art of Beowulf* (Berkeley, 1959); A. C. Bartlett, *The Larger Rhetorical Patterns in Anglo-Saxon Poetry* (New York, 1935); Jean Bloomfield, "The Style and Structure of Beowulf," *RES,* XIV (1938), 396–403.

[8] See William Matthews, *The Tragedy of Arthur* (Berkeley, 1960), which includes a discussion of the structure of *Morte Arthure* and, on pp. 157–177, of the structures of *Awntyrs of Arthur* and *Golagros and Gawane.* E. von Schaubert [note 5 above] discusses the general resemblance of the structure of *Sir Gawain* to the structure of these works.

favorable to this kind of structural variation; the juxtaposition of parallel, opposing elements without an explicit statement of their relations is basically the technique of "dramatic conflict" that, as Hauser writes, dominates "the whole relation of Gothic art to nature and the inner structure of its composition."[9] When the contrast is between the courtly and the churlish or the sacred and the profane—between such completely contrasting characters as Gawain and the Green Knight—the dramatic conflict is late Gothic *par excellence.* We more decorous moderns are sometimes apt to overlook this principle, considering (as museums and photographs sometimes force us to do) only the marvelous statue of the Virgin and overlooking the equally marvelous grotesquerie that exists alongside it, reading the *Inferno* without the *Paradiso* or the tales of the Miller and Reeve without those of the Knight and Man of Law.

Perhaps the one surviving genre of medieval art in which such selective distortion is impossible is that of the illuminated book, the magnificent psalters and books of hours produced by English scribes, mainly of the so-called "East Anglian school," in the late thirteenth and fourteenth centuries.[10] The illuminated page has a fixed form. On the left side or at the top appears the illustration of the religious text. The figures are frontally portrayed, often stiffly hieratic in style. The background is con-

[9] Arnold Hauser, *The Social History of Art,* trans. Stanley Goodman in collaboration with the author (New York, 1957), I, 240. See Charles Muscatine, *Chaucer and the French Tradition* (Berkeley, 1957), pp. 167–173, for a discussion of Gothic form in Chaucer.

[10] The *Gawain*-poet was apparently familiar with these works, for he not only drew on the conventions of painting for his description of Paradise in *Pearl* . . . , he shares with the East Anglian school an interest in heraldry, wild men, and hunting, and his technique of visual description . . . seems to have some affinities with Gothic painting. See Erec G. Millar, Introduction, *English Illuminated Manuscripts of the XIVth and XVth Centuries* (Paris, 1928); Margaret Rickert, *Painting in Britain: The Middle Ages* (Baltimore, 1954), Chap. VI; Joan Evans, *English Art, 1307–1461* (London, 1955), Chap. III; for examples see also the British Museum's *Schools of Illumination, Part* III; *English, A.D. 1300 to 1350* (London, 1921).

ventionalized (usually diapered), and the whole is enclosed within the frame provided by the letter. Surrounding this and the text is the lush foliage characteristic of the East Anglian school. Here the lines are twisting and naturalistic, though the color is not always natural green; blue, purple, and silver may replace the green (as in the Windmill Psalter). At the bottom of the page, competing, as it were, for the reader's attention, is the grotesque—strange, twisted beasts or naturalistically drawn peasants, wild men, or animals frolicking in a natural setting, unconfined by any framing letter. They are almost always in a forest setting, far removed from the decorous scene in which the religious figures appear. They are usually humorous, sometimes indecent, and invariably irreverent or at least unconcerned with the reverent topic at the top of the page. In the good-humored tension between the decorous portrait that illustrates the religious text and the lively grotesqueries one sees the same principle that underlies the contrast between the hunting and temptation scenes or the more obvious contrast in which the grotesque Green Knight holds aloft his bleeding head and whirls to turn upon the shocked and motionless court. Here we have not only the "deux civilisations littéraires" that Pons detected in *Sir Gawain* but also the characteristically Gothic "interplay between the epideictic style of knightly ceremony and the starkly creatural realism that does not shun but actually savors crass effects."[11]

In *Sir Gawain* the juxtapositions are used not only for their local, sometimes crass effects but also as the principal method of communicating meaning. This is what distinguishes structural variation from the use of parallels and contrasts that is essential to any work of art and from apparently similar narrative techniques, such as the *entrelacement* of French romance. In alliterative narratives form has an immediate semantic function that

---

[11] Émile Pons, ed., *Sire Gauvain et le Chevalier Vert* (Paris, 1946), p. 37; Erich Auerbach, *Mimesis,* trans. W. R. Trask (New York, 1957), p. 216.

enables a poet to imply his generalizations and allow his narrative to communicate its meaning without the explicit comments that Chaucer employs. Consequently, when the *Gawain*-poet thought about the meaning of a text, he thought in terms of formal criticism. This sounds more like a modern than a medieval idea, but the *Gawain*-poet's one surviving exercise in critical interpretation is an analysis of form.

This is the "Prologue" to *Patience*. The poet first quotes the Beatitudes from the Gospel of St. Matthew. He then argues for a close relation between poverty and the virtue of patience. This was, of course, a very common idea in the Middle Ages, but the poet's method of proving it was not so common, at least among literary men. When Chaucer's Parson wants to make the point that one should be patient though impoverished, he cites the example of Christ:

> That oother grevance outward is to have damage of thy catel. Theragayns suffred Crist ful paciently, when he was despoyled of al that he hadde in this lyf, and that nas but his clothes.
>
> (*ParsT*, 664)

When Langland wants to make a similar point, he appeals to authority:

> And patriarkes and prophetes and poetes bothe
> Wryten to wissen vs to wilne no ricchesse
> And preyseden pouerte with pacience; the apostles bereth witnesse,
> That thei han heritage in heuene and bi trewe riȝte.
>
> (*PP*, B, X, 340–343)

The *Gawain*-poet appeals neither to examples nor to authority. Instead, he derives his interpretation from a close analysis of the structure of the passage, displaying the keen awareness of the semantic function of form that we might expect from one so imbued with the alliterative tradition as the *Gawain*-poet but that we so seldom find in medieval criticism:

> Bot syn I am put to a poynt þat Pouerte hatte
> I schal me poruay Pacyence, & play me with boþe;

> For in þe tyxte þere þyse two arn in teme layde,
> Hit arn fettled in on forme, þe forme & þe laste,
> & by quest of her quoyntyse enquylen on mede.
>
> *(Pat,* 35–39)

The critic of *Sir Gawain* must acquire the same sensitivity to "forme" as the poet displays in this interpretation of a text, carefully noting what elements "arn in teme layde" and taking account of the meaning this "quoyntyse" produces. . . .

7

CRITICISM OF STYLE: THE NARRATOR IN THE CHALLENGE EPISODE

Marie Borroff

ASSUMING THAT STYLE in narrative poetry manifests itself as the narrating "I"—the fictional being, implied by the language of the poem, by whom the events are reported—let us assess the role of the narrator of *Gawain* in the Challenge Episode, beginning with a summary of the events themselves. The Green Knight rushes into the court during the banquet and opens parley rudely, demanding to know which of those present is the king. The court is frightened at his supernatural appearance, but Arthur speaks. The challenge is presented and at first the court is silent. At this the Green Knight jeers; then Arthur accepts the challenge, but Gawain requests that he be allowed to take his place. The request is granted and he beheads the Knight, who picks up his head and departs, after explaining how Gawain is to go about finding him in a year's time.

Given these events as the material of the story, the particular form they will take—and this is true of all reporting, whether in life or in fiction—will depend on who is narrating them, his attitudes, his interests, and his sympathies. In addition it will

Reprinted from *Sir Gawain and the Green Knight: A Stylistic and Metrical Study* by Marie Borroff, pp. 115–129, by permission of Yale University Press. © 1962 by Yale University. Abbreviations: GDS (Gollancz-Day-Serjeantson edition, 1940); TG (Tolkien and Gordon edition, 1930); *EDD* (*The English Dialect Dictionary*). All quotations from *Sir Gawain* are taken from the GDS edition.

depend on the way his mind and imagination work: any story can be told by one person methodically, by another in random fashion, by one person in detail, by another sketchily, and so on. The events, as mediated by the narrator, cease to be material; they are realized. Story becomes plot. The story of the Challenge Episode could be made into a number of different plots. It could, for example, be treated as an adventure in which the courage and courtesy of Arthur's court were demonstrated in an encounter with the supernatural. This statement, however, would constitute an inaccurate summary of the plot as we have it in *Gawain*. Rather, the Challenge Episode appears to us as a series of humiliations and discomfitures for the court which we feel as more comic than tragic. Despite the fact that the challenge is successfully met, the Green Knight departs from the scene as the victor in a kind of psychological warfare.

His overwhelming presence throughout the episode results in part from the simple fact that whereas he is described at length and in the most minute detail, neither Arthur nor any of his knights is described at all. The only detail of personal description prior to the entrance of the Green Knight is the reference to Guenevere's "yȝen gray" (82). Five lines plus the bob are devoted to the canopy and carpets surrounding her, and a little later on, nine lines plus the bob to the dishes served at the banquet. But the narrator goes into a lavish account of the Green Knight's size, figure, dress, accouterments, horse, coiffure, beard, and axe. It is much as if, in a group painting, one figure were drawn in the style of a Dürer engraving and the others sketched in a few lines. The Green Knight continues to receive the largest share of the narrator's attention throughout the events that follow. The fact that he has much more to say than anyone else aids in making his presence powerfully felt. This, of course, is not the narrator's responsibility (he reports all speeches verbatim); but the actions and gestures of the Green Knight are also given much more space than those of Arthur and the court.

After the challenge is delivered, for example, the narrator begins by telling of the reaction of the assembly:

> If he hem stowned vpon fyrst, stiller were þanne
> Alle þe hered-men in halle, þe hyȝ & þe loȝe
> (301–302)

There follow six lines of description, leading to the jeering speech which in a sense constitutes the climax of the episode: we are told how the Green Knight rolled his eyes, bent his brows, wagged his beard and coughed as a preliminary to speaking. When Arthur accepts the challenge, two lines describe his handling of the axe (330–331), but these are followed by six lines plus the bob, describing the Green Knight's bold confrontation of the expected blow. When Gawain in his turn takes the axe and accomplishes the beheading, four lines are devoted to the Green Knight's gestures of preparation (417–420), six to Gawain's act of striking (421–426), but thirty-three (427–459) to the Green Knight's actions after the head falls. The picking up of the head, the final instructions, and the departure could have been dealt with in half as much space; instead, the narrator tells us of the rolling of the head among the beholders' feet, the glistening of the blood on the green clothing, the "ugly body that bled," and the head's lifting up its eyelids and "speaking with its mouth." The Green Knight continues to dominate the scene ("Moni on of hym had doute," 442) even though the blow he requested has been struck; and the loss of his head is, in fact, dealt with in the narration in such a way that through it he becomes more terrifying than ever. The king and Gawain begin to laugh (463–464) only after the sound of the green horse's hoofs has died away.

The material of the narrative, from the beginning of the poem on, is presented in such a way that certain relationships are tacitly emphasized, those which in another treatment of the same material might have been played down or suppressed altogether. One such relationship appears in what may be considered the first discomfiture of the court by the Green Knight, a discomfiture made possible by the fact that the king is not in his place at table. The narrator's account of the reasons for this behavior has been discussed in detail, and it has been shown that he takes pains to emphasize the part played in it by sheer youthful restlessness. Because Arthur is not in his place, the Green Knight can ask "Wher is þe gouernour of þis gyng?" (224–225) instead of greeting the head of the household as a preliminary to the delivery of the challenge. His question implies, moreover, that the king does not stand out from the rest in appearance or manner. And it is ambiguously, if not rudely, worded (*gyng* is cited by the *OED* from early Middle English on not only in the meaning "the retinue of a great personage" but "in depreciatory sense: a crew, rabble," s.v. *ging, sb.* senses 2, 3c). The minor humiliation undergone by Arthur in not being recognized is thus tacitly presented as deserved. It is the appropriate outcome of his youthful behavior, his "childgered" mannerism. And this behavior in turn is a manifestation of the youthfulness of the court itself, which was earlier described as being in its "first age." The ironic reversal of this detail of the opening description is fully accomplished when the Green Knight, scoffing at the idea of meeting any one of them in single combat, says "Hit arn aboute on þis bench bot berdleʒ chylder" (280).

In a sense the coming of the Green Knight is the exact fulfillment of Arthur's desires as stated earlier. Here indeed is "sum mayn meruayle, þat he myʒt trawe" (94), and it is later "breued . . . ful bare / A meruayl among þo menne" (465–466). But what Arthur had been waiting for was not the marvel itself, but "of sum auenturus þyng an vncouþe tale . . . of alderes, of armes, of oþer auenturus" (93, 95). (*Alder* here surely is the traditional archaic-poetic word meaning "chief, prince or ruler" rather than the more colloquial word "elder."[1]) If someone actually came to the court, it was to be a warrior asking to "join in jousting" with one of his knights. With these expectations the Green Knight is utterly at variance, and his coming produces all the discord foretold by the initial reference to him as "anoþer noyse ful newe." His uncouth appearance and attire have already been discussed, and his manners are unconventional as well. The "gomen" he proposes is unheard of as a mode of knightly combat. It deprives Gawain of the use of sword and shield and involves a humiliating passivity, an inhibition of natural response and action. The Green Knight does in fact descend upon the court with all the irresistible force of a torrent or a ship in full sail, as the metaphorical verb *hales* implies. The implications of the reference to him as "an aghlich mayster" are fully realized. The physical paralysis and silence of the court, even the courteous behavior and quiet courage of the king and Gawain, are overwhelmed by the blustering, rude speeches, the overbearing manner and vigorous gestures, the loud laughter, and the undaunted self-possession, even when headless, of the Green Knight.

With all this, the narrator continues to play his time-honored role, to express, in the words and phrases in which the details are presented, the traditional attitudes of respect and solemnity. Arthur's knights are referred to as *siker knyʒtes* (96), as *aþel frekes* (241), as *burnes* (337), as *renkkeʒ* (432) as the *fre meny* (101), as the *ryche* (362); Arthur himself is "þe stif kyng" (107) and "þe derrest on þe dece" (445). Whatever the relationship between these appellations and descriptions and the facts being narrated, they keep their face value, so to speak, in implying the narrator's manner. At one point, indeed, he explicitly defends the court against the imputation of cowardice.

---

[1] *Alder* "chief, ruler," derives from OE *ealdor,* Anglian *aldor; alder* "elder" from OE *ieldra,* Anglian *aeldra* (*eldra*). TG give the former derivation, GDS the latter. See *OED alder* sb.[2] and *elder* a. and sb.[3]

"I deme hit not al for doute" (246), he says, when the court is too frightened to answer the question as to the whereabouts of their king:

> Bot sum for cortaysye
> Bot let hym þat al schulde loute
> Cast vnto þat wyȝe.[2]
>
> (247–249)

But their silence, prior to this statement, has been the subject of an expanded and emphatic description (242–245), and the form of the defensive statement makes the element of opinion intrusive. "I am sure some of them refrained out of courtesy" is actually less emphatic than "Some of them refrained out of courtesy."

It has already been seen that in the interaction between narrative material and narrative style, the traditional alliterative phraseology is sometimes significantly modified. "Bold on bent" becomes "hardy on hille"; "stif in stour" becomes "stif in stalle." But the traditional phrases themselves may take on an enhanced value as a result of the circumstances of the narration. Such a phrase, in the Challenge Episode, is "burne on bench." This is listed by Oakden as traditional in alliterative poetry (2, 268, s.v. "baroun upon benche"). In origin it is a conventional mode of reference to the retainers at a banquet, and as such doubtless antedates the Middle English period (cf. *Beowulf* 1013a "Bugon þa to bence"—i.e. "went to the banquet-hall"). The phrase is alluded to in the Green Knight's statement "Hit arn aboute on þis bench bot berdleȝ chylder" (280). The knights are literally seated, as is brought out in 242–243 "& al stouned at his steuen, & stonstil seten / In a swoghe-sylence þurȝ þe sale riche." It is Arthur, the only one standing, who answers

---

[2] *Bot,* which begins line 248 in the MS, would seem to be an erroneous repetition, the eye of the scribe having presumably been caught by initial *bot* in the line preceding. The repetition of unstressed words (though usually within a single line) is one of the types of scribal error most prevalent in the *Gawain*-MS; cf., in *Gawain,* lines 95, 182, 1137, etc.

the challenge, and when he prepares to strike the Green Knight with the ax, the latter awaits him as calmly as if "any burne vpon bench hade broȝt hym to drynk / of wyne" (337–338). Gawain then tacitly defends the posture of the court by asking permission to rise: "Wolde ȝe, worþilych lorde . . . Bid me boȝe fro þis benche & stonde by yow þere . . . I wolde com to your counseyl" (343–344, 347). And Gawain defends his fellow knights by alluding to another phrase, phonetically similar but of contrasting significance. It is not seemly, he continues, that the king should undertake the adventure "whil mony so bolde yow aboute vpon bench sytten" (351); there are none stouter of purpose under heaven, "ne better bodyes on bent þer baret is rered" (353). But Gawain's courtesy does not serve entirely to dispel the passive implications of the former phrase.

The narrator of *Gawain,* we may safely say, is richly conscious of the disparity between the reputation for valor and warlike prowess of Arthur's knights and what actually takes place when the Green Knight thrusts himself upon them. But this does not imply that his attitude toward them involves either hostility or contempt. Because he has avoided emphasis on material luxury and worldly power in his depiction of the life of the court, the Challenge Episode is not seen as a rebuke to arrogance or sensual self-indulgence. Arthur and his knights are charmingly youthful and joyous; their pleasures are innocent. And although it is overshadowed by the more conspicuous presence of the Green Knight, Gawain's behavior is exquisitely courteous. His self-possession in requesting that the adventure be allotted to him and in actually dealing the blow indicates clearly that he, at least, had refrained from speaking "for cortaysye" (247) rather than out of fear. In such a passage as 366–371,

> Þen comaunded þe kyng þe knyȝt for to ryse;
> & he ful radly vp ros, & ruchched hym fayre,
> Kneled doun bifore þe kyng, & cacheȝ þat weppen;
> & he luflyly hit hym laft, & lyfte vp his honde,

> & gef hym Goddeʒ blessyng, & gladly hym biddes
> Þat his hert & his honde schulde hardi be boþe,

there is no ironic disparity between the implications of the traditional adverbs *radly,* "with (courteous or befitting) promptness," and *luflyly,* "graciously, in a manner worthy of approval," and the circumstances of the action. Gawain's manner here fully validates the epithet "þe hende," bestowed on him by the narrator when he is talking to the Green Knight a moment later.

There remain to be discussed certain aspects of the fictional narrator which, though manifested in his language, belong to descriptive style rather than to verbal style in the narrowest sense. A full discussion cannot be attempted here, but some remarks may be made, and examples given, under the main headings of actions, space, and descriptive detail.

1. The narrator tends to see actions, whether major or minor, as reciprocal, giving explicit attention to the reciprocating or responding agent even when the response is of no importance to the story line or could be omitted as obvious. The germ of such a tendency may be discerned in the traditional style of alliterative poetry, which provides for the expression of qualities of promptness and readiness in response to commands or requests. But the tendency is sufficiently consistent and systematic in *Gawain* to distinguish that poem from the works of other alliterative poets.[3] The following passages are typical:

> Þen comaunded þe kyng þe knyʒt for to ryse;
> & he ful radly vp ros, & ruchched hym fayre,
> Kneled doun bifore þe kyng, & cacheʒ þat weppen;
> & he luflyly hit hym laft,   (366–369)

---

[3] The extent to which, allowing for differences in purpose and subject matter, these generalizations apply to *Patience, Purity,* and *St. Erkenwald* (and perhaps also *Pearl*) cannot be determined here. Examples from the work of the *Gawain*-poet will accordingly be confined to *Gawain* itself.

Þe fayre hede fro þe halce hit to þe erþe,
Þat fele hit foyned wyth her fete, þere hit forth roled; (427–428)

Þe freke calde hit a fest ful frely & ofte,
Ful hendely, quen alle þe haþeles re-hayted hym at oneʒ
                 as hende, (894–896)

With care & wyth kyssyng he carppeʒ hem tille,
& fele þryuande þonkkeʒ he þrat hom to haue,
& þay ʒelden hym aʒay[n] ʒeply þat ilk;
Þay bikende hym to Kryst, with ful colde sykyngeʒ.
Syþen fro þe meyny he menskly de-partes;
Vche mon þat he mette, he made hem a þonke
For his seruyse & his solace & his sere pyne
Þat þay wyth busynes had ben aboute hym to serue;
& vche segge as sore to seuer with hym þere
As þay hade wonde worþyly with þat wlonk euer. (1979–88)

In its interplay of action and response, the account of Gawain's reception at the castle of Bertilak de Hautdesert contrasts strikingly with a similar passage in *Destruction of Troy:*

Þay let doun þe grete draʒt & derely out ʒeden
& kneled doun on her knes vpon þe colde erþe
To welcum þis ilk wyʒ, as worþy hom þoʒt;
Þay ʒolden hym þe brode ʒate, ʒarked vp wyde,
& he hem raysed rekenly & rod ouer þe brygge;
Sere seggeʒ hym sesed by sadel, quel he lyʒt,
& syþen stabeled his stede stif men in-noʒe.
Knyʒteʒ & swyereʒ comen doun þenne
For to bryng þis buurne wyth blys in-to halle;
Quen he hef vp his helme, þer hiʒed in-noghe
For to hent hit at his honde, þe hende to seruen,
His bronde & his blasoun boþe þay token.
Þen haylsed he ful hendly þo haþeleʒ vch one,
& mony proud mon þer presed, þat prynce to honour; (817–830)

Þai [Jason and his company] bowet to the brode yate or þai bide
   wold.
The Kyng [Æetes] of his curtessy Kayres hom vnto,
Silet furthe of his Citie seriaunttes hym with,
Mony stalworth in stoure as his astate wold;
Than he fongid þo freikes with a fine chere,

> With hailsyng of hed bare, haspyng in armys,
> And led hom furthe lyuely into a large halle,
> Gaid vp by a grese all of gray marbill,
> Into a chamber full choise (chefe) on þere way,
> Þat proudly was painted with pure gold ouer,
> And þan sylen to sitte vppon silke wedis,
> Hadyn wyn for to wale & wordes ynow. (362–373)

Animals and even, in one instance, the inanimate "meat" or food awaiting Gawain become responsive agents in the narrator's imagination:

> He [the boar] hurteʒ of þe houndeʒ, & þay
> Ful ʒomerly ʒaule & ʒelle. (1452–53)

> Bot quen þe dynteʒ hym [the boar] dered of her dryʒe strokeʒ,
> Þen, brayn-wod for bate, on burneʒ he raseʒ,
> Hurteʒ hem ful heterly þer he forth hyʒeʒ,
> & mony arʒed þerat & on lyte droʒen. (1460–63)

> Þe wylde watʒ war of þe wyʒe with weppen in honde,
> Hef hyʒly þe here, so hetterly he fnast,
> Þat fele ferde for þe freke, lest felle hym þe worre; (1586–88)

> [The lord] hit hym vp to þe hult, þat þe hert schyndered,
> & he ʒarrande hym ʒelde, (1594–95)

> Thenne watʒ Gryngolet grayþe, þat gret watʒ & huge,
> & hade ben soiourned sauerly & in a siker wyse,
> Hym lyst prik for poynt, þat proude hors þenne; (2047–49)

> His schalk schewed hym [Gawain] his schelde, on schulder he
>   hit laʒt,
> Gordeʒ to Gryngolet with his gilt heleʒ,
> & he starteʒ on þe ston, stod he no lenger . . . (2061–63)

> & þenne he meued to his mete þat menskly hym keped, (1312)

(In view of this tendency, the meaning "awaited" given for *keped* in GDS' glossary seems preferable to TG's "occupied.")

2. The narrator tends to see a given object or agent in relation to other objects or agents within a limited space. The resultant effect is one of fullness or crowding, with, at times,

a stereoscopic projection and depth in the imagined scene.[4] Again, the tendency is sufficiently marked to distinguish *Gawain* from the works of the other alliterative poets. There is a striking example of it in the description of the New Year's banquet at Arthur's court. The narrator, telling us in traditional fashion of the abundance of the food, says that there was

> Foysoun of þe fresche, & on so fele disches
> Þat pine to fynde þe place þe peple bi-forne
> For to sette þe sylu[eren] þat sere sewes halden,
>   on clothe;
>
> (122–125)

Here the effect depends partly on a realistic limitation in the size of the banquet table. But it depends also on the narrator's explicit reference to *disches, peple, sylueren, sewes,* and *clothe* (cf. "So many dishes that there was scarcely space to set them

---

[4] The effectiveness and importance of the *Gawain*-poet's treatment of space is discussed in detail, though in somewhat different terms, by Alain Renoir in "Descriptive Technique in *Sir Gawain and the Green Knight*," *Orbis Litterarum,* XIII (1958), 126–132. Renoir makes an interesting and revealing analogy between the narrative technique of the *Gawain*-poet, with particular reference to the beheading of the Green Knight, and the use of the camera eye in motion pictures:

> The technique of [the *Gawain*-]poet is to draw a single detail out of a uniformly illuminated scene which is then allowed to fade out in obscurity and of which we may be given an occasional dim glimpse at psychologically appropriate moments. The twentieth century is thoroughly familiar with this device. In effect, it is that most commonly associated with the cinematograph, where the camera may at will focus either upon the whole scene or upon a single detail, while *illumination may be used so as to keep the audience aware of the background against which the action takes place* [italics mine]. We must note that the device is primarily concerned with the utilization of space. (p. 127).

Renoir speaks, again, of "the effective use of both space and motion" throughout the poem, citing as an example Gawain's "first sight of Bercilak's castle, seen through the very same branches which we have so often found on either side of the cinematograph screen under similar circumstances" (p. 131).

down"). This passage may be compared with the account in *Morte Arthure* of the entertainment of the Romans, where the narrator lists one delicacy after another, including

> Flesch fluriste of fermyson with frumentee noble,
> Therto wylde to wale and wynlyche bryddes,
> Pacokes and plouers in platers of golde,
> Pygges of porke-despyne, þat pasturede neuer;
> Sythen herons in hedoyne, hyled full faire;
> Grett swannes ful swythe in silueryn chargeour[e]s,
> Tartes of Turky: taste whan þem lykys!
>
> (180–186)

In the *Morte Arthure* passage the effect aimed at is one of overwhelming splendor, the means being the accumulation of descriptive references without spatial definition. . . .

The same technique is used in the description of the forest into which Gawain rides on his quest for the Green Knight. Here the narrator frames the scene with hills on either side, and then fills it, moving in imagination from far to near, with the great oaks, the hazel and hawthorn bushes tangled together, the rough, hanging moss, and the birds perched in rows on the twigs below which Gawain is riding:

> Hiȝe hilleȝ on vche a halue, & holt-wodeȝ vnder
> Of hore okeȝ ful hoge a hundreth to-geder;
> Þe hasel & þe haȝ-þorne were harled al samen,
> With roȝe raged mosse rayled ay-where,
> With mony bryddeȝ vnblyþe vpon bare twyges,
> Þat pitosly þer piped for pyne of þe colde.
> Þe gome vpon Gryngolet glydeȝ hem vnder. . . .
>
> (742–748)

3a. Descriptive details in *Gawain* are frequently circumstantial, expressing temporary conditions or relationships—e.g., the presence of onlookers—as opposed to attributes inherent in the agent or object. As with the narrator's interest in responsive action, such a tendency can be seen in embryo in the traditional style; specifically, in the stock of alliterative combinations linking persons or qualities with phrases expressing position or place, e.g., "burne on blonk" (Fuhrmann, p. 18) and "bold on bent" (Oakden 2, 268 sv. "bachelors on bent"). But even such phrases as these are often given a specific relevance to circumstances in the style of *Gawain* which is not decreed by tradition, as in "His haþel on hors watȝ þenne" (2065)—i.e., his servant had mounted and was ready to leave with him—or the Green Knight's admonishment to Gawain, "Bolde burne, on þis bent be not so gryndel" (2338).

In each of the following lines one of the strongly alliterating synonyms for "man, warrior" is used in a descriptive detail referring to a group of onlookers or participants who need not have been explicitly mentioned. The result, as with the narrator's treatment of space, is to people or crowd the scene.

& ru[n]yschly he raȝt out, þere as renkkeȝ stoden,	(432)
& hem to-fylched as fast as frekeȝ myȝt loke,	(1172)
Þay ferden to þe fyndyng, & frekeȝ hem after;	(1433)
& he vnsoundyly out soȝt seggeȝ ouer-þwert,	(1438)
Syȝ hym byde at þe bay, his burneȝ bysyde;	(1582)
Here he watȝ halawed when haþeleȝ hym metten,	(1723)

A relative clause or prepositional phrase expressing a circumstantial attribute may combine with its noun to form a periphrastic reference:

Þe gome vpon Gryngolet glydeȝ hem vnder	(748)
Þe burne bode on bonk, þat on blonk houed,	(785)
Þe leude lystened ful wel, þat leȝ in his bedde,	(2006)

The specific relevance of descriptive detail in the poem often makes for the sort of rhythmic continuity or momentum characteristic of the restrictive relative clause, as in the following passages:

Þe bores hed watȝ borne bifore þe burnes seluen	
Þat him for-ferde in þe forþe þurȝ forse of his honde	
so stronge;	(1616–18)

> & went on his way with his wyȝe one
> Þat schulde teche hym to tourne to þat tene place
> Þer þe ruful race he shulde re-sayue.　　　　(2074–76)

Certain lines in which prepositional phrases or relative clauses are separated from the main clause with a comma by GDS could equally well be read without a pause:

> Gawan gotȝ to þe gome with giserne in honde,　　　(375)

> In-to þe comly castel þer þe knyȝt bideȝ
> 　　　　ful stille;　　　　(1366–67)

(TG omit punctuation in 375.)

There is, of course, no question of the *Gawain*-poet's avoidance of descriptive details expressing inherent attributes. Beside those of the type quoted above, we find numerous lines like the following:

> Þat broȝt hym to a bryȝt boure, þer beddyng watȝ noble　(853)

> 　　　　"bi Kryst, hit is scaþe
> Þat þou, leude, schal be lost, þat art of lyf noble!"　(674–675)

> Thenne watȝ Gryngolet grayþe, þat gret watȝ & huge,　(2047)

> Hade hit dryuen adoun as dreȝ as he atled,
> Þer hade ben ded of his dynt þat doȝty watȝ euer.　(2263–64)

But the style of *Gawain* involves a larger admixture of the circumstantial than that of the other alliterative poets.

3b. Descriptive detail in *Gawain,* more often than in the works of the other alliterative poets, expresses what is observed or perceived from a locus within the scene. The relation between descriptive detail and perception may be explicit, as in Gawain's first sight of the lady of the castle, where, after describing her in traditionally superlative terms, the narrator adds the more telling detail that she was "wener þen Wenore, as þe wyȝe þoȝt" (945). Compare, in the Challenge Episode, "Þe stif mon [the Green Knight awaiting a blow from Arthur] hym bifore stod vpon hyȝt, / Herre þen ani in þe hous by þe hede & more" (332–333). . . . On the morning of her first visit to Gawain, the lady is described as she sits on his bed; Gawain, who had been feigning sleep, has just decided to open his eyes:

> Wyth chynne & cheke ful swete,
> Boþe quit & red in blande,
> Ful lufly con ho lete,
> Wyth lyppeȝ smal laȝande.
>
> (1204–07)

Here, chin, cheek, gracious looks, and lips imply the face seen at close range. It is the lips, parted in laughter, to which the hero's gaze is finally drawn, and on which it lingers.

The narrator's adoption of the visual perspective of the central character frequently enhances dramatic suspense, as in the Episode of the Green Chapel when Gawain is awaiting the second stroke of the Green Knight's axe:

> Bot Gawayn on þat giserne glyfte hym bysyde,
> As hit com glydande adoun on glode hym to schende,
> & schranke a lytel with þe schulderes for þe scharp yrne.
>
> (2265–67)

Here the blade is described as Gawain sees it from below. Compare, in an otherwise dramatic account of the battle between Gawain and Modred in *Morte Arthure,* "He schokkes owtte a schorte knyfe, schethede with siluere" (3852), where neither combatant would presumably be looking at the sheath. The effectiveness of the above-quoted lines from *Gawain* is heightened by the expansive reference to the descent of the blade. The content of the adverbial clause, which occupies an entire line, is superfluous, but the drawing out of the instant of suspense is psychologically valid from the point of view of the person concerned.

In the account of the third and final stroke in the same episode, there are, as one might expect, a number of verbal parallels to the beheading of the Green Knight in the Challenge Episode. "He [the Green Knight] lyftes lyȝtly his lome & let hit doun fayre" (2309) echoes "Let hit doun lyȝtly lyȝt on þe naked" (423), and "Þe scharp schrank to [Gawain's] flesche þurȝ þe schyre grece" (2313) echoes "Þat þe scharp of þe schalk schyndered þe bones, / & schrank þurȝ þe schyire grece, & sc[h]ade hit in twynne" (424–425). There is a further parallel in that the narrator in both passages refers to the sight of blood, but it is a parallel with a difference. In the beheading scene the Green Knight's blood is said to have "blykked on þe grene" (429) of the headless trunk—i.e., it is seen by the spectators. In the Episode of the Green Chapel, Gawain sees his own blood as it falls to earth over his shoulders to "blenk on þe snawe" (2315).

The choice of a particular word to express the content of the descriptive detail is sometimes important in effects of this kind. On the morning of her second visit to Gawain, we are told that the lady "commes to þe cortyn & at þe knyȝt totes" (1476). *Toten* had in Middle English the meanings "to protrude, stick out" (see *OED* s.v. *toot* v.[1] sense 1) and "to peep, peer" (sense 2). The figurative meaning "to look inquisitively; to pry" (sense 2b) is earliest cited from Gower. The word has descended into Northern dialects in the meanings "to peep and pry about" (see *EDD* s.v. *toot* v.[2] sense 1) and "to jut out; to project; . . . to shoot above the ground, as corn, etc." (sense 3). Its meanings make it particularly apt for the line in question. Gawain is awake, ready to greet the lady when she arrives (see line 1477). *Totes* expresses the thrusting in of her head through the curtains as seen by the man in the bed; it also suggests her intrusiveness, her unwelcome "peeping" at Gawain in the privacy of his bedchamber. Compare the use of *loke* "to look" in similar position in the line in 478–479 "& hit [the axe] watȝ don abof þe dece, on doser to henge, / Þer alle men for meruayl myȝt on hit loke."

The same precision is shown in the use of *lyft* and *kay*, both meaning "left (side or hand)," in two lines in neither of which the choice of word is compelled by the alliteration. In describ-

ing Gawain's journey in quest of the Green Chapel, the narra-
tor tells us that "Alle þe iles of Anglesay on lyft half he haldeʒ"
(698). Here, *lyft* (as opposed to *west*) expresses Gawain's
point of view. But when Gawain prepares to strike the behead-
ing blow, we are told that "Þe kay fot on þe folde he be-fore
sette" (422). Here, *lyfte* could equally well have been used.
But *kay,* like *toten,* must have been a colloquial word for the
Gawain-poet; it has descended into Northern dialects in such
compounds as *key-fisted* "left-handed," and *key-neive* and
key-paw "the left hand." (See *EDD* s.v. *key* adj. senses 1(3),
(6), and (8); cf. *OED* s.v. *kay, key,* a.) "Þe kay fot" thus has
the immediacy of the language one would use to refer to one's
own hand or foot in everyday situations. Compare the use of
lyfte in alliterating position in the description of the green girdle
as worn by Gawain: "& þe blykkande belt he bere þeraboute,
/ A-belef as a bauderyk, bounden bi his syde, / Loken vnder
his lyfte arme" (2485–87). Here the point of view is not
Gawain's own, but that of the one looking at him.

The above-discussed features of style manifest themselves in
the poem as what might be called the characteristic mode of
imagination of the narrating "I," who is here also the narrating
"eye." In general, the narrator of *Gawain* tends to imagine
agents and objects as they assume particular relationships within
a limited space (and in limited time). He tends also to adopt
the point of view of the character central in a given narrative
passage as that character responds to the circumstances of the
action. The result is vividness, but it is vividness of a special
kind. When it is visual, it depends as much on the exact appro-
priateness of what is seen, by whom, and from where, as on
the color, texture, or other intrinsic sensory or aesthetic quali-
ties of the object. It is the vividness of the frozen stream that
"henged heʒe ouer [Gawain's] hede in hard ysse-ikkles"
(732), rather than of those streams that "thro' wavering lights
and shadows broke, / Rolling a slumbrous sheet of foam be-

low" in the landscape of "The Lotos-Eaters." In recognizing the dramatic implications of the successive details of the narrative, the reader is pulled in imagination into the world of the poem and experiences it as a reality.

In the Challenge episode, as later in the poem, the narrator's attitude toward the hero is one of affection. And in this episode Gawain shows himself superior to the rest of the court (the king excepted) in his response to an unfamiliar, trying, and seemingly dangerous situation. As a result of this response, he is to be singled out for sore trials of chastity, of courtesy, and finally of courage. In the first there is no real question of failure. The second, conducted concomitantly by the lady in the bedchamber scenes, is the more subtle, the more suspenseful, and the more amusing of the two, though the hero's courtesy, like his chastity, is successfully maintained throughout. It is in the third that, showing himself less hero than human, he falls short, and as a result, abandons courtesy too for a few moments in an acrimonious outburst of antifeminism. In the account of these trials, as in that of the Challenge episode, the elements of discomfort, frustration, and annoyance inherent in each situation will be realized to the full, and the extent to which Gawain falls short of the ideal, by implication, clearly defined. But through it all, the narrator's time-honored attitudes of solemnity and deference, mixed with a genuinely felt affection, will be maintained.

This story and the way it is told—the "what" and the "how" of the narration—must, for the purposes of a study of style, be considered as two different things. The historical study of style reveals that in *Sir Gawain and the Green Knight,* the verbal expression of the story is thoroughly traditional, to an extent that is more and more fully apparent as one becomes more familiar with the other extant works belonging to the same tradition. But in *Gawain* the traditional features of style do not serve the traditional purposes. They become devices for the production of an effect in which the narrator—the presiding, interpreting "I," with his emotions and attitudes, his manner, and his particular mode of imaginative perception—is all-important. In the last analysis what this narrator has to tell and the way in which he chooses to tell it are one.

8

AN ECHO TO THE SENSE:
THE PATTERNS OF SOUND IN
SIR GAWAIN AND THE GREEN KNIGHT

Alain Renoir

BECAUSE LITERARY CRITICS generally agree with Émile Pons that *"Sir Gawayne and the Green Knight* is not only the most beautiful Arthurian poem in English but one of the most vivid works of Arthurian literature of all countries and of all times,"[1] the visual aspect of this work has been the object of repeated investigation. Within the past few years, Francis Berry has suggested that the vividness in question is due to descriptions in which "the experience is actualized in the muscular images and rhythms, in the firm grasp of concrete particulars";[2] Laura Hibbard Loomis has attributed it to the poet's "habit of close observation and an exceptional sense of form, proportion, and design";[3] and Werner Habicht has shown that the descriptive technique of certain passages is comparable to that of the

Reprinted, by permission of author and editors, from *English Miscellany,* XIII (1962), 9–23. All quotations from *Sir Gawain* are from the Gollancz edition, *EETS,* O.S. no. 220 (London, 1940); spelling normalized by author.

[1] Émile Pons, ed., *Sire Gauvain et le Chevalier Vert* (Paris, 1946), p. 15 (my translation).

[2] Francis Berry, "Sir Gawayne and the Grene Knight," in *The Age of Chaucer,* ed. Boris Ford, Pelican Books A290 (London, 1954), p. 149.

[3] Laura Hibbard Loomis, see above, p. 20.

painter Giotto.[4] I have myself argued at some length that the basic descriptive technique in the poem is analogous to that of the cinematograph.[5]

More recently I have pointed out the presence throughout the poem of a relationship between the visual descriptions and the various states of mind attributed either explicitly or implicitly to the principal character.[6] In general, when Gawain feels physically secure, he is depicted as proportionally equal to or larger than his immediate surroundings, and he is made to occupy a place in the upper half of the picture with which we are presented; whenever he feels insecure, the ratio is likely to change so as to make him proportionally smaller than his immediate surroundings, and he is moved to the lower half of the picture. The purpose of the present essay is to investigate what James R. Kreuzer has termed the "powerful . . . patterns of sound"[7] in the poem and to argue the existence of such a conjunction between these and the sense of key passages that the sounds and silences which we are asked to imagine parallel and reinforce the effects of the visual descriptions.

In the following argument, the term *sound* is not used in reference to intelligible human speech as such, although it is occasionally used in reference to incoherent manifestations of the human voice. Thus understood, sounds serve two specific purposes in *Sir Gawain:* (1) they contribute to the tone of certain scenes, and (2) they emphasize, and occasionally help the reader guess, Gawain's state of mind at relevant points in the narrative. They sometimes perform both functions together.

---

[4] Werner Habicht, *Die Gebärde in englischen Dichtungen des Mittelalters* (München, 1959), p. 149 ff.

[5] Alain Renoir, "Descriptive Techniques in Sir Gawain and the Green Knight," *Orbis Litterarum,* XIII, 126 ff.

[6] Alain Renoir, "The Progressive Magnification: an Instance of Psychological Description in *Sir Gawain and the Green Knight*," *Moderna Sprak,* LIV (1960), 245–253.

[7] James R. Kreuzer, *Sir Gawain and The Green Knight* (New York, 1959), p. xli.

We need not dwell at great length on the first function, for it is simply that which auditory imagery may be expected to fulfill when used functionally in a sophisticated work of literature. We must note, however, the exceptional mastery with which it is carried out in *Sir Gawain*.

For the sake of reference, it will be helpful to recall the gist of the poem. The narrative begins with a description of the New Year festivities in King Arthur's hall at Camelot. Suddenly an almost gigantic Green Knight rides into the hall and dares anyone present to behead him and receive a return blow a year and a day later. Gawain takes up the challenge and beheads the Green Knight, who then tells him to seek a certain Green Chapel on the appointed date, and gallops away holding his severed head in his hand. Nearly a year passes, and Gawain sets out on his quest for the Green Chapel. After a long and arduous journey, he arrives at the castle of Bercilak de Hautdesert, where he learns of the proximity of the Green Chapel, and accepts an invitation to stay until New Year's Day. On the three consecutive days, Bercilak goes hunting from sun up to sun down. Gawain, who must recuperate from the hardships of his journey, remains at the castle, where each morning he enjoys but resists the amorous advances of his host's beautiful wife. Because on the first evening he and Bercilak had agreed to exchange henceforth whatever each of them might win during the day, Gawain receives each evening the catch of the hunt and in return gives his own take to his host: one kiss the first day, two on the second, and three on the third. On the third morning, however, the amorous lady gives her guest not only three kisses, but also a green girdle which supposedly makes its wearer invulnerable. Because he fears his coming encounter with the Green Knight, Gawain breaks his agreement and hides the girdle from Bercilak. On the next morning he rides to the Green Chapel, where the Green Knight, who turns out to be Bercilak himself, merely nicks him on the neck for having kept the girdle and declares him the best of all knights.

Gawain, smarting under the shame of having been found untrue to his word, returns to Camelot, where his peers agree to wear henceforth a green belt to commemorate his adventure.

The opening feast at Camelot is a very gay affair. We are told that it lasts "ful fiften dayes / With alle the mete & the mirthe that men couthe a-vyse" (44–45). The carefully selected and sharply defined images with which we are presented bring vividly to life the innumerable courtly entertainments in which a multitude of carefree and merry guests constantly takes part amidst the splendor of the royal palace. We see the noblemen joust with each other during the day (41) and dance with the ladies at night (47); we see them hold hands and exchange gifts (67); we see the most renowned knights of the Round Table surround Queen Guenevere to sit at table under a rich canopy (77); we see the silver dishes before them (124), as well as staggering quantities of the most elegant foods (121) and beverages (129). In effect, the poet selects all the relevant details which connote elegance, wealth, and revelry, and makes us see them with quasi-pictorial exactitude.

Elegant revelry conducted on a grand scale, however, is one kind of human activity which artists have seldom succeeded in depicting sympathetically through visual imagery alone; this is perhaps why Watteau chose to paint the *embarcation* for Cythera rather than the subsequent revelries which his famous painting allows us to foresee. An example from the silent motion pictures will illustrate my point. David W. Griffith's *Intolerance* is unanimously considered one of the greatest films of all times, but it must nevertheless be considered a dismal failure in one respect, for the scenes of revelry at the royal palace in Babylon are perfectly ludicrous. In order to convey the regal grandeur of the festivities, Griffith shot the entire sequence on a scale whose magnitude had never been attempted before and has seldom been matched since. Yet, even with the accompanying music which recent editors have added, the sequence falls flat: the very contrast between the supposed uproars of the swarming multitudes and the actual silence of their performance is simply too grotesque to evoke anything but amusement on the part of the audience.

In this respect, the *Gawain*-poet is luckier than Griffith: if he cannot actually reproduce the appropriate sounds, he can at least force his audience to imagine them; and he avails himself of the opportunity to the highest degree. Indeed, he has no sooner sketched visually the mirthful activities of his protagonists than he qualifies them in respect to sound: "Such glaumande gle glorious to here, / Dere dyn vp-on day, daunsyng on nyghtes" (46–47). As King Arthur enters both the poem and the hall, a few lines later, the ovation which he receives is described in terms that render it almost audible:

> Loude crye wats ther kest of clerkes & other,
> Nowel nayted o-newe, neuened ful ofte.
>
> (64–65)

Thus the atmosphere of joy conveyed by the visual images is emphasized by the auditory images with which we are presented.

Just as the poet emphasizes the mood of merriment by making us imagine the appropriate sounds, so he emphasizes fear and astonishment by making us imagine utter silence. No sooner has the semigigantic Green Knight entered the hall and asked to speak to "The gouernour of thys gyng" (225) than the merrymaking turns to silence and stillness:

> & al stouned at his steuen, & stonstil seten
> In a swoghe-sylence thurgh the sale riche;
> As al were slypped vpon slepe so slaked hor lotes
> in hyghe.
>
> (242–245)

It is significant that the actual decapitation takes place in utter silence with one single exception: the poet allows Gawain to wield the axe with such power that it not only goes all the way through the green man's neck but continues on its course until it sinks into the floor (426), thus punctuating the episode with the one thud we are made to imagine.

The poet likewise uses sound as a dramatic means to bring the gruesome episode to an end. The Green Knight has picked up his head and mounted his horse. We see his bleeding trunk twist fitfully in the saddle (440–441) as his solitary voice rings through the dead silence of the motionless hall to remind Gawain of their agreement and enjoin him to seek the Green Chapel a year hence. With the last word, his voice rises to a bloodchilling roar as he jerks his horse around and gallops away in a thunder of clattering hooves:

> With a runisch rout the raynes he tornes,
> Halled out at the hal-dor, his hed in his hande,
> That the fyr of the flynt flawe fro fole houes.
> (457–459)

The frightening combination of sounds makes the exit final, and the poet may now appropriately ask, "What thenne?" (462).

Sounds in *Sir Gawain* are particularly effective when used to emphasize a contrast between two situations. Consider, for instance, the first temptation of Gawain by Bercilak's wife. Her husband has risen long before sunrise to lead his hunting party to the fields. The preparations for the hunt take place in the atmosphere of excitement and confusion that suits the situation. Within only twelve lines (1126–37) the castle awakens; the masters call their grooms, who saddle the horses, load the hunting bags, and prepare the equipment; the hunters don their outdoor garments, jump in the saddle, grab the reins, and gallop away. Bercilak himself eats a sop in all haste, hardly takes time to hear a quick Mass, and is off to the fields. We may easily imagine the multitude of noises that accompany the commotion. But the poet is not content with letting us guess the sounds from the action; on the contrary, he explicitly brings in the two sounds that most emphasize the wild and energetic nature of this action. At the precise instant that Bercilak gallops off, we are made to hear the peals of the hunting horns: "With bugle to bent-felde he buskes by-lyue" (1136). And immediately thereupon, we see the pack of excited hunting dogs racing through the fields, and we hear their quasi-demoniac barking mingling with the repeated blasts of the horns:

> Thenne thise cacheres that couthe, cowpled hor houndes
> Vnclosed the kenel dore & calde hem ther-oute,
> Blwe bygly in bugles thre bare motes;
> Braches bayed therfore & breme noyse maked,
> And thay chastysed & charred, on chasyng that went;
> A hundreth of hunteres, as I haf herde telle,
> > the best;
> > To trystors vewters yod,
> > Couples huntes of kest,
> > Ther ros for blastes gode
> > Gret rurd in that forest.
>
> (1139–49)

It is not long before the hunters uncover a herd of deer; and, as they shoot them down, the sorrowful braying of their victims mingles with the baying of the dogs and the blasts of the horns to awaken the echoes of the neighboring cliffs:

> What! thay brayen & bleden, bi bonkkes thay deyen,
> & ay rachches in a res radly hem folwes,
> Hunteres wyth hyghe horne hasted hem after,
> Wyth such a crakkande kry as klyffes haden brusten.
>
> (1163–66)

At this point, we abandon Bercilak to the cacophonous raptures of his destructive sport, and we turn our attention to Gawain. The contrast is radical. Whereas all is clamor and motion with Bercilak, all is stillness and quiet with Gawain as he peacefully enjoys the leisure of lying in bed while the sunlight silently plays on the walls of his room:

> & Gawayn the god mon in gay bed lyges,
> Lurkkes quyl the day-lyght lemed on the wowes,
> Vnder couertour ful clere, cortyned aboute.
>
> (1179–81)

But Gawain's repose is exactly as precarious as that of the deer in the forest where the hunt is going on. Just as Bercilak is hunting in the fields, his wife is hunting in the castle; but whereas the object of his hunt is wild game, the object of hers is Gawain himself. Not only are the objects of the two hunts different, but so are the methods: whereas the deer in the woods may be tracked down, cornered, and felled by brute force, Gawain in the bedroom can be made to fall only through the subtlest wiles; and the sounds that accompany the two activities are designed to emphasize this difference. To symbolize its energetic and brutal nature, the poet has begun the hunt in the fields with repeated blasts of the horn. He now begins the hunt in the bedroom with a sound that dramatically contrasts with the thunder of the hunt in the fields and sets the atmosphere for the amorous chitchat which follows: "A littel dyn at his dor" (1183). With this, the lovely temptress may tiptoe to the bedside of her prospective victim. The remainder of the scene is all courtliness and delicacy, and we are asked to imagine no louder pattern of sound than that of the discreet laughter concomitant to an elegant flirtation. When the lady finally leaves the room, the poet once again insists on the quietness of her actions: "Ho dos hir forth at the dore with-outen dyn more" (1308).

Sounds, however, are most masterfully used in the poem when they serve as cues to Gawain's state of mind. Let us return to the opening scene at Camelot. The atmosphere of mirth, we recall, is conveyed as much by the sounds which we are asked to imagine as by the visual images with which we are presented. At the beginning, Gawain is in no way distinguished from the other knights, so that the sounds tell us the same thing about him as they do about everybody else. However, he does not long remain merely another member of the multitude. As the guests are called to dinner, he is distinguished with a special mark of honor. Not only is he seated among the greatest lords at the elevated end of the table, but his place is next to

Queen Guenevere herself. At this point, it is reasonable to suppose that Gawain feels at least some urge toward momentary pride at the great honor conferred upon him.[8] We are never explicitly told whether it is so; but it is significant that he not only occupies the upper part of the picture with which we are presented, but that he has no sooner sat down than we are made to hear the blasts of the instrument most symbolic of pride—the trumpet. Since the poem was certainly intended for oral delivery,[9] we must note the strikingly onomatopoeic quality of the vocabulary as the trumpets sound their first blasts and the other instruments follow:

> Then the first cors come with crakkyng of trumpes,
> Wyth mony baner ful bryght that ther-bi henged,
> Nwe nakryn noyse with the noble pipes,
> Wylde werbles & wyght wakned lote.
>
> (116–119)

The music brings the opening scene to a close with a sudden intensification of the atmosphere of general elation. The sounds so clearly symbolize the union of regality and merriment that, we are told, "mony hert ful highe hef at her towches" (120). Thus the stage is set to emphasize by contrast the silence and dismay that will spread over the hall only sixteen lines later with the entrance of the Green Knight.

As he appears in the poem, Gawain is a civilized and thoroughly courtly knight. He obviously delights in the elegant

---

[8] The supposition that at this point the poet expects us to assume at least a touch of pride in Gawain is born out by his own statement that Gawain is subject to that sin; we are told later in the poem that Gawain has accepted the Green Knight's challenge "for angardes pryde" (681). For the suggestion that the first fit of the poem emphasizes Gawain's pride much more than we have hitherto realized, I am indebted to a yet unpublished paper, entitled "The Christian Paradox of *Sir Gawain and the Green Knight*," delivered by Mr. Bernard S. Levy at the 1960 annual meeting of the Philological Association of the Pacific Coast.

[9] The poet introduces his story with the statement, "I schal telle it . . ./ with tonge" (31–32).

festivities of the court and in his social intercourse with his peers. But now he must set out on his quest for the Green Knight and exchange the lot of a knight at court for that of a knight errant. Although he has all the courage and determination required for the successful performance of knight-errantry, the concomitant removal from the court and the company of men has not the least attraction for him. Quite on the contrary, we are told explicitly that the prospect "hym no gomen thoght" (692), and his utter loneliness is emphasized over and over again. Here we read that "Hade he no fere bot his fole" (695), there we are reminded that his journey through a strange country has taken him away from all his friends:

> Mony klyf he ouer-clambe in contrayes straunge;
> Fer floten fro his frendes fremedly he rydes.
>
> (713–714)

On the day of Christmas Eve, the contrast between the hardships he must undergo and the festivities in which he so eagerly took part the year before is emphasized by further insistence upon his utter loneliness: "Bi contray cayres this knyght tyl kryst-masse euen, / al one" (734–735). A few lines below, we find him crossing a weird and desolate forest. The scene is dominated on either side by towering hills (742), and Gawain at the very bottom must make his way through clumps of gigantic oaks (745) that dwarf him into utter insignificance. Considering what we already know about his lack of enthusiasm for the wilderness, we may easily guess his reaction to his own plight. But the poet is much too skillful a narrator to leave such important information to chance; he is likewise much too subtle a craftsman to spoil the delicacy of his narrative with an explanation. Instead, he allows one continuous, mournful sound to break the ghostly silence and suggest Gawain's state of mind far more effectively than an elaborate dissertation. The trees are covered, he tells us, "With mony bryddes vnblythe vpon bare twyges, / That pitosly ther piped for pyne of the colde" (746–747). This is a masterstroke of narrative technique. By using this visual and auditory image to cue us to his character's emotions, the poet has gone one step beyond Shakespeare himself, who in *Sonnet 73* mentions only "Bare ruin'd choirs where late the sweet birds sang."

With the device discussed here, the poet has won our sympathy for Gawain, and he may now mention his anguish and allow us to hear his appeal to Christ for help:

> The gome vpon Gryngolet glydes hem vnder
> Thurgh mony misy & myre, mon al hym one,
> Carande for his costes, lest he ne keuer schulde
> To se the seruyse of that syre, that on that self nyght
> Of a burde wats borne, our baret to quelle;
> & therefore sykyng he sayde, "I be-seche the, lorde,
> & Mary, that is myldest moder so dere,
> Of sum herber ther heghly I myght here masse
> Ande thy matynes to-morne, mekely I ask,
> & ther-to prestly I pray my pater & aue
>   & crede."

> He rode in his prayere
> & cryed for his mysdede,
> He sayned him in sythes sere
> & sayde "Cros-Kryst me spede!"
>
> (748–762)

Just as contrasting patterns of sounds are used to emphasize the difference between hunting in the field and hunting in the bedroom, so they are used to emphasize significant changes of mood in Gawain. We have mentioned earlier that on the evening of the third hunt he says nothing of the green belt he has received that morning, thus failing to his agreement with Bercilak. But the breach of faith rankles, and he shows a telling eagerness to cut short Bercilak's fiendish insistence to prolong the discussion of the day's activities:

> "I-nogh," quoth sir Gawayn,
> "I thonk yow, bi the rode."
>
> (1948–49)

We may assume him to be both relieved and overjoyed when the episode is finally over, for his success in keeping the protective girdle will supposedly insure his surviving the stroke which the Green Knight is to deal him on the next day. The sounds which suddenly burst out to break up his conversation with Bercilak are precisely those that best evoke this state of momentary elation:

> With merthe & mynstralsye, wyth metes at hor wylle,
> Thay maden as mery as any men moghten.
>
> (1952–53)

The last sound we hear that evening is appropriately the carefree laughter of the women:

> With laghyng of ladies, with lotes of bordes,
> Gawayn & the gode-mon so glad were thay bothe.
>
> (1954–55)

Gawain's sense of security, however, lasts only as long as the laughter of the women. In the darkness and solitude of his own room, his victory of the evening seems somewhat less significant, for the supposed protective quality of the girdle remains to be demonstrated, while his breach of faith has earned him at least Purgatory if he should die. Indeed, no sooner has Gawain been "blythely brought to his bedde" (1990) than the poet hints, "yf he ne slepe soundyly, say ne dar I" (1991). In accordance with his own statement, he does not immediately tell us how soundly Gawain sleeps, but the violent contrast between the minstrelsy and laughter of a few lines earlier and the next sound we hear is more revealing than any explicit commentary:

> The werbelande wynde wapped fro the hyghe
> & drof vche dale ful of dryftes ful grete.
>
> (2004–05)

Gawain has clearly traded his mood of merriment for one of anxiety, and we now learn that "thagh he lowkes his liddes,

155

ful lyttel he slepes" (2007). It is no wonder then, that he, who spent half of the preceding three mornings in bed, feels now compelled to imitate Bercilak and get up before sunrise (2009).

It is appropriately as Gawain reaches the Green Chapel and the end of his quest that we encounter the most dramatic instance of conjunction between sound and sense. The guide whom Bercilak had lent him has gone back after issuing the warning that the place is inhabited by a being of monstrous size who inexorably kills all those who come within his ken. As Gawain cautiously walks around to inspect the chapel, which turns out to be a weird, hollow mound covered with grass, he begins losing his confidence, "Debatande with hym-self quat hit be myght" (2179). The conclusion he reaches leaves no doubt concerning his state of mind:

> "We, lorde," quoth the gentyle knyght,
> "Whether this be the grene chapelle?
> Here myght abaute myd-nyght
> The dele his matynnes telle."
>
> "Now i-wysse," quoth Wowayn, "wysty is here;
> This oritore is vgly, with erbes ouer-growen;
> Wel bisemes the wyghe wruxled in grene
> Dele here his deuocioun on the deueles wyse;
> Now I fele hit is the fende, in my fyue wyttes,
> That hats stoken me this steuen, to strye me here;
> This is a chapel of meschaunce—that chekke hit by-tyde!
> Hit is the corsedest kyrk that euer I com inne."
>
> (2185–96)

The sense of security which the green girdle gave Gawain the preceding morning is now totally gone. Despite his renowned courage and his knightly training, the thoughts to which he has just given voice show him slowly falling prey to terror as he imagines the approach of a supposedly inevitable death. Once again, the poet abruptly marks a change in the course of the action with the help of a sound that echoes Gawain's innermost feelings. The knight is expecting decapitation, and the sound we hear is appropriately that of a whetting stone sharpening a cutting instrument. Furthermore, just as his terror would amplify the sound, so the grinding which we hear is utterly out of proportion with reality:

> Thene herde he of that hyghe hil, in a harde roche,
> Biyonde the broke, in a bonk, a wonder breme noyse.
> Quat! hit clatered in the clyff as hit cleue schulde,
> As one vpon a gryndelston hade grounden a sythe;
> What! hit wharred & whette as water at a mulle.
> What! hit rusched & ronge, rawthe to here.
>
> (2199–2204)

The comparison of the grinding sound to the whetting of a scythe bears out my suggestion that the incident is at least partly intended to convey something of the emotional turmoil in which Gawain finds himself in the face of death. Because of the terms of his agreement with the Green Knight, Gawain knows—and so do we—that the instrument that is being sharpened is nothing else than a battle-axe. The scythe, however, is the weapon with which painters traditionally equip the allegory of death for the purpose of mowing down her victims. The original audience of the poem may be assumed to have been completely familiar with that allegory,[10] so that the mention of a scythe rather than of an axe must have left little doubt in their minds that Gawain had given up hope of surviving the Green Knight's return-blow. As in the case of the other episodes discussed here, the poet now puts into words what we have only been allowed to guess thus far:

> Thenne "bi Godde," quoth Gawayn, "that gere as I
> [trowe,
> Is ryched at the reuerence me, renk, to mete
>   bi rote;
>   Let God worche; we loo,
>   Hit helppes me not a mote.

[10] The gruesome representation of the allegory of death which the fourteenth century could see on the pages of manuscripts and on the walls of religious buildings has been illustrated by Istvan Kozaky, *Geschichte der Totentänze* (Budapest, 1944), II, iii ff.

> My lif thagh I for-goo,
> Drede dots me no lote."
>
> (2205-11)

The patterns of sound in this preface to the final meeting of Gawain and the Green Knight are symbols of their respective external behaviors throughout the poem. Whether Bercilak gallops off with his head in his hand, leads a hunting party to the fields, or grinds a battle-axe, he is consistently a tumultuous and clamorous creature. By contrast, whether Gawain accepts a challenge, repulses amorous advances, or anxiously awaits for his head to be lopped off, he always remains an outwardly composed and properly quiet-spoken knight.

In one respect *Sir Gawain and the Green Knight* is a circular poem, for it ends precisely where it begins. The opening scene takes place at Camelot immediately after an initial mention of the fall of Troy; the closing scene likewise takes place at Camelot immediately before a concluding mention of the fall of Troy. Like the action, the atmosphere is the same at the beginning and the end. The first scene is one of rejoicing, and the first sounds we hear are those of merriment. The last scene is likewise one of rejoicing. Despite the incident of the green girdle, Gawain has regained his self-confidence, and the last sounds we hear are again those of merriment:

> The kyng comfortes the knyght, & alle the court als
> Laghen loude ther-at.
>
> (2513-14)

9

STRUCTURE AND SYMMETRY IN
SIR GAWAIN

Donald R. Howard

NO ONE WHO reads *Sir Gawain and the Green Knight* fails to notice its elaborate, symmetrical structure. Everywhere in the poem is balance, contrast, and antithesis. Things are arranged in pairs—there are two New Year's days, two "beheading" scenes, two courts, two confessions; or in threes—three temptations, three hunts, three kisses, three strokes of the axe. These intricacies are unobtrusively integrated with events and themes; and perhaps just for that reason, critics have taken note. of them only piecemeal and in passing, often with reference to the poem's mythic or symbolic content.[1] In what follows I intend to examine the narrative units of *Sir Gawain* which are based upon structural parallels, and to suggest in what way they coincide with the divisions of the poem marked by the ornamented

Reprinted, by permission, with some minor changes, from *Speculum*, xxxix (1964), 425–433, published by the Mediaeval Academy of America. Some of the ideas in this essay have been developed in the author's *The Three Temptations: Medieval Man in Search of the World* (Princeton, 1966), Chap. v.

[1] Morton W. Bloomfield in *"Sir Gawain and the Green Knight:* An Appraisal," (see above, Chapter II) has pointed to the need for detailed analysis of the poem's structure. Some pertinent comments may be found in Charles Moorman, "Myth and Mediaeval Literature: *Sir Gawain and the Green Knight,"* MedStud, xviii (1956), 164–169, and in Francis Berry, *"Sir Gawayne and the Grene Knight,"* in *The Age of Chaucer,* ed. Boris Ford, Pelican Books A290 (London, 1954), pp. 152–155.

and colored capitals of the manuscript. To do so, however, I shall have to turn first to the symbolism of the poem; for what I wish to argue is that its most protracted structural parallel depends upon the juxtaposition of two symbols, the shield and the girdle.

I.

Everyone from Mary McCarthy to C. S. Lewis has expressed caveats about literary symbolism, and it is true, symbol-hunting is an easy game with no particular criteria of corrigibility. In the study of medieval literature there is the added problem of a vast body of symbolism based on the four-level method of interpreting Scripture.[2] It is reassuring, therefore, to have at least one medieval work in which the symbols are identified as such by the author. No one has ever questioned the fact that the pentangle shield and the green girdle in *Sir Gawain and the Green Knight* are symbols. They are neither "Freudian" nor "patristic." Rather, the author tells us in lines 619–665 what the pentangle means, and there is precedent in medieval lore for that symbolic meaning. Likewise with the magic girdle: when Gawain keeps it at the end of the poem he says in so many words that it is to be a "syngne of my surfet" to remind him of the "faut and þe fayntyse of þe flesche crabbed."[3]

These two symbols are juxtaposed and paired, so that their meaning, to use Northrop Frye's language, comes about through the centripetal force of their relationship within the

---

[2] With respect to *Sir Gawain*, see Hans Schnyder, *Sir Gawain and the Green Knight: An Essay in Interpretation,* Cooper Monographs, 6 (Bern, 1961). While Schnyder grants (p. 74) that "the poem does not simply consist of a series of allegorical situations pedantically and painstakingly strung together," he treats dozens of recondite symbols in the poem without ever acknowledging the humorous tone, and devotes a chapter to the temptations without ever mentioning the girdle.

[3] Ll. 2433–36. References are to the edition of J.R.R. Tolkien and E.V. Gordon (Oxford, 1930).

whole literary structure.[4] Gawain's journey to the Green Chapel, we know, is made in two stages. Hence there are two descriptions of the arming of the knight, one when he leaves Arthur's court (536–669), the other when he leaves Bercilak's castle (2011–41). The earlier passage begins with Gawain's statement of his indifference to his destiny—"Quat schuld I wonde? / Of destinés derf and dere / What may mon do bot fonde?" (563–565); it ends with the description of the shield. The later passage, however, ends with a description not of the shield but of the girdle, which Gawain wears "to save himself."

Thus the girdle, within the symbolic structure of the poem, becomes a substitute for the shield. By shield I mean the shield itself, not its painted allegory. Critics often treat the shield and its pentangle device as a single object, which of course they are. Yet the symbolism of shield and girdle is symbolism of a different kind from that of the pentangle. The pentangle has an *assigned* symbolic value; it is put into the poem in order to stand for an abstraction, like Sansfoy and Sansloy, or Sin and Death. It tells us that Gawain is the "pentagonal man," the ideal knight.[5] The shield and girdle, however, take their symbolic meanings from the situation, the uses they are put to, the attitudes and emotions which people show towards them, and their juxtaposition one against the other. They remain just as much girdle and shield as Desdemona's handkerchief remains a handkerchief or Eve's apple an apple. While

---

[4] See *Anatomy of Criticism* (Princeton, 1957), pp. 82–94. That the shield and girdle stand in relation to each other is recognized by Robert W. Ackerman, "Gawain's Shield: Penitential Doctrine in *Gawain and the Green Knight*," *Anglia*, LXXVI (1958), 265, and by Richard H. Green, "Gawain's Shield and the Quest for Perfection," *ELH*, XXIX (1962), 137.
[5] On the pentangle, see Vincent F. Hopper, *Medieval Number Symbolism* . . ., Columbia Univ. Stud. in Eng. and Comp. Lit., 132 (New York, 1938), pp. 124–125, and Edgar de Bruyne, *Études d'esthétique médiévale,* II: *L'époque romane,* Rijksuniversiteit te Gent, Werken uitgegeven door de Faculteit van de Wijsbegeerte en Letteren, 98 (Bruges, 1946), pp. 349–350; also Green, pp. 129–135. On the shield, see Green, pp. 126–129 and Schnyder, pp. 53–54.

the pentangle is a painted sign—it appears on the knight's cote-armor as well as on his shield[6]—the shield and girdle are real objects and function in the poem as living, articulate symbols, dynamically paired.

The pentangle shield of course evokes the chivalric ideal. As part of the knight's armor, it is not surprising that it has symbolic meaning, for a knight's garments and gear, like a priest's vestments, were often given symbolic values.[7] Yet the description of the arming of Sir Gawain gives no symbolic meaning to anything *but* the pentangle. All his articles of clothing and armor are described in the most worldly terms—they are of costly silk, of bright fur, of well-worked and highly polished steel adorned with gold. His helmet, the last garment he puts on (kissing it as a priest might kiss the stole), has a silk cover embroidered with the best gems and encircled with costly diamonds. His garments and armor are also *useful*—they are "alle þe godlych gere þat hym gayn schulde" (584). The poet has concentrated all his powers on the lush description and saved the symbolism until the end, where it is more pointed and dramatic. By arranging his material in this way, he has underscored an essential fact: that a knight's valor is dependent on worldly means. The practice of chivalry presents the knight with the problem of using the world's goods for worldly ends and yet adopting those virtues which will keep him from loving the world itself.

After hearing Mass, Gawain puts on his helmet and takes up the shield (the manuscript at this point makes a subdivision with a colored capital).[8] On its inside is the image of the

---

[6] See line 637.

[7] On the symbolism of the knight's garments, see Edgar Prestage, "The Chivalry of Portugal," in *Chivalry: A Series of Studies to Illustrate Its Historical Significance and Civilizing Influence,* ed. Edgar Prestage (New York, 1928), p. 145; A.T. Byles, "Medieval Courtesy Books and the Prose Romances of Chivalry," ibid., p. 192; Sidney Painter, *French Chivalry: Chivalric Ideas and Practices in Mediaeval France* (Baltimore, 1940), pp. 83–84.

[8] See Tolkien and Gordon, p. viii.

Blessed Virgin, which will remind Gawain of her five joys and so renew his courage. On its outside is the pentangle or "endless knot," representing Gawain's perfection in his five senses and his five fingers, his faith in the five wounds of Christ and the five joys of the Virgin, and his possession of the five knightly virtues—franchise, fellowship, purity, courtesy, and pity.[9] (These virtues, as Professor Engelhardt has shown,[10] correspond in a general way to the chivalric virtues of piety, valor, and courtesy, and so represent his religious, military, and courtly obligations.) Hence the shield, with its images on either side, functions in two ways—to the knight as a devotional reminder, to the world as an emblem of his inner moral perfection. It is at base a worldly object, a part of his warlike gear, designed at once to protect his body and remind him of his immortal soul, so that it suggests at once his knightly valor and his spiritual indifference to destiny. To the world, the shield shows what spiritual strength lies beneath Gawain's rich trappings; to Gawain, it shows what ultimate spiritual meaning lies beneath the world's bright lures. Yet it is to have this devotional and spiritual meaning precisely in those moments when he is most the knight, when he is most given to worldly deeds and most reliant upon the shield as a made object. It thus points to the proper attitude for a knight: to be indifferent to one's life in the world and yet preserve it, to use the world well and yet love it little.[11]

*　　　*　　　*

After the temptations, when Gawain is ready to leave the

[9] Ackerman (*Anglia*, LXXVI, 254–265) suggests that the reference to the five wits would have called up fourteenth-century writings on auricular confession, so that the passage is consistent with the later theme of penitence.

[10] George J. Engelhardt, "The Predicament of Gawain," *MLQ*, XVI, (1955), 218–225.

[11] On the Christian and "otherworldly" aspects of the chivalric code, see Painter, Chap. 3, and F. Warre Cornish, *Chivalry* (London, 1908), pp. 218–219. See also Henry Osborn Taylor, *The Mediaeval Mind: A History of the Development of Thought and Emotion in the Middle Ages*, 2 vols. (London, 1930), I, 545–551.

SIR GAWAIN AND THE GREEN KNIGHT

castle for the Green Chapel, the poet again describes the arming of the knight. This time, however, he says nothing about the shield; instead, he ends by explaining why Gawain wears the girdle:

> Bot wered not þis ilk wyȝe for wele þis gordel,
> For pryde of þe pendauntez, þaȝ polyst þay were,
> And þaȝ þe glyterande golde glent vpon endeȝ,
> Bot for to sauen hymself, when suffer hym byhoued,
> To byde bale withoute dabate of bronde hym to were
>   oþer knyffe.
>
> (2037–42)

As the shield is emblematic of Gawain's knightly virtue, the girdle is emblematic of his fault. The whole movement of the story hangs upon his yielding to temptation, accepting the girdle, and having his failing revealed to him. In the end, Gawain himself makes the girdle a symbol of his "surfet" and of the weakness of the flesh. Now a girdle was an ordinary article of clothing, a belt or cincture from which one hung objects like keys or a purse. Because of its function, it was a convenient symbol for worldliness—the Oxford English Dictionary in fact reports such a metaphorical usage in the fifteenth century. *This* girdle, however, has the added lure of being rich and finely wrought in its own right: it is made of green silk, embroidered about the edges, and hung with pendants of highly polished gold.[12] More than that, it has powers of its own—not merely an emblematic meaning, like that of the shield's device, but remarkable "costes þat knit ar þerinne" (1849), magical properties to save the wearer from being slain. The author carefully reminds us that Gawain accepts the girdle for these powers, not for its richness. He goes so far as to tell us what the knight thought before accepting it:

> Þen kest þe knyȝt, and hit come to his hert,
> Hit were a juel for þe jopardé þat hym iugged were,

---

[12] See ll. 1830–33, 2037–39, 2430–32.

When he acheued to þe chapel his chek for to fech;
Myȝt he haf slypped to be vnslayn, þe sleȝt were noble.
(1855–58)

And Gawain, when he proposes to wear it as a memento of
his failing, himself denies any interest in either its worth or
its beauty:

"Bot your gordel" quoþ Gawayn "God yow forȝelde!
Þat wyl I welde wyth good wylle, not for þe wynne
  golde,
Ne þe saynt, ne þe sylk, ne þe syde pendaundes,
For wele ne for worchyp, ne for þe wlonk werkkeȝ,
Bot in syngne of my surfet I schal se hit ofte,
When I ride in renoun, remorde to myseluen
Þe faut and þe fayntyse of þe flesche crabbed,
How tender hit is to entyse teches of fylþe . . ."
(2429–36)

Gawain has taken the girdle, then, not to own it for its value
or wear it for its beauty, but simply to save his life.[13] It is as
worldly an object, and used for as worldly an end as the shield;
but unlike the shield, it is magical, it is used solely for a selfish
reason, and its acceptance requires that he act dishonorably
either to the lady or her husband if he is to keep it. He is guilty
not because he desires "to sauen hymself," but because in order
to do so he uses worldly means in the wrong way.

Even after he has taken the girdle, however, the knight con-
tinues to profess submission to God's will. When tempted by
his guide to flee he declares, "Ful wel con dryȝtyn schape /
His seruaunteȝ for to saue" (2138–39), and again, "I wyl nauþer
grete ne grone; / To Goddeȝ wylle I am ful bayn, / And to
hym I haf me tone" (2157–59). So, when he sees the Green
Chapel, he says, "Let God worche! . . . My lif þaȝ I forgoo, /

---

[13] John Burrow in "The Two Confession Scenes in *Sir Gawain and the
Green Knight*" (*MP*, LVII [1957], 73–79) has pointed out that Gawain
twice confesses to covetousness (ll. 2374–86, 2507–08) but his extrava-
gance is corrected and the sin specifically denied (ll. 2366–68, 2429–32).

Drede dotʒ me no lote" (2208–11). In these utterances we must not think him hypocritical. While he has taken the girdle and presumably held some hope for its efficacy, he has not deserted, but compromised, the chivalric ideal and its religious requirements. He is, in fact, never wholly sure of the girdle's powers. At the first stroke of the axe he flinches; and on the third stroke, when his neck is nicked, he bounds up and positions his shield.

Gawain's indifference to "destinés derf and dere" is, we need to remember, the self-abnegation not of the cloistered monk but of the active knight. "What may mon do bot fonde?" (565) he had asked—what can one do but *try*. He is admirably suited to put his destiny to the test: he is devoted to the articles of faith and has the virtues appropriate to the ideal Christian knight. The problem is to maintain the fine balance between this religious ethos and the unavoidable necessity of using worldly means to preserve life and accomplish knightly deeds. Hence he accepts the girdle not for any active pride which revolts against God, nor for avarice, nor covetousness, nor for vainglory, but for instinctive self-preservation, the central, involuntary worldliness of fallen man, through which even the best is easily tempted. This perfectly understandable weakness, however, leads him into other transgressions—the breaking of his oath to the lord, the false confession, the last failure of courtesy to the Green Knight. Once he has upset that finely balanced indifference to the world, those of the chivalric virtues which govern worldly action become in part unattainable. The poem suggests in this way how the worldly aims of chivalry and the other-worldly aims of the Christian life are ideally interrelated, but, for fallen man, incompatible.

II.

The poet suggested these distinctions by treating as symbols articles which were naturally part of his story. The girdle and shield are juxtaposed as two kinds of worldliness: the girdle an illicit and self-centered means of holding on to life; the shield an allowable, self-abnegating use of the world's goods in the service of the highest Christian ideals. These two symbols, paired so that they reflect the moral choice which confronts the hero, initiate two sequences which form a major structural parallel in the poem. The main action, beginning with Gawain's departure in the second division, falls into two stages—the events at the castle, and those at the Green Chapel.[14] The one comprises Sections II and III; the other, Section IV. No one, I think, has noticed that these two sequences are matched by an elaborate parallelism. The same kinds of events, in exactly the same order, occur in either part, and they center upon the three temptations in the first sequence and the three strokes of the axe in the second, with a confession following in each. These parallel contrasts are used artistically to distinguish Gawain's temptation and fall from his punishment and pardon. We shall see this best if we represent the contrasts in diagram:

Sections II–III	*Section IV*
(1) Arming of the knight, and description of the shield (536–669)	Arming of the knight, and description of the girdle (1998–2041)
(2) Journey to the castle (670–762)	Journey to the Green Chapel (2069–2159)

[14] Dale B. J. Randall in "A Note on Structure in *Sir Gawain and the Green Knight*" (*MLN,* LXXII [1959], 161–163) points out also that the Green Knight is the fiendish challenger at the beginning and end, but the genial host in the middle. The three parts correspond to those I have outlined, the "prologue," and the two parts of the major action. Such a triple structure was pointed out by Sylvan Barnett ("A Note on the Structure of *Sir Gawain and the Green Knight*," *MLN,* LXXI [1956], 319), who remarks on its consistency with the pattern hunt-temptation-hunt, with the three temptations, three hunts, three strokes of the axe, and so on.

(3) Description of the castle (763–810)

Description of the Green Chapel (2160–2211)

(4) Three temptations (1126–1869)

Three strokes of the axe (2212–2330)

(5) Confession to priest (1876–1884)

Confession to Green Knight (2378–2438)

This structural design coincides with the four manuscript divisions marked by ornamental capitals, the four "sections" of the poem observed in editions. Now the last three of these are subdivided by small ornamented capitals, so that the whole falls into nine units.[15] These nine units seem to be based on a principle of suspense; they mark off blocks of information. The four major divisions, on the other hand, mark the major episodes of the story—the opening scene, with the beheading episode and challenge; the passing of a year, and Gawain's journey to the castle; the temptations; and the second "beheading" scene, followed by the explanation and Gawain's return to court. The opening scene is kept as a single unit with no internal division —a most important prologue to the mission which Gawain must undertake. The work begins and ends with a reference to the fall of Troy and the founding of Britain, so that the events at Arthur's court are seen in the perspective of history as a point out of the past to which the reader draws up close and then away.[16] This sense of the sweep of time is matched within the poem by the lines on the passing of the year, at the beginning of the second division (491–535), which divide the prologue from the main action—the first New Year's feast with its be-

[15] See Laurita Lyttleton Hill, "Madden's Divisions of *Sir Gawain* and the 'Large Initial Capitals' of *Cotton Nero A.x*," *Spec,* XXI (1946), 67–71. Mrs. Hill argues that the size of the capitals is without significance.

[16] Randall, pp. 161–163, points out that the frame at the beginning and end reverses the order of the three elements—"þe sege," Brutus, and Arthur's court.

heading episode from the journey which Gawain must make a year later.

The second division of the poem is therefore a kind of inter-mezzo between the challenge and Gawain's journey. It comprises the description of the year's passing, Gawain's preparations to leave, the description of his armor with the passage on the pentangle, his voyage through the wilderness, and his arrival at the castle. The smaller capitals of the manuscript make two divisions within it, one beginning with the description of the shield (619), the other with his arrival at the castle (763). In the castle, a great dinner is set with many dishes and fine sauces, which Gawain calls a feast; it is a fish dinner, though, since Christmas Eve is a fast day, and he is drolly reminded that these culinary splendors are a penance—"Þis penaunce now ȝe take, / And eft hit schal amende" (897–898). After dinner the company hears evensong, and in the chapel Gawain sees for the first time the beautiful young lady with her ugly, aged companion.[17] On the next day there is a true Christmas feast; after it Gawain learns that the Green Chapel is nearby, and agrees that while waiting to leave he will exchange what he wins in the castle for what the lord wins hunting. Throughout, there is a fine balance of contraries: the revolution of the seasons, the warlike shield and its religious emblem, the unpleasant journey and the agreeable life of the castle, fasting and feasting, youth and age, beauty and ugliness, and at last the agreement to give what each has gained.

This tendency to match and contrast things is a dominant feature of the poem's style. It is, with respect to the purely verbal element, a feature encouraged by alliterative verse; a dozen examples come to mind—"bliss and blunder," "brittened and brent," "stad and stoken." And as we have seen, it sustains the

---

[17] For the principle of description by contrast in this passage, see Derek A. Pearsall, "Rhetorical 'Descriptio' in *Sir Gawain and the Green Knight*," *MLR*, L (1955), 129–134.

structural unity not only in the two beheading scenes but in the parallels, diagrammed above, between the events at the castle (Sections II–III) and those at the chapel (Section IV). These parallels contribute to the almost ritual symmetry of the whole, and they give to the later sequence a dreamlike aura of familiarity. Each of them contrasts in its own way, and each contrast contributes to the mystery and wonder of the final scene:

(1) In both parts, the arming of the knight before the journey is described in detail. In the earlier passage, the description ends with the lines on the pentangle shield. But when Gawain leaves the castle for the Green Chapel, the shield is not mentioned; instead the passage ends with a description of the girdle and a reminder that he is wearing it not for avarice or vainglory, but only to save his life.

(2) In both parts, he must undertake a journey. In the earlier journey there is positive danger from beasts and giants; there is cold, and hardship. In the shorter journey to the Green Chapel there are no physical dangers, but there is a spiritual one: his guide tempts him to flee. The description of the mist which hovers about the place and of the streams flowing through it creates an atmosphere of eerie uncertainty, very different from the explicit perils of the earlier passage: here, the perils are to come at the *end* of the journey.

(3) In both parts, the building is described as the knight comes upon it. The castle is on a knoll, surrounded by a park, and is built in the very newest style of late fourteenth-century architecture.[18] It is so new, and so idealized, that it seems almost illusory; its pinnacles, the author tells us, seemed as if cut out of paper (802).[19] The Green Chapel, on the other hand, is

[18] See Tolkien and Gordon, pp. 94–95.
[19] See Robert W. Ackermann, " 'Pared out of paper': *Gawain* 802 and *Purity* 1408," *JEGP*, LVI (1957), 410–417. Ackerman shows that the line refers to a custom of serving food on festive occasions covered or crowned with paper decorations in such shapes as that of a castle. Cf. Chaucer, *Parson's Tale*, X. 444.

ancient and gnarled, in part subterranean—such a place as the devil at midnight would say his matins in—like a cave or the crevice of an old crag, overgrown with grass. It is at the fork of a roaring stream, and the air is split with the ominous, and comic, whirring of a grindstone.

(4) The three temptations are paralleled by the three strokes of the axe. The temptations are carried out with an exuberant humor in which the daily hunting and the exchange of winnings serve as humorous parallels. The hunts themselves contrast with the temptations in intensity and aggressiveness, and the animals hunted suggest those qualities which Gawain must conquer— timidity, ferocity, and cunning.[20] The relation between Gawain and the lady reverses the courtly love code, in which the God of Love was said to be irresistible; indeed, the lady offers to be the knight's servant (1240).[21] The enviable but ridiculous position of the hero was a familiar one, to be sure, but it is heightened by the ritual exchanges. The kisses increase in number daily. The whole is recounted in a tone of suppressed mirth; while there is great suspense over the outcome of the temptations, the reader is encouraged to feel that he really knows what is going on. The lord's replies on receiving the kisses are richly ambiguous, for it is never wholly clear whether or not he knows what his wife has been up to. And the romping style of the passage makes the reader feel that he knows something of the *kind* of outcome, though he knows no details.

But at the Green Chapel, the three strokes of the axe are short and suspenseful. We know something is going to happen; we hear a noise, *as if* someone were grinding a scythe! But

[20] For the latter point, see John Speirs, *Medieval English Poetry: The Non-Chaucerian Tradition* (London, 1957), pp. 236–237. On the hunting scenes, see Henry L. Savage, *The "Gawain"-Poet, Studies in His Personality and Background* (Chapel Hill, 1956), pp. 31–48.

[21] On the treatment of the situation here as a reversal of courtly love, see J. F. Kiteley, "The *De Arte Honeste Amandi* of Andreas Capellanus and the Concept of Courtesy in *Sir Gawain and the Green Knight*," *Anglia,* LXXIX (1961), 7–16.

when Gawain gets under the axe we are completely in the dark. Even when his neck is nicked on the third stroke and he bounds up in self-defense, we are puzzled. When he accepted the girdle, we knew exactly what had happened; here, we are more confused than ever. We know the facts, but they make no sense.

(5) The explanation follows at once. As soon as Gawain's fault is revealed to him he flares up at the knight, flinging the girdle at him. Then he confesses his fault. This confession, as John Burrow has shown, parallels his confession to the priest after Gawain has taken the girdle. That earlier confession was really invalid; but in the second confession (though made to the Green Knight) he is genuinely contrite, he makes an honest confession (2379–86), he promises to do better (2387–88), and he does public penance by wearing the girdle. The court's judgment of his sin, however, is far less severe than his own—he twice confesses covetousness, although this is specifically denied in the poem. He wears the girdle as a sign of the weakness of the flesh, and the rest of the court join him in wearing a green band across their chests. Agreeing to do so, the king comforts him and the rest laugh.

Whatever else it may suggest, I hope this analysis of the narrative structure shows that the significant manuscript divisions are the ornamented capitals which mark the four major divisions. The five small capitals which mark subdivisions do not systematically correspond to narrative units. They seem to serve for emphasis, and were probably placed in accord with the author's—or scribe's—sense of dramatic rhythm. One precedes the description of the shield (619); another marks Gawain's arrival at the castle (763). In the third section, one marks the beginning of the second temptation (1421), and another follows Gawain's confession (1893). In the fourth section, there is a small capital at the beginning of the "beheading" scene (2259). If we divided the poem into nine sections (without regard to the size of the capitals), its structure and symmetry would be obscured.

All of this lends significance to a fact which has generally been ignored: at each of the three internal divisions marked by the larger capitals, the scribe left one ruled space, and through each of these spaces the illuminator extended the red ornamentation across the page in an identical design. There is no similar spacing or ornamentation elsewhere within the text of *Sir Gawain* or the other three poems preserved in the same manuscript. Hence both scribe and illuminator performed definite actions which made the four larger capitals different in kind from the smaller ones.

The poem's elaborate parallelism, with its multiple contrasts, helps produce the gamelike, ironic tone of *Sir Gawain*. Its effect is comic. The ritual balance of incidents does, in the end, what comedy always does—it purges extremes of conduct and brings the reader comfortably back to a norm; it restores the *status quo*. Gawain returns to the starting place, and, however chastened, is greeted with laughter which dispels his sobriety. The symbolism of shield and girdle suggests an essential and inescapable conflict between chivalry and Christianity; but this conflict is treated throughout in a spirit of amused and ironic detachment, as if the poet meant to suggest that these contrarieties of medieval thought, being irreconcilable, should be taken in good humor as a condition of life in an imperfect world. The mysterious and marvelous, which in tragedy remain ultimately incomprehensible, are here explained rationally away; we are asked not so much to *feel* the hero's experience as to think about it, to understand. The symmetrical world of the poem is at once unreal and substantial—far in the past and idealized, and yet plainly the world of real human conduct, of uncertainty and self-deception. It is too neatly balanced to be like the flux of history itself, yet it is an unpredictable world full of surprises; and, from the long view, it is ordered and right.

10

GAWAIN'S SPEECHES AND THE POETRY OF "CORTAYSYE"

A. C. Spearing

. . . I HAVE TRIED to show that for the poet the central interest in the poem is not the Green Knight but Gawain and the *cortays* Arthurian civilization he represents. But even if this is accepted it may still be felt that, whatever the poet's conscious interests, the imaginative center of his poem remains the Green Knight, and that the poem's poetry springs from him. In order to combat this view, it will finally be necessary to carry out some further critical analysis, by which it may be shown that, however impressive the poetry of muscular action that surrounds the Green Knight, there is another kind of poetry, at least as impressive, centering in Sir Gawain. There is, I believe, a poetry of *cortaysye* in *Sir Gawain and the Green Knight* as well as a poetry of muscular energy. For an illustration of this, let us look at Gawain's first speech in the poem, the speech in which, after Arthur has accepted the Green Knight's challenge and prepares to deal the blow, Gawain rises and begs to be substituted for the King:

> "Wolde ye, worthilych lorde," quoth Wawan to the kyng,
> "Bid me bowe fro this benche, and stonde by yow there,

Reprinted from *Criticism and Medieval Poetry* by A. C. Spearing, pp. 38–45, by permission of Messrs. Edward Arnold. © 1964 by A. C. Spearing. All quotations from *Sir Gawain* are from Tolkien and Gordon's revised edition (Oxford, 1930); spelling normalized by author.

That I wythoute vylanye myght voyde this table,
And that my legge lady lyked not ille,
I wolde com to your counseyl bifore your cort ryche.
For me think hit not semly, as hit is soth knawen,
Ther such an askyng is hevened so hyghe in your sale,
Thagh ye yourself be talenttyf, to take hit to yourselven,
Whil mony so bolde yow aboute upon bench sytten,
That under heven, I hope, non hagherer of wylle,
Ne better bodyes on bent ther baret is rered.
I am the wakkest, I wot, and of wyt feblest,
And lest lur of my lyf, quo laytes the sothe,
Bot for as much as ye ar myn em I am only to prayse,
No bounté bot your blod I in my bodé knowe;
And sythen this note is no nys that noght his yow falles,
And I have frayned hit at yow fyrst, foldes hit to me,
And if I carp not comlyly, let alle this cort rych
      bout blame."

                                                  (343–361)

It will be seen that the purpose of this speech is to move to-
wards a particular action—the substitution of Gawain for
Arthur as the Green Knight's opponent—but to do so without
giving any possible offense. A key word in it is *vylanye* (345),
for *vylanye* is the opposite of *cortaysye;* just as *cortaysye* means
in one sense the polite behavior appropriate to a courtly per-
son, so *vylanye* means the offensive behavior appropriate to a
vilain, a peasant. In both terms moral status is connected with
social status, in accordance with the aristocratic structure of
medieval society. It is *vylanye* above all that Gawain must avoid,
and he does so, so far as the plain sense of the passage is con-
cerned, by deferring successively to Arthur ("worthilych lord"),
to Guinevere ("my legge lady"), and, at the very end, to the
whole court. He argues that the Green Knight's challenge is
foolish, and hence not suitable to be taken up by the King him-
self, and that Arthur's court is full of men brave enough to take
it on themselves. Thus Gawain avoids claiming to be the only
worthy opponent; indeed, he says that he is a suitable oppo-
nent only because the loss of his own life would matter least.

And then, after all this, he puts his own claims, again in the most self-effacing way: he is Arthur's nephew (indeed, that is his only title to consideration), and he is the first to ask the boon of the King. The actual content of the speech, then, is supremely *cortays;* but Gawain's *cortaysye* is expressed most fully in the *way* in which he says what he says. The content of the speech can be easily translated into modern English, but the manner of expression (which is what turns the speech into a dramatic poem of *cortaysye*) is completely lost in translation. This may be illustrated by comparing the original with the modern translation by Mr. Brian Stone—a version chosen not because it is particularly bad, and certainly not because I think it would be easy to do better, but simply to show how the very essence of the passage is to be found in its detailed phrasing, so that it demands from the reader or listener a subtlety of response which can be represented in writing only by the most minute critical analysis.

> "If you would grant, great lord," said Gawain to the King,
> "That I might stir from this seat and stand beside you,
>   Be allowed without lese-majesty to leave the table,
>   And if my liege lady would likewise allow it,
>   I should come there to counsel you before this court of nobles.
>   For it appears unmeet to me, as manners go,
>   When your hall hears uttered such a haughty request,
>   For your great self to go forward and gratify it,
>   When on the benches about you so many bold men sit,
>   The best-willed in the world, as I well believe,
>   And the finest in the field when the fight is joined.
>   I am the most wanting in wisdom, and the weakest, I know,
>   And loss of my life would be least, in truth.
>   My only asset is that my uncle is my king;
>   There is no blessing in my body but what your blood accords.
>   And since this affair is so foolish that it should not fall to you,
>   And I first asked it of you, make it over to me;
>   And if I speak dishonourably, may all the court judge
>   Without blame."[1]

[1] *Sir Gawain and the Green Knight,* trans. B. Stone, The Penguin Classics L92 (London, 1959).

One of the first things one notices on looking at the original passage closely is the presence of a number of peculiarly circumlocutory phrases. Gawain does not simply ask the King's permission to rise and give him advice, he begs the King to *command* him to rise: "Wolde ye, worthilych lorde, . . . Bid me bowe fro this benche." Again, he does not merely ask the Queen's permission, but hopes that she will not be positively displeased if he rises: "And that my legge lady lyked not ille." The significant indirectness of both these addresses is lost when they are translated into the more straightforward "If you would grant" and "would likewise allow it." A second noticeable aspect of the original passage is the length and complexity of its sentences. The manuscript is simply broken into lines and stanzas, but according to modern conventions the passage may reasonably be divided into three sentences only (as by Tolkien and Gordon in their edition), and each of the three is full of subordinate clauses. The complexity of the syntax suggests the subtlety of the relationships that Gawain is establishing between a number of independent factors: the King's position, the Queen's position, the nature of the challenge, his own relationship to the King, the possible touchiness of the other leading nobles, and so on. These various and potentially opposing forces are woven by Gawain into a momentarily stable equilibrium, so that a particular action may follow. One observes how in the first sentence the main point—the wish of Gawain to offer advice to the King—is delayed until the very last line by a pair of conditional clauses (*If* the King would command it, *if* the Queen did not dislike it . . .), with a consecutive clause sandwiched between them (*So that* I might come forward without *vylanye*). Similarly in the last sentence the crucial request (Make it over to me) is delayed by subordinate clauses (*Since* the request is foolish, *since* I was the first to ask for it . . .), and immediately qualified by a further condition (*If* I am speaking unsuitably . . .). The sense one has in moving through the passage is of the skirting of a series of obstacles, the overcoming or evading of one difficulty after another: the syntax seems to wind itself along, to move two steps sideways for every step forward. This effect is heightened by the profusion of parenthetic phrases inserted before the main point of each clause is reached. For example, at the very beginning we are held up for the principal verb of the first conditional clause until the beginning of the second line, through the insertion of the polite address to the King and the poet's explanation of who is speaking to whom. There are parentheses and subordinate clauses even within the subordinate clauses. Throughout the speech we are delayed by phrases such as "as hit is soth knawen," "Thagh ye yourself be talenttyf," "I hope," "I wot," "quo laytes the sothe." The translator, even where he retains these, loses the main part of their effect by changing their position slightly: for example, in line 352, even though the phrase "I hope" is lengthened to "as I well believe," its delaying effect is lost because it is moved from the middle of the line to the end. Exactly the same thing happens to "I wot" in line 354. The effect of the passage is gained or lost precisely in such minute details as these.

To suggest that Gawain's *cortaysye* is expressed in this way through tiny syntactical effects may make it sound rather bloodless. This would be a mistaken impression, however; for it is in fact very close to the physical—as close as the Green Knight's bluffness. This is particularly apparent in the use, twice in this passage, of the single word *body*. In line 353, where the translation has "And the finest in the field when the fight is joined," we find in the original "Ne better bodyes on bent ther baret is rered." The nobles are good fighting men in a realer sense than belongs merely to Gawain's politeness: they are so in a directly physical sense which has vanished in the translation. And, even more strikingly, in line 357 the translation has "There is no blessing in my body but what your blood accords," while the original reads "No bounté bot your blod I in my bodé knowe." Here the translation retains the word *body,* but once again the original line contains a physical conception which the translator has lost. For the *Gawain*-poet, Arthur's blood runs

in Gawain's veins in a quite literal sense: the family relation-
ship is conceived of as completely physical, and so what worth
Gawain possesses is Arthur's not hyperbolically or metaphori-
cally, but in simple truth. The modern translator is using a lan-
guage which rejects such simplicity, and with his "what your
blood accords" he weakens it into something not quite physical
and not quite metaphorical. This is a matter of language, as
well as of what a particular poet does with it. Fourteenth-
century English falls naturally into such physical conceptions of
events, and more recent English does not. The change might be
illustrated vividly by a comparison of one of Dryden's "transla-
tions" from Chaucer with its original; but here a single example;
from *The Wife of Bath's Tale,* must be enough. In Chaucer,
the Queen tells the knight, "Be war, and keep thy nekke-boon
from iren" (*Canterbury Tales,* III 906), using an idiom in which
the idea of execution is presented in terms of its physical con-
stituents—the iron blade and the bone it will shatter. The
equivalent line in Dryden runs: "Beware, for on thy Wit de-
pends thy Life"—and here the concrete has been completely
replaced by the abstract.

We have seen from our analysis of Gawain's first speech how
his character is declared as soon as he appears in the poem,
partly by what he says, but still more by the way in which he
says it. The extremely complex manner of expression, full of
qualifications and delays, is typical of Gawain in the situations
which most test his *cortaysye*. We can find it again, for exam-
ple, in the speech he makes in the second bedroom scene, after
the Lady has twice referred to him as *cortays* and suggested
that he ought to display his *cortaysye* in teaching her "sum
tokenes of trweluf craftes" (1528). Instead he displays his
cortaysye in a further show of sinuous politeness, a politeness
here devoted not to achieving action, as in the first example, but
to evading the action that the Lady would force upon him:

> "In goud faythe," quoth Gawayn, "God yow foryelde!
> Gret is the gode gle, and gomen to me huge,
> That so worthy as ye wolde wynne hidere,

And pyne yow with so pouer a mon, as play wyth your knyght
With anyskynnes countenaunce, hit keveres me ese;
Bot to take the torvayle to myself to trwluf expoun,
And towche the temes of tyxt and tales of armes
To yow that, I wot wel, weldes more slyght
Of that art, bi the half, or a hundreth of seche
As I am, other ever schal, in erde ther I leve,
Hit were a folé felefolde, my fre, by my trawthe."

(1535–45)

Here he begins with polite exaggerations of phrasing, playing
"so worthy as ye" against "so pouer a mon," and suggesting
that any attention she gives him must be a trouble to herself
and the greatest of pleasures to him. Then, in the second part
of this single long sentence, after the semicolon, he uses exactly
the same syntactical devices as in his first speech, delaying the
completion of the sense until the last line by a series of noun
and adjectival clauses. Further delay is caused by the insertion,
as before, of polite qualifying phrases such as "I wot wel," "bi
the half," and "other ever schal." Finally, having reached the
main clause with the guileful internal assonance and alliteration
of "folé felefolde," he at once adds two further qualifying
phrases, as if to muffle its force. As in his first speech, the line
of sense winds its way stealthily through a series of obstacles:
this is what the poet means when he tells us that in his dealings
with the Lady Gawain "ferde with defence" (1282). We can
hardly be surprised that, by the parallelism of hunting and bed-
chamber scenes, he is eventually compared with the "wylé" fox,
twisting and turning as Sir Bercilak hunts him on the third day.
By way of contrast, we might compare Gawain's manner of
expression with the Green Knight's way of talking in a charac-
teristic speech of his. It is what he says when he makes himself
known to Gawain at the Green Chapel:

"Gawayn," quoth that grene gome, "God the mot loke!
Iwysse thou art welcom, wyye, to my place,
And thou hats tymed thi travayl as truee mon schulde.
And thou knowes the covenauntes kest uus bytwene:
At this tyme twelmonyth thou toke that the falled,

And I schulde at this Nwe Yere yeply the quyte.
And we ar in this valay verayly oure one;
Here ar no renkes us to rydde, rele as uus likes.
Haf thy helme of thy hede, and haf here thy pay.
Busk no more debate then I the bede thenne
When thou wypped of my hede at a wap one."

(2239–49)

The most obvious comment on this is that it is completely different from Gawain's speeches. The Green Knight's bluffness is expressed through a series of short sentences, usually linked by "and"—by coordination as opposed to the elaborate subordination of Gawain's idiom. Where Gawain's speeches are full of conditional and subjunctive verbs, the verbs here are most often in the simple present or past indicative, or else, significantly, in the imperative: "*Haf* thy helme of thy hede, and *haf* here thy pay." Where Gawain is subtle, the Green Knight is brusque: in both cases, character is expressed through syntax rather than through imagery.

The speeches I have chosen for analysis are fairly typical of their speakers, though naturally cases can be found where Gawain is brusque and paratactic, or the Green Knight subtle. Again, the insertion of qualifying phrases of the "I wot" or "bi the half" type is characteristic not simply of Gawain's speech, but of Middle English verse in general, and especially of alliterative verse. These phrases . . . belong to a style which still has its roots in a tradition of oral composition, and their original function is to fill a gap in rhythm and alliteration while enabling the poet to think ahead and his listeners to catch up with him. But in some of Gawain's speeches these conventional devices are put to an expressive purpose, in a way which is original as well as conventional. It is at least clear, I think, that, so far as the poetry of the poem is concerned, the Green Knight does not have things all his own way. I hope it is also clear that the modern critical method of close reading can be applied to this medieval poem with some profit, even though it must be directed to characteristics of style different from those with which most modern critics have been concerned.

11

THE ART OF
SIR GAWAIN AND THE GREEN KNIGHT

Theodore Silverstein

A ȝere ȝernes ful ȝerne, and ȝeldeȝ neuer lyke.

I.

THAT *curiosa felicitas* WHICH IN a distinguished literary epoch yet distinguishes the art of *Sir Gawain and the Green Knight* nowhere appears more happily than in the stanzas on the passage of the seasons which bridge the first two parts of the poem.[1] One of the few supposed additions by the poet himself to the données of the story he is telling,[2] the stanzas illustrate, in their freshness, their wit, and their shaping of general convention to particular case, the technical mastery which marks the poem throughout. Tightly woven into the fabric of the plot, they bring to bear on one of its critical moments a group of topics and verbal devices from poetic tradition, rhetoric, and philosophy—and do so with an ease that, despite their ornamental character, hastens rather than impedes the unfolding drama. Having chopped off the head of the terrible Green Knight, who picks it up and with it takes his leave, Gawain can

---

Reprinted, by permission of the University of Toronto Press, from the University of Toronto Quarterly, xxxiii (1964), 258–278.

[1] Lines 491–535.
[2] See ed. Tolkien and Gordon (Oxford, 1925), xvi.

only await the passage of the year before setting out for his own, more permanent, decapitation. The stanzas on the seasons both get us through the year and interpose a check to overt action that joins and clashes with their inward speed to produce a restlessness which deepens our anxiety for the hero as his peril comes upon him.

The poet gives us our first intimation of things to come at the end of the head-chopping scene itself. That clue occurs, as does much else of significance in the poem, in the final rhyming quatrain of a stanza, embodied, moreover, in one of the few *sententiae auctoris* which our poet allows himself. The knight's green head has been severed by a blow, it has rolled about like a ball on the floor, bleeding, among Arthur's guests, it has reminded Gawain of his promise to submit twelve months hence to like ordeal, and it has vanished with its mounted owner out the door. The pause which ensues would be awkward at any party, and this is, besides, the merry Christmas season, when Arthur welcomes wonders. He hastens to comfort Guenevere and carry on the feast: like Belshazzar our courteous king is, after all, a host. But there is also the courteous Sir Gawain. What of him at this moment of youth and jollity? In answer the poet suddenly abandons narrative to intervene in his own poem with solemn admonition:

> Now þenk wel, Sir Gawan,
> For woþe þat þou ne wonde
> Þis auenture for to frayn
> Þat þou hatȝ tan on honde.
> (487–490)

Thus the episode comes to an end which is no end, with a gaiety that is no gaiety. Our hero is in trouble and we know it.

The admonition is significant in another way. It is one of a pair of statements which, with what in a ballad might be called incremental repetition, forms a sort of envelope within which the stanzas on the seasons are enclosed. When the year has passed and the seasons have run their course, the poet tells us, once again at the emphatic end of a stanza:

> And wynter wynde3 a3ayn . . .
> Till Me3elmas mone
> Wat3 cumen wyth wynter wage;
> Þen þennke3 Gawan ful sone
> Of his anious uyage.
>
> (530–535)

The difference within similarity is instructive. Our hero has no further need of admonition. The time for action only too soon is here, right now. Sir Gawain is in trouble and he knows it.

What makes the difference between the admonition and its echo is exactly the group of stanzas on the seasons that lies between them, when the world turns full circle with scarcely a word of Gawain and his friends. The effect derives from the power of indirection which produces a growing anxiety by silence, even as it is formally eloquent in a brilliant but conventional piece of ornamentation. That formality is evident from the way the stanzas begin. According to the *artes poetriae* one of the proper ways of making a start is by aphorism or *sententia*,[3] and the passage gives us aphoristic utterance enough:

> Gawan wat3 glad to begynne þose gomne3 in halle,
> Bot þa3 þe ende be heuy, haf 3e no wonder;
> For þa3 men ben mery in mynde quen þay han mayn drynk,
> A 3ere 3ernes ful 3erne, and 3elde3 neuer lyke,
> Þe forme to þe fynisment folde3 ful selden.
>
> (495–499)

More than that, the poet appears to use another artistic device, that color of rhetoric called *annominatio*.[4] This consists, in one

---

[3] See, e.g., Geoffrey de Vinsauf, *Poetria nova*, vv. 126 ff. and esp. 180 ff. (ed. E. Faral, *Les artes poétiques du xiie et du xiiie siècle* [Paris, 1923], 201–203); and *Documentum de arte versificandi*, i. 10–17 (ed. Faral, 267–268).

[4] Geoffrey de Vinsauf, *Summa de coloribus rhetoricis*, ed. E. Faral, 323. Cf. 93–97.

version, of a use of different words having at the same time similar form or sound: "A ȝere ȝernes ful ȝerne, and ȝeldeȝ neuer lyke." The "native" alliterative pattern of the first half-line is, with its three rather than two head rhyming words, perhaps a little heavier than usual but not unique in the poem, which elsewhere also follows a like practice in order to establish an emphasis or some other particular effect. Here it introduces a syllabic repetition with change that is the essence of *annominatio.* In addition, *ȝere, ȝernes,* and *ȝerne,* words of different Anglo-Saxon origin that have fallen together phonetically by *Gawain's* time, are meant to yield a punning cross play with each other. They thus furnish an example of yet another figure, *traductio,* similar words or syllables with different meaning.[5] The yearly changes of seasons, as the Latin encyclopedists tell us, are denominated *curricula* because the seasons run, *quod currunt.*[6] Hence in *Gawain* the "ȝere ȝernes ȝerne" owing to its nature and its name. But something in addition is also being suggested by our poet. Since the nicely chosen *ȝernes* can represent either of two Anglo-Saxon verbs, *ge-irnan* (*gerinnan*) or *girnan* (*giernan*), the phrase may mean two different things at once; as if we were to say, the year runs running, or the year yearns yearning. So the punning play between the separate words is redoubled by the double sense of the whole. Nor does the wit reach its terminus in this line. There follows shortly after, more openly eliciting our crooked smile, the charming but less complicated jugglery with Lent:

> After Crystenmasse com þe crabbed lentoun,
> Þat fraysteȝ flesch wyth þe fysche and fode more
> symple.
>
> (502–503)

---

[5] Faral, 96.
[6] E.g., Isidore of Seville, *Etymologiae,* ed. Lindsay (Oxford, 1911), v. xxxv, i; and Rabanus Maurus, *De universo,* x, xi, in Migne, *PL,* cxi, 302BC.

And we have reached the body of the stanzas.

This artful introduction is more than sleight of hand intended to display an artist's virtuosity. With respect to the plot, its aphorisms have a particular significance because they bear the burden of the poet's chief intention: what he describes at length is the swiftly changing year—an elaborate and moving piece of nature poetry; what he means to imply is the threat of mutability with its unknown perils lying in the future. If he speaks no word of Gawain as the year submits uneasily to change, it is we who sense the connection with the hero's dilemma. And we sense it, first of all, from the peculiar character of the aphorisms themselves.

No one seems to have bothered with those aphorisms. Yet their sources and their literary histories are the direct clues, not only to what our poet may have read, but also to what at this point he is saying and how he makes us feel it by a subtle and precise manipulation.

The entire opening passage of five lines which we have been considering is a single aphoristic statement, admonitory in character like the previous admonition which it develops. Its indirection shows in its being now addressed, not to Gawain like its sober predecessor, but to us, who must gradually feel what Arthur's court must feel and what Gawain himself must come to wrestle with. Within its general statement two particular *sententiae* are quoted, which control both the statement and everything that is to follow after. The first is an adaptation of a half-line from Proverbs XIV. 13:

> *Gawain: Bot þaȝ þe ende be heuy* haf ȝe no wonder . . . .
> *Vulgate:* extrema gaudii luctus occupat
> *English: the ende* of myrth is *heuynes.*[7]

[7] This is the reading of the Great Bible of 1539, and Tavener's (1539), Cranmer's (1540), Matthew's (1549), and Coverdale's (1551) are like it. The Wycliffite versions are closer to the Latin: "and the endis of ioȝe weiling ocupieth"; "and morenyng ocupieth the laste thingis of ioye" (ed. Forshall and Madden [Oxford, 1850], III, 22).

The second, linked with the punning *annominatio* on the year, is translated from the Latin of Cato's moral distichs:

> *Gawain:* A ȝere ȝernes ful ȝerne, and ȝeldeȝ neuer lyke,
> Þe forme to þe fynisment foldeȝ ful selden
> *Cato:* non eodem cursu respondent ultima primis

in which *cursus* also supports the play on ȝere and ȝernes.[8] What is significant for the *Gawain* poet's technique in both cases is his suppression of the words which precede each quotation in its original, and his substitution of others fitting it to its context:

> *Gawain:* Gawan watȝ glad to begynne þose gomneȝ in halle,
> Bot þaȝ þe ende be heuy, haf ȝe no wonder
> *Proverbs:* Risus dolore miscebitur, et extrema gaudii luctus occupat
> [Laughter shall be mingled with sorrow, . . .]
> *Gawain:* A ȝere ȝernes ful ȝerne, and ȝeldeȝ neuer lyke,
> Þe forme to þe fynisment foldeȝ ful selden
> *Cato:* Cum fueris felix, quae sunt adversa caveto:
> non eodem cursu respondent ultima primis.
> [When you are happy, beware of misfortunes:]

Both capture perfectly the situation at Arthur's festive court; both express the change which it portends, the second with an

---

[8] Cato, I. 18 (ed. J. W. and A. M. Duff, *Minor Latin Poets* [Loeb Lib., 1934], 598). *Gawain's* line
"For þaȝ men ben mery in mynde quen þay han mayn drynk"
also has the sound of an aphorism, something like "Corde laetantes cum magnum sunt potantes," "Animi jocosi dum magnum sunt vinosi," or "Quamquam corde luditur quando magnum bibitur," but I have not found it. See, however, *Florilegium Gottingense*, no. 331 (ed. Ernst Voigt, in *Romanische Forschungen*, III [1887], 311), with its apt last hemistich:
> Dum bibitur uinum, dum luditur ante caminum,
> Tunc surgunt risus, stultis tunc est paradisus.
> [While wine is drunk, while there is revelry before
> the fireplace, / Then laughter rises, then it is a
> paradise for fools.]
And cf. I Samuel XXVI.36–37, II Samuel XIII.28, and Esther I.10.

address, not to hero but to audience, paralleling the negative admonition, "haf ȝe no wonder," added by the poet to the first. If he has deliberately left these clauses out as still another trick of indirection, their absence can only strengthen their effect with the reader who remembers his Bible and his Cato.

In the Middle Ages that memory was often enough reinforced by the special uses these *sententiae* were put to. Change of fortune, mutability, the turn of joy to sorrow were the contexts that elicited their quotation. Thus the crucial second verse of Cato's distich turns up, paraphrased, in one of the many *De contemptu mundi* poems that circulated in the twelfth century and later, the rhymed *Carmen paraeneticum ad Rainaldum,* which warns us of the bitterness that follows worldly joys:

> Postea finitur nec dulcis jam reperitur.
> Sed fit amara nimis, *non aequans ultima primis,*
> Et graviter pungit miseros quos primitus ungit.[9]

[Once worldly joy is ended its sweetness no more returns.
But it becomes very bitter, the end unequal to
the beginning,
And sorely vexes the miserable ones whom at first it anoints.]

In the prose *De contemptu* of Innocent III, Proverbs XIV. 13 appears in similar use, together with a verse from Ecclesiasticus (XI.27) that parallels the first line of Cato. What makes the passage peculiarly intriguing for the situation in our poem is its illustration of the Book of Proverbs' point by the sudden disaster that comes upon the prosperous sons of Job as they sit at table happily, eating and drinking wine:

Semper enim mundanae laetitiae tristitia repentina succedit. Et quod incipit a gaudio desinit in moerore. Mundana quippe felicitas multis amaritudinibus est respersa. Noverat hoc qui dixerat: *"Risus dolore miscebitur, et extrema gaudii luctus occupat* [Prov. XIV]." Experti sunt hoc liberi Job, qui cum comederent et biberent vinum in domo fratris sui primogeniti, repente vehemens ventus irruit a

---

[9] Printed among Bernard of Clairvaux's works in Migne, *PL,* CLXXXIV, 1309C.

regione deserti, et concussit quatuor angulos domus, quae corruens universos oppressit [Job I]. Merito ergo pater aiebat: "Versa est in luctum cithara mea et organum meum in vocem flentium [Job xxx]."
. . . Attende salubre consilium: *"In die bonorum non immemor sis malorum* [Eccli. XI.27]."[10]

[For sudden sorrow always follows worldly joy: what begins in gaiety ends in grief. Worldly happiness is besprinkled indeed with much bitterness. He knew this who said, "Laughter shall be mingled with sorrow, and mourning takes hold of the end of joy (Prov. XIV)." The children of Job experienced it when they ate and drank wine in the house of their first-born brother, for suddenly a strong wind rushed out of the desert and struck the four corners of the house, which fell in and crushed them all (Job I). Rightly then did the father say, "My harp is tuned to mourning and my organ into the voice of those that weep (Job xxx." . . . Attend to the wise counsel: "In the day of good things, be not unmindful of evil things (Eccli. XI.27."]

In Chaucer this is the passage the Man of Law must surely have in mind in the tragic second section of his Tale, since he translates its two key biblical quotations, along with an addition of its own (*Attende salubre consilium*), also to introduce a banquet that turns to disaster and death:

> O sodeyn wo, that evere art successour
> To worldly blisse, spreynd with bitternesse!
> The ende of the joy of oure worldly labour!
> *Wo occupieth the fyn of oure gladnesse.*
> *Herke this conseil for thy sikernesse:*
> *Upon thy glade day have in thy mynde*
> *The unwar wo or harm that comth bihynde.*
>
> For shortly for to tellen at o word,
> The Sowdan and the Cristen everichone
> Been al tohewe and stiked at the bord.
>
> (421–430)

But the *Gawain*-poet, if he had read the *Carmen* or the words of Innocent, also had in mind some other works as well. He had access to an English text of Proverbs less literally like the

---

[10] I, XXIII, "De inopinato dolore," Migne, *PL,* CCXVII, 713CD.

Latin which it rendered and similar to the subsequent transla-
tions of the Bible leading to the language of the Authorized
Version:

> Gawain: Bot þaȝ þe ende be heuy, haf ȝe no wonder
> Authorized Euen in laughter the heart is sorrowfull; and
> Version: the end of that mirth is heauinesse.

As for the Cato, the opposite is true: he evidently knew it also
in a version closer to the original than the *Carmen's,* since
that paraphrase fails to keep the metaphor of running (*cursu*)
which matches his word play with the year.

The importance of the word play, beyond the game of wit,
lies in the function of the aphoristic verse which it embellishes:
"A ȝere ȝernes ful ȝerne, and ȝeldeȝ neuer lyke." What the
verse promises the following lines fulfill; the seasons run with
speed and restless conflict. When the seasons come to an end,
moreover, the verse reappears, transmuted by a theme that
speaks the somber mood these stanzas have induced: the in-
exorable recession of all presentness into past. The theme
touched the Roman Seneca,[11] and it moved that other unknown
fourteenth-century Englishman who reminds us in the Vernon
Manuscript that the world is but a phantom:[12]

> Whon Men beoþ muriest at heor Mele,
> [w]iþ mete & drink to maken hem glad,

[11] *Epistulae morales,* XLIX, esp. 2–3: "Infinita est velocitas temporis,
quae magis apparet respicientibus. . . . Quicquid temporis transît, eodem
loco est; pariter aspicitur, una iacet. *Omnia in idem profundum cadunt"*
[Infinitely fast is the speed of time, which those who are looking behind
see more clearly. . . . That time that is past is all in the same place;
it is all perceived in the same way, it lies together. All things fall into
the same deep gulf]. Cf. the Senecan epigram "Omnia tempus edax
depascitur, omnia carpit" [Greedy time devours all, plucks all to pieces],
in *Anthologia latina,* ed. Baehrens, *Poetae latini minores,* IV, (Leipzig,
1882), 55; and Ovid, *Meta.,* XV, 234–236: "tempus edax rerum . . ." [time,
greedy for all].

[12] Ed. Carleton Brown, *Religious Lyrics of the XIVth Century* (Ox-
ford, 1924), 143.

[W]iþ worschip & with worldlich wele,
Þei ben so set þey conne not sade; . . .
Þis day, as leef we may be liht,
Wiþ al þe murþes þat men may vise,
To Reuele wiþ þis buirdes briht,
Vche mon gayest on his gyse;
At þe last hit draweþ to night,
Þat slep most make his Maystrise.
Whon þat he haþ I-kud his miht,
Þe morwe he boskeþ vp to rise,
Þen al draweþ hem to fantasy[s]e.
    Wher he is bi-comen, con no mon say—
And ȝif heo wuste þei weore ful wise—
    For al is tornd to ȝester-day.

And so, with the whirling of the year, the *Gawain*-poet returns
again to the verse that he began with, adding now the note of
poignancy:

And þus ȝirneȝ þe ȝere in *ȝisterdayeȝ* mony.

II

The superbly mobile stanzas which the aphorisms control
are incomparable of their kind in Middle English:

Forþi þis ȝol ouerȝede, and þe ȝere after,
And vche sesoun serlepes sued after oþer:
After Crystenmasse com þe crabbed lentoun,
Þat fraysteȝ flesch wyth þe fysche and fode more symple;
Bot þenne þe weder of þe worlde wyth wynter hit þrepeȝ,
Colde clengeȝ adoun, cloudeȝ vplyften,
Schyre schedeȝ þe rayn in schowreȝ ful warme,
Falleȝ vpon fayre flat, flowreȝ þere schewen,
Boþe groundeȝ and þe greueȝ grene ar her wedeȝ,
Bryddeȝ busken to bylde, and bremlych syngen
For solace of þe softe somer þat sues þerafter
        bi bonk;
    And blossumeȝ bolne to blowe
    Bi raweȝ rych and ronk,
    Þen noteȝ noble innoȝe
    Ar herde in wod so wlonk.

> After, þe sesoun of somer wyth þe softe wyndeȝ,
> Quen ȝeferus syfleȝ hymself on sedeȝ and erbeȝ;
> Wela wynne is þe wort þat waxes þeroute,
> When þe donkande dewe dropeȝ of þe leueȝ,
> To bide a blysful blusch of þe bryȝt sunne.
> Bot þen hyȝes heruest, and hardenes hym sone,
> Warneȝ hym for þe wynter to wax ful rype;
> He dryues wyth droȝt þe dust for to ryse,
> Fro þe face of þe folde to flyȝe ful hyȝe;
> Wroþe wynde of þe welkyn wrasteleȝ with þe sunne,
> Þe leueȝ laucen[13] fro þe lynde and lyȝten on þe grounde,
> And al grayes þe gres þat grene watȝ ere;
> Þenne al rypeȝ and roteȝ þat ros vpon fyrst,
> And þus ȝirneȝ þe ȝere in ȝisterdayeȝ mony,
> And wynter wyndeȝ aȝayn, as þe world askeȝ,
>   no fage,
>   Til Meȝelmas mone
>   Watȝ cumen wyth wynter wage . . . .

(500–533)

What circumstances suggested these stanzas to our poet? Tolkien and Gordon mention lines of "lyrical tone" as beginning the divisions of romances in the French and they cite *Kyng Alisaunder* as well as *Arthur and Merlin,* where the verses have to do with indicating time lapse or simply the season of the year.[14] This reminds us that the very presence of such stanzas would seem to be conventional in a fourteenth-century English romance. But it misses nearly everything else: it does not provide their nexus with the aphorisms, the march and interplay of their details, nor their sensitive relation to the narrative.

What, besides genius and a pretty vernacular convention, gave rise to and fashioned these "lyrics"? Was our poet, as it were, a Wordsworthian romantic with an English taste for Nature feelingly observed? Perhaps he was, but if so that predilection also gathered nourishment elsewhere. Gollancz, with

---

[13] Tr. "loosen," "fall," from ON *lauss.* Gollancz's reading (ed. EETS, O.S., no. 210 [London, 1940]), as contrasted with Tolkien and Gordon's *lancen*—"fly." See Gollancz's note to the line.

[14] xvi, n. 2.

his usual sharp eye, observing in them the special role of wind and of weather, relates the stanzas to the winter-summer conflict widely known in popular mythology.[15] Loomis carries the observation further by making that conflict integral to the argument itself in a reconstructed Welsh precursor of the story.[16] If these hypotheses are sound, then the writer of the *Gawain* may have found some reference to the seasons in his source as he began to set his poem down. But two new conditions now transformed their character: first and most important, the narrative, at the hands of whatever intermediary, no longer personified their conflict as a combat between two quasi-human foes; the new plot was literal and not allegorical, for the English poet, indeed, the basis of a serious comedy that turned upon chivalresque distinctions and the Christian knightly nature of Sir Gawain. As a result the seasons themselves, divested of any older mythical disguise, now also functioned differently: as literal circumstance, but embodied in a piece of rhetoric, in character both an ornament and a device to discipline emotion.

The second condition was the existence of a body of verse and prose currently available to the poet dealing with the turning of the year, which paralleled in many ways the popular mythology yet added to it particular nuance and permitted its adjustment to the new necessity. Some of the verse, by theory and practice, also furnished a poetic lexicography and a certain amount of substantive detail. As a whole the various interrelated traditions emphasized both the naturalistic qualities of the seasons and the months—the conflict of those qualities, their connection with the progress of the crops, the relation of the seasons with sun and constellations, with wind and storm, with generation, growth, and decay. In addition, they exhibit at certain of their moments a philosophic interest in the theme of mutability, metaphorizing the passage of the year as the trou-

---

[15] Gollancz, note to Ʒrepeʒ in l. 504.
[16] *Wales and the Arthurian Legend* (Cardiff, 1956), esp. 80 ff.

bled worldly life of man with winter at the end as death. Their discriminated patterns can easily be discerned in the literature of debate between winter and summer, in the prose accounts of the Latin encyclopedists, in the epithetic descriptions of the seasons in the *artes poetriae,* and in the moralistic verse from Boethius to Marbod of Rennes and after that set a tone in consonance with the *Gawain*-poet's purpose.

From their rich and apt materials, made magic with inimitable skill, our poet shaped his "lyrics" on the seasons.

The conflict of winter and summer is a persistent medieval genre, whose examplars survive, Latin and vernacular, in France, Germany, and England from the Carolingian era to the fifteenth century and beyond.[17] Unlike the *Gawain* it depends for its being on the device of personification, as does the allegorical combat acted out in the folk customs described by Jacob Grimm[18] and by Loomis in his reconstruction of the Welsh. Distinct, however, from the folk combat, the events of the literary *conflictus* consist of talk not deeds, since the situation is typically not a tournament but a *causa,* with a judge (*Ratio, God*) who renders judgment as in a court of law. Such a *causa* need not everywhere be limited to discourse. Thus a similar situation arises in the Fourth Fable of the Roman Avianus, which had an active long career in the Middle Ages and was known in England in the thirteenth-century version by Alexander Neckam.[19]

---

[17] The best general account of this literature is in H. Walther, *Das Streitgedicht in der lateinischen Literatur des Mittelalters* (Quellen u. Unters. z. latein. Philol. des Mittelalters, Bd. V. 2 [München, 1920]), 34–46 and (texts) 191–211. For further bibliography of the seasonal poetry, of which the *conflictus* is a part, see L. Biadene, " 'Carmina de Mensibus,' di Bonvesin de la Riva," *Studi di Filologia romanza,* IX (1903), 1–130, esp. 81 ff. Cf. G. Morici, "La poesia della stagione," *Nuova antologia,* CXXXII (1893), 479–515; and R. van Marle, *Iconographie de l'art profane au m.a. et à la ren.,* II (La Haye, 1932), 314–340, esp. figs. 358–359 (11 and 12 c.).

[18] *Deutsche Mythologie,* II (4e Ausgabe, ed. Meyer [Berlin, 1876]), 631–658, esp. 641 ff.

[19] For this history and the MSS and texts see L. Hervieux, *Les fabulists latins* (Paris, 1894), III.

In it Phoebus (Sol) and Boreas (Ventus) contend as to which is the more powerful, and Jupiter and the "Stars" pass judgment in the end. Yet with this case the contending parties supplement their talk by the evidence of an actual demonstration: Boreas blows, brings on clouds and thunder, wintry cold and wet; Phoebus dries the rain and quietly sends down his warmth. In the *conflictus* poetry the talk which is its action grows from the condition of the classical eclogue, on which its fictional format evidently draws. Debate rather than deed is its regular procedure. Even here, however, there are evidences of contact with the allegorical action of the popular traditions. A highly wrought thirteenth-century version of the *conflictus,* extant in a manuscript at Göttingen, stays within the limits of the format yet brings to talk descriptions of the individual months as knightly henchmen, though their powers are never exercised in fact.[20] On the other hand, the wind's and weather's turbulence set loose twice by the *Gawain* stanzas in keeping with the desired effect of active nature actively observed, also occurs in the Göttingen *conflictus* as a part of its setting for the *causa*:

Phebus libram perlustrabat	media temperie
et autumpnus autumnabat	uaria congerie,
quod Ceres, quod Bachus dabat	de nature serie . . . .
Qui dum tractant de potenti	rerum compugnancia,
reges duo uehunt uenti	summa cum iactancia
compugnantis elementi	septos elegancia,
istum glacie rigenti,	hunc ignis flagrancia.[21]
[Phebus shone his way through Libra	moderate in his temperature,
Autumn ripened fields and vineyards	with their varied garniture,
Grain and grape as gods had granted	out of nature's furniture . . . .
While they thus discoursed together	of the warring state of things
Winds bore up with mighty conflict	on their agitated wings,

---

[20] Walther, 191–203, esp. 191 and 194.
[21] Ibid., 191.

> Each distinguished as contender   in the war, a pair of kings:
> One leads on the rigid frost and   one the flaming fire brings.]

Gollancz[22] has suggested that the twin turbulences in the *Gawain* represent the equinoctial gales; since the Göttingen *conflictus* takes place when the sun is in the sign of Libra, its turbulence would seem to be a kind of poetic shorthand on this occasion for the autumn equinox. Whether the *conflictus* borrowed such details from Celtic or Germanic custom, or that custom reflects a literary convention vulgarized, remains a crucial question not readily resolved. *Das Folk* does not necessarily always come first, and nothing is more obvious, from classical reference and a learned play with words not unlike some of our English poet's, than the "literary" nature of the Göttingen elaboration and of other surviving specimens of the same genre. At the moment, of course, this speculation does not really matter. What does matter is the survival from contemporary *conflictus* of a capital detail whose relevance as analogue to the *Gawain* text is plain.

The progress of the argument in the *conflictus* established for each of the two chief seasons a convention of particulars that occurs with regularity in the literature of this sort and finds its place in other poetry that uses the *conflictus* for its topoi and its language. The convention is founded on naturalistic considerations similar to those that form the base for *Gawain,* but none of it is exactly like what our poet's stanzas develop. That winter is cold, its weather cloudy and wet, its nature suitable to the aged, its moral analogues sobriety and prudence; that summer brings flowers and crops, that it is gentle and warm, that it is suitable to youth and gaiety; these are all the expected lines of discourse. That, on the contrary, winter's virtues are injuries to all, to laity and spiritual, to gentlemen and rustics alike; that summer's virtues may in fact be disadvantages, its boon to youth may bring lasciviousness, its heat may be too

[22] Note to l. 504, with ref. to l. 2000.

hot, its dry too dry, its warmth recruit the inconvenient insect, its breeze permit the plague that only winter's storm can extirpate; these are the counter-arguments of each contending party against the other.[23] None of this, embedded as it is in polemics and moral recrimination, exhibits anything of the freshness of our poet's seeing eye. If the poetry of spring and love and daisies which flourished from the twelfth century onward drew upon this conflict for metaphor and topos, it did so with a freedom that abandoned mere polemics and transformed recrimination into plangency and laughter.

The very oppositions of the argument, moreover, would seem to have fixed two characteristics of the *conflictus* which generally deny another basic quality of the *Gawain* stanzas: an emphasis on the hostility of the seasons as against their speedy ordered cyclic movement, and an almost exclusive concern with winter and with summer as against the natural round of all the four. These are characteristics that the popular mythology also seems to stress, especially in its earlier stages, and the Welsh (and even English) examples analysed by Loomis apparently offer no exception. Yet valid evidence does survive, though briefly, that the literary *conflictus,* even in its stress on opposition, extended its active cast of characters to comprehend all the year's four seasons. It occurs in a German work roughly contemporary with the *Gawain,* Johannes Teppel's *Der Ackermann aus Böhmen.* There God begins his judgment in the case of the Ploughman versus Death with words whose reference to what may now be called the *altercacio quatuor temporum* [dispute of the four seasons] no editor has ever seemed to notice:

Der lenze, der sumer, der herbest, und der winter, eie vier erquicker und handhaber des jares, die wurden zwifertig mit grossen kriegen. Ir jeder rümte sich, un wolte jeglicher in seiner würkung der beste sein. Der lenze sprach, er erquickte und machte güftig alle früchte; der sumer sprach, er machte reif und zeitig alle früchte; der

---

[23] Cf. the texts in Walther.

herbest sprach, er brechte und zechte ein beide in stedel, in keller
und in die heuser alle früchte; der winter sprach, er verzerte und
vernutzte alle früchte und vertribe alle gifttragende würme. Sie
rümten sich und kriegeten faste; sie hetten aber vergessen, das si sich
gewaltiger herschaft rümten.[24]

[Spring, summer, autumn, and winter, the strengthening and ad-
ministrative four of the year, were divided with great quarrels. Each
boasted a desire to be the best in his operation. Spring said that he
revived all the fruits and made them grow. Summer said he ripened
all the fruits and in time. Autumn declared he picked and sorted all
the fruits in storage bins, the cellar, and the house. Winter said he
ate and used all the fruits and drove away all the poisonous worms.
They boasted and almost fought; but they had forgotten they were
extolling a more powerful authority.]

And spring and summer, excluded from the action though they
are, figure as *alumpni*[25] in the Göttingen exemplar, which also
does not fail to sound the echo of a further crucial philosophic
topos: the harmony in conflict of the running of the year:

Yemps:
"Cursu quidem sumus pares,   impares effectibus:
dies tui salutares,   mei spumant noctibus;
nostris fauent omnes una   contrarietatibus,
currunt secla, sol et luna   congruis metatibus."[26]

[Winter:
In our courses we are like though   unlike in the consequence;
Days with you are bright and   mine are dark with turbulence.
    tranquil,
Yet all shape a single happy   order of our difference;
Sun and moon and seasons run with   even measured congruence.]

The march across the *Gawain* stanzas, which strikes us very
strongly, of the different elemental *qualitates* of the seasons—

---

[24] Cap. xxxiii, ed. Krogmann (Wiesbaden, 1954), 138. See nn., 216.
Cf. ed. A. Bernt and K. Burdach (Berlin, 1917), 83–84 and (nn.) 400;
ed. A. Hübner (Leipzig, 1937), 43 f. and (nn.) 62; ed. K. Spaulding
(Oxford, 1950), 28 and (nn.) 74–75; and M. O'C. Walshe (London,
1951), 43 and (nn.) 73–74.
[25] Walther, 202, St. 105.
[26] Ibid., 192, St. 14.

cold and dry, cold and wet, warm and wet, warm and dry—
though implied, is not a deliberate feature either of *conflictus*
or of popular mythology. Its natural home lies among the cos-
mological summaries from Isidore of Seville to William Caxton.
Whatever special sense we have of that march as we read the
poet's lines, we also feel when we scrutinize the current cos-
mologies. Guillaume de Conches illustrates their character in
this respect in an expanded section of his twelfth-century
treatise *De philosophia mundi,* which offers every fundamental
motif of the passage of the seasons.[27] In it *qualitates,* the sun's
movement through the Signs, turbulence and wind, crops and
human life, variety within the forward progress, all appear or
are implied in a direct account of nature as it acts, detached
from personification and talk. The drift within each separate
season, moreover, and the linkage with what precedes and fol-
lows, underlines the current round of *tempora* and months in
qualitative terms that also have their cousinship to *Gawain.*
Various texts of the literary *conflictus* as well, with all the special
interests of their genre, show in coincidences with Guillaume and
his kind, how a poetry of the changing year could be affected by
such common philosophic learning.

Even so we need not hang too heavily on the cosmologist's
prosy words. Philosophy is, after all, philosophy, and poetry is
another sort of thing. *Gawain*'s author found among his fellow
poets and his continental predecessors, beyond the *conflictus,* a
definite though sometimes less defined concern for the seasons'
qualitates, marching along with that philosophic interest, but
in language and particulars closer to his fresh and artful lines.

With respect especially to diction, and to some extent to the
features of a nature "naturally" presented, the contemporary
English alliterative verse is witness to the currency of a body of
conventions on which our poet evidently drew. For the time of
spring and summer in particular, *Winner and Waster,* the *Parle-*

---

[27] II, xxvi-xxvii, Migne, *PL,* CLXXII, 67–70.

ment of the Thre Ages, and a dozen romances and lyrics all
bear the mark variously of that currency. Thus the *Parlement*
poeticizes May in a language nicely comparable to *Gawain*'s:

> In the moneth of maye when mirthes bene fele
> And the sesone of somere when softe bene the wedres
> Als I went to the wodde my werdes to dreghe . . . .
>
> The dewe appon dayses donkede ful faire
> Burgons & blossoms & braunches full swete
> And the mery mystes full myldely gan falle . . . .
> And the throstils full throly threpeden in the bankes.[28]

Even the dust at summer's end, another season, which our poet
might have witnessed directly for himself, finds its analogue in
a somewhat older narrative that he knew, Laȝamon's thirteenth-
century *Brut,* where it appears in a lively battle metaphor:

> *Gawain:* He dryues wyth droȝt þe dust for to ryse,
> Fro þe face of þe folde to flyȝe ful hyȝe . . .
> *Brut:* Swa þode doð on felde þenne he þat dust heȝe
> aȝiueð from þere eorðe . . . .[29]

But most of the surviving vernacular examples, whatever their
literary charms, are limited in their bearing on our poem: a
single season, a setting, a striking metaphor, breeze and dew
and boughs and birds and leaves. Beside them we must put, to
fill the picture out, not only the history of the *curriculum an-
norum,* whose patterns we have looked at in philosophy and
conflictus, but also another Latin poetry, which, preoccupied
with literary technique, yet links the active detailed life of
nature with the themes of the qualities of the seasons. The
mixture appears in the formalized *descriptiones loci* offered for
instruction by the *artes poetriae.* We may cite an apt example

[28] Ed. Gollancz (Roxburghe Club, no. 132 [London, 1897]), I, vv.
1–14. Similar language occurs, for example, in such pieces of about
the year 1400 or earlier as *Morte Arthure* (vv. 313, 3248, 3750), *De-
struction of Troy* (vv. 2368, 7997, 9639), the *Siege of Jerusalem* (v.
624), and *Lenten ys come* (vv. 2, 28).
[29] V. 27645.

from Matthew of Vendôme, which combines a presentation of
a recognizable scene with a clear preoccupation with the quali-
ties of spring, the generative union of moisture and of warmth:

> Donandi transgressa modum, sibi nulla reservans,
> Purpurat ornatu floridiore locum.
> Tellus luxuriat crinito gramine, gramen . . . .
> Comprimit et brevitas auris amica placet.
> Non infestat aquas solis calor, immo teporem
> Ramorum series orbiculata fovet.
> Humor, amicitiae solis sua jura maritans,
> Destinat in florum fructificare comas.
> Altera gratuitas superest, cumulantque decorem
> Organicae studio garrulitatis aves.[30]
> [Having passed all limit of giving, retaining nothing for itself,
> (Spring) brightens the scene with beautiful flowers.
> The earth luxuriates in long-haired grass, grass . . . .
> . . . and its congenial shortness delights the breezes.
> The heat of the sun does not trouble the waters; rather
> Its circular course kindles a gentle warmth in the branches.
> Moisture, joining its laws to the friendship of the sun,
> Chooses to fructify in the leaves of flowers.
> Spontaneity takes precedence over all else, and singing birds
> Increase the loveliness with their zealous chattering.]

Artificial as this may seem beside the effective freshness of the
Parlement and the freshness and energy of the *Gawain,* it yet
marks out an area in which nature poetry of this sort could work.
It is supplemented in Matthew by another illustration, not of a
single time of year but of all the seasons, and on this occasion
not by an amplified account but its contrary, *abbreviatio.* The
technical problem here involved also arises in the *Poetria nova*
of Geoffrey de Vinsauf, who gives us several full-blown pas-
sages on spring and winter, then illustrates the means by which
their characteristic acts may be shifted to the verbs and the
verbs themselves be chosen for their particular suggestive vivac-

[30] Faral, 148.

ity.[31] Thus winter, according to Geoffrey, should we wish to emphasize its capacity for harm:

> Semper hiems *inhiat* duris praedura tyrannis,
> Imperio cujus *contristant* aera nimbi,
> *Excaecat* caligo diem, *parit* aura procellas,
> Nix *claudit* stratas, *transfigit* bruma medullas,
> Grando *flagellat* humum, glacies *incarcerat* undas.[32]

> [Oppressive winter is ever envious of those stern tyrants;
> At his command the clouds sadden the air.
> Mist blinds the day, wind creates tempests,
> Snow blankets the ground, wintry cold pierces the marrow,
> Hail beats the land, ice imprisons the waves.]

Matthew solves the problem with an *abbreviatio* whose power of evocation depends on the reader's knowledge of the complicated seasonal traditions and its skillful use of epithetic method. Its parallel occurs in the widely known philosophic fiction by Bernardus Silvestris, the *De mundi universitate,* where the yearly vicissitudes of the seasons are stated in a distich whose verbs carry the burden of the elemental qualities:

> Viderit: unde vices rerum, cur aestuat aestas,
> Siccitat autumnus, ver tepet, alget hiems.[33]
> [He will have seen: whence the vicissitudes of things,
> why summer heats,
> Autumn dries, spring warms, and winter cools.]

Matthew gives us a comparable distich, but with a single modification for autumn which adds to the series of the qualities a reference to a second series, namely, the working of all the seasons on the crops:

> Sunt partes anni bis binae: ver tepet, aestas
> Aestuat, autumnus *vina dat,* alget hiems.[34]

---

[31] Ibid., 221 ff.

[32] Vv. 802–806; Faral, 222.

[33] II, x, 39–40, ed. Barach and Wrobel (Bibliotheca philosophorum m.a., no. I [Innsbruck, 1876]), 56. Cf. Horace, *Odes,* IV, vii, 9–12.

[34] Faral, 147.

[The parts of the year are twice two: spring warms,
Summer heats, autumn gives wine, winter cools.]

He thus redoubles by this simple substitution both the evocation of the seasonal traditions and the concentrated power of his lines.

The point of such observations is this: that the substance of the traditions of the turning of the year by *Gawain's* time had entered into the current world of verse and that even the most formidable formalist could be concerned with their significant and lively representation. If nothing quite comparable to our poet's lively lines survives from the vernacular of his time, he found hints enough elsewhere, both substantive and technical, on which to base his own poetic practice.

The richness of the passage in the *Gawain* resides largely in the number of expectations it fulfills. Little among its patterns or descriptive details can have been per se very original in its day. Its effectiveness derives from its energy, and its energy from its adjustment to the plot and the aptness of its technical devices. Matthew creates a springtime as evocative, perhaps, and even more elaborate in sensuous appeal, but it seems a conscious artifice beside the *Gawain*. The spring and early summer of the *Parlement of the Thre Ages* may be as charming and as "natural" but is static in comparison with our poet's movement. The difference is that they are only settings; his stanzas are the statement of an issue in the plot, implying the peril and unquiet of its hero. But there is also something else to be remarked. Our poet has learned, along with *annominatio* and punning, to capture speed and restlessness especially with his verbs. Geoffrey de Vinsauf and Matthew did not, of course, first discover the device; it occurs throughout the history of Western poetry, consciously in much of the current Latin verse as an aspect of wit and ornament, and the English alliterative style itself had long bred encouragement of the practice. No other contemporary English poet, however, uses it with such sustained yet delicate deliberation. In *Gawain* the year runs, the seasons sue each after the other, the weather fights with winter, the rain sheds in showers, Zephirus gently blows, the dew drops, autumn hastens and hardens and drives the dust to rise, the heavens wrestle with the sun, the leaves loosen, the grass grays, the harvest ripens and rots. Later, in a wintry passage that supplements the stanzas we have been examining, nature once again performs as vigorously in verbs:

> Now neȝeȝ þe Nw ȝere, and þe nyȝt passeȝ,
> Þe day dryueȝ to þe derk, as dryȝtyn biddeȝ;
> Bot wylde wedereȝ of þe worlde wakned þeroute,
> Clowdes kesten kenly þe colde to þe erþe,
> Wyth nyȝe innoghe of þe norþe, þe naked to tene;
> Þe snawe snitered ful snart, þat snayped þe wylde;
> Þe werbelande wynde wapped fro þe hyȝe,
> And drof vche dale ful of dryftes ful grete.
>
> (1998–2005)

Among these lines "Þe snawe snitered ful snart, þat snayped þe wylde" is a little *tour de force* of sharp-set verb and vowel-shifting *annominatio,* though some of the others run it very close. But perhaps the most arresting line of all catches at our fancy in the earlier stanzas, when the winter begins to turn to spring. With the addition of rhetorical antithesis, "Colde clengeȝ adoun, cloudeȝ vplyften," in a figure that recreates forever the lifting vastness of a moving sky in March.

Virtually nothing in these stanzas is what present-day scholarship has come to call personification allegory,[35] but they bring to external nature a metaphorical life whose possibilities had been explored as grammatical machinery by Geoffrey de Vinsauf and by Matthew of Vendôme in his verb-centered *abbreviatio.* And now the difference which strikes us is not a matter simply of history and tradition, of convention and device, but the operation of a high poetic talent. The two Latin writers are schoolmasters at best, with a gift for penning propaedeutic

---

[35] See M. Bloomfield, "A Grammatical Approach to Personification Allegory," *MP,* LX (1963), 161–171.

verse. They were, however, with others of their kind, instructors to several distinguished literary generations. The author of the *Gawain* may also know their texts or the principles their textbooks recommend, but, like the English writers of his own alliterative milieu, he also is a poet and a great one. He stands among the greater poets of our language and is very nearly the greatest poet in Middle English. The association of *Gawain's* stanzas with mutability and death is also part of the seasonal traditions. *Tempus fugit,* a fear of dying, temptation, and *Weltschmerz* had long been interacting emotional commonplaces. Life itself from the moment of our birth, Seneca tells us, is but a natural progress to the grave.[36] Its symbols are the ending of each day in night and of all the seasons in winter. In a world beset by vicissitude and danger, *virtus* is the only valid guide, the virtuous deed per se its own reward. An eloquent passage in which the Roman moralist sounds this unyielding note might also be the outline—if indeed it is not our poet's source—for what in fact proves to be the nature of the larger part of Gawain's strenuous journey:

Seneca: Est videlicet magna in ipso opere merces rei et ad adliciendas mentes hominum ingens honesti potentia . . . . Sed illud intuere, an ad istam virtutem, quae saepe tuta ac facili aditur via, *etiam per saxa et rupes et feris ac serpentibus obsessum iter fueris iturus.*[37]

[36] *Epistulae morales,* xxx, 10 (ed. R. M. Gummere, Loeb Library, I, 217).

[37] *De beneficiis,* IV, XXII, 2–4 (ed. J. W. Basore, Loeb Library, III, 250). Cf. *Epistulae morales,* CVII (ed. Loeb Lib., III, 226). For further association of seasons, vicissitudes, and *virtus,* see, among others, *Epistulae,* XCIX, 9–10 (ed. Loeb, III, 134). That our poet is actually paraphrasing "moral Seneca" is, in terms of access, very likely. The Roman is cited by Chaucer on occasion and his influence, considerable throughout the Middle Ages, was strong in France and England during the twelfth through fourteenth centuries. For a summary of that influence see Sandys, *A History of Classical Scholarship* (3rd ed., Cambridge, 1921), I; index, *s.n.* Seneca the younger; the indexes in Webb's ed. of John of Salisbury's *Policraticus* (Oxford, 1909) and *Metalogicon* (1929), in D.E. Sharp, *Franciscan Philosophy at Oxford in the Thirteenth*

[It is clear that the great reward for an act is in the act itself, and that virtue has enormous power to affect the minds of men. . . . But consider this: whether (or not) you would travel toward this virtue, which often is approached by a safe and easy way, even though the road lay over rocks and precipices, and was infested with savage beasts and serpents.]

Gawain: Mony klyf he ouerclambe in contrayeȝ straunge,
Fer floten fro his frendeȝ fremedly he rydeȝ . . . .
Sumwhyle wyth wormeȝ he werreȝ, and with wolues als,
Sumwhyle wyth wodwos, þat woned in þe knarreȝ,
Boþe wyth bulleȝ and bereȝ, and boreȝ oþerquyle,
And etayneȝ, þat hym anelede of þe heȝe felle.

(713–723)

Contemporary romance, both English and French, sometimes takes its hero through a difficult terrain swarming with the terrors of the bestiaries; thus our poet, no doubt, is also making use of still another current convention. That terrain, as Finlayson has recently well observed, is related to the otherworld of the dream visions.[38] But Gawain is not acting in a dream like the speaker in Thomas of Usk and the alliterative *Morte Arthure,* nor does he flee from danger as in the *Morte Arthure,*[39] nor does he move in fear even with the reassurance of a guide

Century (Oxford, 1930), in B. Hauréau, *Notices et extraits* (Paris, 1890 ff.), 6 vols. in Manitius, *Geschichte der Lat. Lit. des Mittelalters,* 3e Tiel (München, 1931), in Albertanus of Brescia, *Liber consol. et consil.,* ed. Thor Sundby (London, 1873); and C. H. Haskins, *Studies in the History of Mediaeval Science* (2nd ed., Cambridge, Mass., 1927), 373. Passages from the dialogue *De remediis fortuitorum,* ascribed to Seneca and made up in part of passages from his works, are used by *Der Ackermann aus Böhmen*: see Chaps. XII, XX, XXII, and Krogmann's notes, 190, 198, 200. Many other contemporary pieces, Latin and vernacular, quote the Roman but such quotation has yet to be catalogued.

[38] "Rhetorical 'Descriptio' of Place in the Alliterative *Morte Arthure,*" *MP,* LXI, (1963), 1–11, esp. 7 ff.

[39] Ibid., 3. "Thurghe Þat foreste *I flede,* thare floures whare heghe, For to fele me *for ferde* of tha foule thyngez." (*Morte Arthure,* vv. 3236–37).

as in Machaut's *Le dit dou lyon*.[40] He climbs cliffs, he wars with worms and beasts, displaying, though alone, the fortitude of the Senecan protagonist.

A poem attributed to Bede, though probably very much older, and extant in manuscripts of the tenth to fourteenth centuries, combines the speedy changing of the seasons and the recession of all worldly things in time with the poignant themes of mutability from Ecclesiastes iii:

> Omnia tempus agit, cum tempore cuncta trahuntur.
> Alternant elementa uices et tempore mutant . . .
> Tempora sunt florum, retinet sua tempora messis,
> Sic iterum spisso uestitur gramine campus.
> Tempora gaudendi, sunt tempora certa dolendi.
> Tempora sunt uitae, sunt tristia tempora mortis.
> Tempus et hora uolat: momentis labitur aetas.
> Omnia dat tollit minuitque uolatile tempus.
> Ver aestas autumnus hiems: redit annus in annum.[41]
> [Time moves all, as all things are drawn along by time.
> Changes alter the elements and pass away with time . . . .
> There is a time for blossoms; the harvest keeps its own time;
> So in time the meadow is covered with thick grass.
> There is a time for rejoicing, a time for grieving.
> Times of life, sad times of death.
> Time and the hour fly; the lifetime of a moment slips by.
> Winged time gives, takes, and limits all.
> Spring, summer, autumn, winter: the year returns in a year.]

Boethius sounds the ancient theme of changing day and seasons to symbolize man's life subject to the shifting fortunes of temporality, and the medieval commentators, and afterwards the allegorists, took the matter up with a no less definite insistence. Those whose cupidity commits them to this unstable enterprise are characterized as *anxii,* their journey as burdened by *angus-*

---

[40] Ibid., 9. " 'Venez hardiement, biau sire! / Car vous estes en mon conduit.' " [Come boldly, good sir! / For you are in my company.] (*Le dit dou lyon, vv.* 348–349, ed. Hoepffner, II [*SATF,* 1911], 171).

[41] "Incerti carmina varia," LVIII, I, ed. Baehrens, V (1883), 349–350.

tia.[42] In an elegy quite typical of its age the twelfth-century Henry of Settimello expatiates upon human misery, that turns in mortal turning with the changes of the weather:

> Sic solet arboreas Boreas evolvere frondes,
>> sic rota mortales, sic aqua seva rotam.
> Nunc calor ignitus, nunc frigus membra gelatum,
>> nunc, hostilis ei, sudor aquosus habet.[43]
> [So the Northwind is used to rolling over the leafy branches,
>> so the wheel rolls over mortals, and so the savage water
>>> rolls the wheel.
> Now fiery heat, now freezing cold,
>> now watery sweat—each hostile to him—covers his limbs.]

At another place, with a quatrain that reminds us of both Guillaume de Conches and Bernardus Silvestris' distichs and Matthew's, Henry distills in tears the seasons' qualities as fortune shifts and death stands in the offing:

> Temporibus cunctis ieiunus prosperitatis,
>> morte minante, minis asperiora gemo.
> Ver dedit inditium, febrem mala contulit estas,
>> nutrit autumpnus, frigida pascit hiems.[44]
> [Deprived at all times of good fortune,
>> and with death threatening, I bemoan things harsher than threats.
> Spring showed the symptoms, evil summer brought on the fever,
>> autumn nourishes it, and cold winter feeds it.]

Three centuries later and in England Peter Idley, the sensible

---

[42] *De cons. philos.,* II, m. iii and pr. iv, esp. 69–71; and *Saeculi noni auctoris in Boetii cons. philos. commentarius,* ed. E. T. Silk (Amer. Acad. Papers and Monographs, IX [Rome, 1935]), 80, I. 22–81, I. I; and 84, II. 15–20. The commentary is not ninth century but contains materials from Guillaume de Conches and others of a later period. Hans Schnyder (The Cooper Monographs, no. 6 [Bern, 1961], 46 ff.) calls attention to the allegories. His interpretation of *Sir Gawain* raises issues which will be dealt with by the present writer in an essay on Gawain's quest.

[43] *Elegia, sive de miseria,* ed. A. Marigo (*Scriptores latini m.a. italici,* no. I, [Patavii, 1926]), 35, vv. 209–212.

[44] Ibid., 34, vv. 167–170.

heir of all this homiletic passion, could turn the weather figure
to the profit of his son:

> Ofte it is seyn in a longe way
> Somtyme the wedir fresshe and faire of hewe,
> Now duste, now rayne, now sande, now clay,
> Now fresshe, now foule, now oolde, now newe;
> So in a longe lyffe man may not eschewe
> Aduersitees, troble, angre, and disease,
> Daily enfirmytees, and grete vnease.[45]

But Peter's mood is stiffening, not lacrymose like Henry's, and
the sense of swift inevitability is not anywhere in it.

Within what might be called the topos of the *tempora
annorum* the assimilation of wintertime to death occurs often
enough to constitute a specialized convention. That icy season's
natural barrenness no doubt gave origin to the theme. Accord-
ing to the cosmological writers, winter is to be equated with
decrepitude, and the point had long been present to the medi-
eval mind from the discourse of Pythagoras in Ovid.[46] Jacob
Grimm remarks, with a handful of instructive folk examples,
the frequent substitution of death's name for winter's in the
popular Germanic mythology.[47] Christian moral poetry likewise
adumbrates the kinship, as the influential bishop-poet Marbod
of Rennes with these verses on the seasons testifies:

> Quis quod deccurit per tempora quatuor annus,
> Veris temperiem distemperet acrior aestas,
> Quae mox autumno sibi succedente fugatur,
> Quem glacialis hiems violento frigore pellit?
> Ver aperit fructus, quos fervida decoquit aestas;
> Maturos legit Autumnus, sed bruma recondit
> Annum concludens, *gelidaeque simillima morti*

---

[45] *Instructions to His Son,* ed. Charlotte D'Evelyn (MLA Monographs,
no. VI [1935]), 104, vv. 1380–86.
[46] Guillaume de Conches, *Philos. Mundi,* II, xxvi, Migne, *PL,* CLXXII,
67D; and Ovid, *Meta.,* on the four seasons: XV, 199 ff., esp. 212–213.
[47] *Deutsche Mythologie,* II, 639 ff.

Decutit arenti marcentes arbore frondes.[48]
[Why is it that the year runs on through four seasons,
That the harsher summer disturbs the mildness of spring,
Which soon is chased away, pursued herself by autumn,
Whom icy winter then beats down with violent cold?
Spring opens the fruits which the hot summer spoils;
Autumn gathers the ripe ones, but winter lays them by,
Concluding the year, and very much like icy death
Knocks off the withering limbs from the drying tree.]

The lines could be a kind of partial paraphrase of *Gawain's,* whose hero must go questing forth in the fatal winter season; their subject, like that of *Der Ackermann aus Böhmen* and many another *Poema de morte,* is man's old *querela* with the harsh uncertain certainty of death.

III.

To the contemporary reader of the *Gawain,* therefore, the bridging stanzas would by the very nature of their substance have brought a certain accustomed expectation. The introductory aphorisms suggest it and the changing seasons, seasoned with nostalgia, lead us to its brink by other inherited conventions. When at the end of the year Sir Gawain thinks at last of his necessary journey, why does it now seem to him *anious*? Because, as he faces up to it, he realizes that the road is bound to be hard? "Mout estoit li chemins *enioz* et rude de roches et de montaignes" [Many of the roads were tedious and rugged with rocks and mountains]. Is it because the time of year is winter and winter is wet and cold, as Gautier de Metz observes?

Que [l'hiver] est frois et pluvieus
Plus que l'autres et *anieus*.
[That season (winter) is cold and wet,
More than the others, and vexing.]

[48] *De bono mortis,* Migne, *PL,* CLXXI, 171CD. Cf. Ovid, *Meta.,* xv. 153 ff.

The answer, of course, to both these qusetions is Yes, for the season is indeed the stormy winter, and the road, no road at all, will be painful and difficult to follow. But these, after all, are the more ordinary concomitants of a quest. Is it, beyond such physical considerations, an even greater trouble, the moral temptations that lie in wait for fortitude and honor, with sudden death lurking on the way and certain death standing at the Green Chapel in the end?

Death and moral peril are the greater threats, and both are in the hero's mind, and Arthur's and his court's, and in the mind of poet and reader alike. The formal arming of Sir Gawain for his quest, another established convention of chivalresque romance, is accompanied by the one deliberate allegory in the poem, an allegory whose purpose is to state in advance the Christian knightly nature of the hero, as a counter to the perils that the world may bring to him. Christian though the details are of Gawain's moral virtues, Seneca would have recognized the principle. When the time to go at last arrives our hero yet delays a while his leaving, till after Michaelmas, beyond all Hallows' Day, until at last he reaches All Souls. On that day he departs,[49] the day when the Church was wont to offer prayers in behalf of all its faithful dead. Together with the aphorisms at the beginning of the stanzas on the seasons, nothing provides evidence more literal than this of the poet's intent to nourish our anxiety nor the power of indirection by which once more he feeds it. Trouble seems sure, death very likely, and the bridging verses have carried us across the brink to the opening of another strange adventure. If aphoristic verse and moral commonplace, *conflictus* and "lyric" nature poetry, have furnished our author with the matter for this moment in his story, it is he who has given them their peculiar energy by forming them to the issues of his plot.

As for Sir Gawain, how can he possibly forsee that his weary

---

[49] Ll. 532, 536, 566.

way will lead him to a bedroom and a lady; that his tiny slip with her, elicited by courtly love's decorum, will rest, not on love, but on fear, his troubled fear brought from dream to daylight as death seems suddenly at hand; that the upshot of the challenge by the terrible Green Knight will turn out to be, not his decollation, but a nick on the neck to suit the tiny nature of his slip; that society will forgive him, both enemy and friend, but he, however, will not forgive himself; that no one else indeed will take his sense of failure seriously; that what to him will come to seem an overwhelming sin, will only generate laughter in the world which understands these matters, the very world which bred him and sent him on his way, the elegant knightly world of Arthur's court?

This is the stuff that comedy is made of, serious comedy, and Gawain is its hero and its victim. The world wags wittily, turns its worldly wit against his perhaps excessive sensibilities. If it runs too swiftly with winter at its heels, there is always indoors, as Horace once remarked, with comfort and warmth and wine and laughter.

And besides, in due course, the year will turn again, amen, *in secula seculorum.*

PART FOUR:

CHARACTERS AND SETTING

12

THE KNIGHT WHO CARED FOR HIS LIFE

J. F. Kiteley

AT THE END of *Sir Gawain and the Green Knight* the reader feels that Gawain has, in all essentials, come triumphantly through his severe testing at the hands of Bercilak and his wife —and yet Gawain himself is ashamed. While we, with Arthur's court, think that his adventure should indeed be "acorded þe renoun of þe Rounde Table,"[1] Gawain broods over his point of failure. What precisely is it? Bercilak states it quite clearly:

> Bot here yow lakked a lyttel, sir, and lewté yow wonted;
> Bot þat watȝ for no wylyde werke, ne wowyng nauþer,
> Bot for ȝe lufed your lyf; þe lasse I yow blame.[2]

Gawain is under no illusions as to his exact weakness—"Corsed worth cowarddyse and couetyse boþe!"[3]—and he repeats this in similar terms on his return to Camelot:

> Þis is þe bende of þis blame I bere in my nek,
> Þis is þe laþe and þe losse þat I laȝt haue,
> Of couardise and couetyse þat I haf caȝt þare.[4]

A study of Gawain's character in French and Middle English

Reprinted, by permission of author and editor, from *Anglia,* LXXIX (1962), 131–137.
[1] *Sir Gawain and the Green Knight,* ed. J.R.R. Tolkien and E.V. Gordon (Oxford, 1925), l. 2519.
[2] *Gawain,* ll. 2366–68.
[3] *Gawain,* l. 2374.
[4] *Gawain,* ll. 2506–08.

romance makes the reader aware of the fact that many of the knight's traditional traits reappear in *Gawain*. Monsieur E. Pons, in fact, says that one of the great achievements of the *Gawain*-poet is ". . . d'avoir de tant de portraits gauviniens discordants et de silhouettes allant jusq'au burlesque, dégagé un caractère nouveau de Gauvain cohérant et viable, suffisamment individualisé pour que nous le voyions devant nous différent de chacun de ses prototypes . . ." [to have drawn, from so many conflicting portraits of Gawain and from sillhouettes ranging all the way to the burlesque, a new character of Gawain, consistent and viable, individualized enough for us to see him before us distinct from each of his prototypes . . .].[5]

The passage which deals with the symbolism of the Pentangle is the only "set" piece of description of Gawain's character. The "fifth five" is the only specific statement of his virtues, for elsewhere we see his character depicted dramatically as the story progresses. The virtues ascribed to Gawain in this passage make an impressive list:

> Þe fyft fyue þat I finde þat þe frek vsed
> Watȝ fraunchyse and felaȝschyp forbe al þyng,
> His clannes and his cortaysye croked were neuer,
> And pité, þat passeȝ alle poynteȝ, þyse pure fyue
> Were harder happed on þat haþel þen on any oþer.[6]

and yet only one of them (clannes) does not appear elsewhere in romance associated with Gawain. Of course, there is much in his character in *Gawain* which is completely original, in the sense that he acts in the idiosyncratic way of a human being, but it is unlikely that the poet was not influenced by the current ideas about such a well-known knight.

For this reason, it is interesting to enquire whether, in other romances, Gawain was depicted as a knight who cared for his life. There is, perhaps, a hint of such a weakness in four Middle

---

[5] Émile Pons, *Sire Gauvain et le Chevalier Vert* (Paris, 1946), p. 80.
[6] *Gawain*, ll. 651–655.

English romances where Gawain fights a battle without a swift
and clear-cut victory. He is, of course, usually victorious: his
life is seldom in danger because of his marked superiority over
his opponents. He is certainly killed in the *Morte Arthure* by
Mordred, but his death is in many ways the result of an acci-
dent: he has wounded Mordred severely, and is just about to
administer the *coup de grâce* with a "shorte knyfe" when the
weapon slips on Mordred's mail; his adversary takes immediate
advantage of this and cleaves through his helm to his brain.
Elsewhere we may detect a willingness to accept an honorable
draw when the outcome of a joust is in doubt, and especially
when he is wounded. This cannot always be accounted for by
his courtesy in battle.

In his joust with Sir Priamus in the *Morte Arthure,* he is
very harsh and taunting in his words, and gives every indication
of a fight to the finish. When Priamus wounds him, however,
and boasts that the blood will not stop flowing from the
wound, he is quick to ask how the blood may be staunched,
while still maintaining an outward bravado. He readily gives
Priamus leave to prepare himself for his end when Priamus
makes this a condition of informing Gawain about the remedy:

> Thow betydes torfere of thowe hyene turne,
> Bot thow telle me tytte, and tarye no lengere,
> What may stanche this blode þat thus faste rynnes.[7]

This occurs in a romance which depicts Gawain as the warrior
knight, the headstrong man of action who strikes off the head
of his chief tormentor when sent as an emissary to Rome,[8] the
brave leader to whom the thought of retreat is anathema:

> Thane sais syr Gawayne, "so me God helpe!
> We hafe bene chased to daye, and chullede as hares,

[7] *Morte Arthure,* ed. G. Perry, EETS, no. 8 (New Ed. 1871), ll.
2582–84.
[8] *Morte,* ll. 1352–54.

Rebuyked with Romaynes appone þeire ryche stedez,
And we lurkede undyr lee as lowrande wreches!"[9]

Golagros and Gawayn is a romance composed very much to
the honor of Gawain; great emphasis is placed on his court-
liness and good manners. It is he who gains, where Kay has
failed, food and troops for Arthur through his courteous
speech. The courtesy shown by him to his vanquished oppo-
nent, Golagros, transcends mere good manners when he is pre-
pared to undergo the transitory shame of being apparently
taken prisoner in order to save Golagros from everlasting loss
of reputation in the eyes of his people. The fight between
Golagros and Gawain is prolonged, and the fortunes sway from
one knight to the other. Gawain's victory is not swift and clear-
cut; Arthur is very anxious for Gawain and twice prays for him:

> " . . . Lord, as thow life lent to levand in leid,
> As thow formit all frute, to foster our fude,
> Grant me confort this day,
> As thow art God verray!"—
> Thus prais the King in affray,
> For Gawayne the gude,[10]

as well he might when we read of Golagros' spirited resistance—

> His scheild he chopit hym fra,
> In tuenty pecis and ma;
> Schir Wawane writhit for wa,
> Witlese and woud.[11]

Certainly Gawain's mercy to Golagros is praiseworthy, but there
is a marked contrast between his harsh warlike words earlier in
the fight:

> Than he carpit to the knight, cruel and kene,
> "Gif thou liffis thi life, lely noght to layne,
> Yeld me thi bright brand, burnist sa bene;"[12]

---

[9] *Morte* ll. 1443–46.
[10] *Golagros and Gawayne,* ed. Sir F. Madden, Bannatyne Club (Edin-
burgh, 1839), St. lxxiv, ll. 8–13. See also St. lxxviii, ll. 7–8.
[11] *Golagros,* St. lxxv, ll. 10–13.
[12] *Golagros,* St. lxxx, ll. 6–8.

and his milder words when Golagros has refused to submit, and has declared his intention of fighting until he dies:

> Schir Gawayne tretit the knight to turn his entent,
> For he wes wonder wa to wirk hym mare wugh.[13]

(This, of course, is before Golagros has revealed his reasons for fighting to the death.) Gawain's behavior is above criticism, but there is this implication of a desire to end the combat then and there: one wonders if the mild words would have been spoken when he was fresh and not battle-scarred.

There is a prolonged fight in *Ywain and Gawain* when the two heroes joust with each other because of mistaken identities. The conduct of the fight exemplifies the finest qualities of chivalrous conduct. When it is obvious that, however long they fight, the outcome of the joust is unlikely to be decisive, they yield to each other. Gawain is clearly pleased to accept this honorable draw, and we learn that he is sorely wounded:

> Sir Gawayne said: "Sir, sertanly,
> Þou ert noght so weri als I;
> For, if we langer fightand were,
> I trow, I might do þe no dere.
> Þou ert no thing in my det
> Of strakes, þat I on þe set."[14]

We should also note that the two knights have not recognized each other when they are reconciled, and so this cannot have influenced the truce.

The Jeaste of Syr Gawayne does not depict a particularly attractive Gawain. The action consists of Gawain's dalliance with a beautiful damsel being interrupted successively by her father and her three brothers. Gawain is portrayed as the amorous knight, possessing little sense of moral rectitude; he fights the father and the first two brothers, overcoming them easily, and then resumes his dalliance without any apparent qualms.

---

[13] *Golagros,* St. lxxxiii, ll. 3–4.
[14] *Ywain and Gawain,* ed. G. Schleich (Oppeln und Leipzig, 1887), ll. 3363–68.

The third brother, Brandles, is made of sterner stuff, and they fight a prolonged battle.

> They fought together with suche yre,
> That after flamed out the fyre,
> They spake of no mercye.
> Thus full longe than gan they fyght,
> Tyll at the laste they wanted lyght.[15]

Not only is the joust evenly contested, but we also learn by implication that Gawain is wounded:

> They fought together, those knightes good,
> Throughe theyr haburgeons ran out the redde blode,
> That pytte yt was to see.[16]

Gawain is very quick to accept Brandles' suggestion that the fight should be postponed because of the darkness:

> "I holde," sayd Gawayne, "by milde Marye!
> And thus we make an ende."[17]

He endeavors to accept Brandles' terms in a face-saving manner, but his tone is very different from his sarcastic and taunting remarks to the two brothers whom he defeats easily:

> "What," sayde Gawayne, "ys that youre boast greate?
> I wonde youe woulde haue foughten tyll ye ssweate,
> Ys youre strenght all done?"[18]

May we not have a hint in these four instances that Gawain, the invincible man of arms, cared for his life? Whenever Gawain is placed in the position of being likely to lose his life, he is ready to come to terms with his opponent. This situation, naturally enough, happens infrequently, but when it does we cannot explain it away merely by saying that the exigencies of the plot

---

[15] *The Jeaste of Syr Gawayne,* ed. Sir F. Madden, Bannatyne Club (Edinburgh, 1839), ll. 452–456.

[16] *Jeaste,* ll. 449–451.

[17] *Jeaste,* ll. 483–484.

[18] *Jeaste,* ll. 275–277.

demand that Gawain should not be killed. Such a situation need never be allowed to arise. Again, only in *Golagros* is this characteristic used for the positive commendation of Gawain. One suspects, in fact, that the romancers may have come across some trait of the knight based ultimately upon his mythic origin, a trait which became less clear through the passing of time and the increasing popularity of the knight.

Miss J. L. Weston, while not always a safe guide, is clearly supported by facts when she notes that "One of the most striking characteristics of Gawain, and one which may undoubtedly be referred to the original conception of his character, is that of the waxing and waning of his strength as the day advances and declines."[19] "The original conception of his character" is a reference to his possible existence in far-off times as a solar hero. Several passages in French and English romances mention this trait, of which three may be quoted as typical. The earliest one is that in the First Continuation of Chrétien's *Conte del Graal:*

> Hardemens et force doubloit
> Toustans puis ke midis passoit,
> Por voir, a monsignor Gauvain,
> Tout en devons estre certain;
> Quant le clartés del jor faloit
> Icelle force tresaloit
> Et de miedi en avant
> Le recroissoit tot autrement.[20]

[Indeed, Sir Gawain's boldness and strength redoubled after midday: we can be certain of that. When daylight waned his strength ebbed, and before midday it flowed back to him forthwith.]

In the English stanzaic romance, *Le Morte Arthur,* we learn that

> Than had syr gawayne such a grace,
> An holy man had boddyn that bone,

---

[19] J. L. Weston, *The Legend of Sir Gawain,* Grimm Library VII (London, 1897), p. 12.
[20] *Conte del Graal,* ed. C. Potvin (Mons, 1866–1871), ll. 19139–46.

> Whan he were in Any place,
> There he shuld batayle done,
> Hys strength shulld wex in suche A space,
> From the vndyr-tyme tylle none . . . .[21]

Of several passages in Malory, one notes:

> But Sir Gawayne, fro hit was nine of the clok, wexed euer strenger
> and strenger, for by than it cam to the howre of noone he had three
> tymes his myght encresed . . . So whan it was past noone, and whan
> it drewe toward evynsonge, sir Gawayns strength fyebled and woxe
> passyng faynte, that unnethe he myght dure no lenger . . . .[22]

It might well be that the characteristic willingness of Gawain to
accept a draw (albeit an honorable one) when a fight is pro-
longed is ultimately to be connected with his mythic origin and
the fluctuating nature of his strength.

Gawain accepts the girdle from Bercilak's wife only when he
learns of its power to protect life:

> Þer is no haþel vnder heuen tohewe hym þat myȝt,
> For he myȝt not be slayn for slyȝt vpon erþe.[23]

We may always dismiss Gawain's acceptance of the girdle as
just another example of the poet's lifelike portrayal of his hero
(as indeed it is in its context). At the same time, the presence
of other traditional traits of Gawain in this romance makes one
suspect that his "cowarddyse," too, may have its roots in some
far distant part of the "legend" of Sir Gawain, the knight who,
on more than one occasion, cared for his life.

[21] *Le Morte Arthur*, ed. J. D. Bruce, EETS, no. 88 (1903), St. ccclii,
ll. 1–6.
[22] *Morte D'Arthur*, ed. E. Vinaver (Oxford, 1947), i. p. 161, ll. 1–8.
[23] *Gawain*, ll. 1853–54.

13

A NOTE ON THE
GREEN KNIGHT'S RED EYES

Robert B. White, Jr.

CERTAINLY ONE OF the most awesome figures in all of English literature is the remarkable Green Knight who clattered on horseback into King Arthur's court, right up to the dais, intimidating the King and his entire court of heroes, one New Year's Day long ago. Not the least striking characteristic of this knight is his greenness, which extends not only to the man himself but also to his garments, his stirrups, his ominous axe, and even his horse. Much has been written concerning the significance of this knight, his extensive greenness, and the contrasting gold of his ornaments; no one, however, seems to have noted what is in some ways the most striking detail of all the Green Knight's coloring, his "rede yȝen" that "he reled aboute" (line 304).[1] Amid all of the attention that has been directed toward the striking hyperbole of greenness in the description of this figure, these red eyes seem to be the one contrasting detail to have gone unnoticed and unexplained.

The hyperbolic use of symbolic colors, the greenness, and the knight himself have all been traced through various sources and analogues back to similar motifs in much earlier legends, gen-

Reprinted, by permission of author and editors, from *English Language Notes,* II (1965), 250–252.
[1] *Sir Gawain and the Green Knight,* ed. Sir Israel Gollancz, EETS, no. 209 (London, 1938), 11.

erally Celtic in origin.[2] The correct interpretations of the greenness and of the figure characterized by it have been the crux of an extensive and, at times, turbulent scholarly debate. In spite of all the effort which has been expended on the problem of the greenness, however, it still remains without a full and satisfactory resolution. The Green Knight's red eyes, on the other hand, do not appear in the various sources and analogues proposed for this poem, nor have they been traced back to any significant motifs in the folklore and mythology of prehistory. They are probably, it would seem, one of the details which the *Gawain*-poet himself contributed to this poem; and they constitute a meaningful detail.

One need not look far to discover the general symbolic significance of red when it appears in early literature; it was generally associated with blood, cruelty, and violence.[3] In the case of the Green Knight and his red eyes, however, it is possible to be much more specific. Just as the lank hair, the beardless face, and the high voice of Chaucer's Pardoner would have been indicative of his inner nature, or as the gap between Alice of Bath's teeth would have disclosed her amorous inclinations, so to the medieval reader the red eyes of the Green Knight would probably have been indicative of an important portion of his character.

The Middle Ages based the "science" of physiognomy, with which one could read with great detail the character of any man simply by observing his physical characteristics, on Plato's theory regarding the forming from within of Matter by Idea, or of the Body by the Soul. The interpretation of the personalities of Chaucer's Pilgrims through their physical characteristics has

[2] Seldom mentioned is the comparable hyperbolic use of red in the description of the ominous three red men in "The Destruction of Da Derga's Hostel," see Tom Peete Cross and Clark Harris Slover, eds., *Ancient Irish Tales* (New York, 1936), pp. 102–103, 122.

[3] See Don Cameron Allen, "Symbolic Color in the Literature of the English Renaissance," *PQ*, xv (1936), 88–89, for various examples.

yielded rich rewards, yet this approach has seldom been applied to other figures in medieval literature.

In order to simplify the theory of physiognomy in its application to individual persons, the philosophers of the Middle Ages digested the rules for applying this science into handbooks, the most popular of which seems to have been the *Secreta Secretorum.* This manual indicates in one version that "If eghen be Reed, he þat hauys hem ys coraious, stalworth, and myghty."[4] This description certainly applies to the Green Knight, but the comments in another version of the same handbook seem even more to the point: "And tho that haue eyen y-colorid like rede wyne, ben dysposyd to woodnesse, y-likenyd to bestes whych may not be daunted. And tho that haue eyen like ly of fyre brandynge and sprakelynge, bene angry and shamles, y-lykenid to houndes"; and "he that hath rede sparkelynge eyen, his fierse and corageous."[5] The interpretation of the Green Knight's red eyes which these three comments have suggested is strongly reinforced by still another comment from the manual of physiognomy by Lydgate and Burgh:

> Eeyen also / which be lightly mevyng,
> visage long / with oute mesure,
> Off hasty man / untrewe and levyng,
> Be signes Evident / and tooknys I the sure;
> Colour reed / Causyd of blood pure,
> Is signe of strengthe / and greet manlynesse,
> Which to fight / gevith greet hardynesse.[6]

---

[4] *Three Prose Versions of the Secreta Secretorum,* ed. Robert Steele, EETS, E.S. 74 (London, 1898), 115.

[5] Ibid., pp. 230, 233. In connection with the "eyen like ly of fyre brandynge and sparkelynge," it is interesting to note the description of Wrath in Lucifera's train (*Faerie Queene,* I, iv, 33):

> His eyes did hurle forth sparkles fiery red,
> And stared sterne on all, that him beheld.

[6] *Secrees of Old Philisoffres,* ed. Robert Steele, EETS, E.S. 66 (1894), 82.

Thus, to those knights seated at King Arthur's banquet table and to the fourteenth-century readers of this poem, these red eyes, it seems, would have conveyed specific information concerning the Green Knight which has gone unnoticed by modern readers. The Knight himself in his striking coloring and great size certainly appears as a formidable opponent; but the strength, courage, and manliness, which "to fight / gevith greet hardynesse," all indicated by his red eyes, make the hesitation of Arthur and his knights even more understandable.

14

THE ROLE OF THE GUIDE IN
SIR GAWAIN AND THE GREEN KNIGHT

Paul Delany

SIR GAWAIN'S JOURNEY from Bercilak's castle to the valley of
the Green Chapel has been a curiously neglected incident in
Sir Gawain and the Green Knight. In 1935 Elizabeth M.
Wright drew attention to the function of Gawain's guide as an agent
of the Green Knight: "in pursuance of his policy of frightful-
ness he [the Green Knight] primes the guide to do his best to
scare Sir Gawain beforehand by tales of ruthless murders com-
mitted by the giant he is about to meet. The guide is to try and
tempt the knight to break his plighted word."[1] Sir Israel Gol-
lancz suggested that the guide is probably the Green Knight
himself in a different shape.[2] I wish here to examine the role of
the guide and his relationship to the themes of the poem, and
to evaluate Gawain's performance in the temptation offered
him by the guide.

That the guide is really the Green Knight in disguise can be
denied, but not disproved. The denouement of the poem fails
to explain the role of the guide, just as it fails to give us the

Reprinted, by permission, from *Neophilologus*, XLIX (1965), 250–255.
[1] Elizabeth M. Wright, "Sir Gawain and the Green Knight," *JEGP*,
XXXIV (1935), 160.
[2] *Sir Gawain and the Green Knight*, ed. Sir I. Gollancz, EETS, O.S.
210 (London, 1940), p. xxxvi. Line references in my text are to this edi-
tion.

explicit cause of Morgan le Fay's hatred for Guenevere. In support of Gollancz's theory one could argue that the guide and the Green Knight affect a similar manner of speech—a mixture of boorishness and joviality—and that both are dashing horsemen. Here, for example, is the Green Knight's exit from Arthur's court:

> With a runisch rout þe rayneȝ he torneȝ,
> Halled out at þe hal-dor, his hed in his hande,
> Þat þe fyr of þe flynt flaȝe fro fole houes.
>
> (457–459)

This may be compared with the guide's abandonment of Sir Gawain:

> Bi þat þe wyȝe in þe wod wendeȝ his brydel,
> Hit þe hors with þe heleȝ as harde as he myȝt,
> Lepeȝ hym ouer þe launde & leueȝ þe kynȝt þere
> al one.
>
> (2152–55)

But Gawain also indulges in this kind of bravado when he leaves Arthur's court (see lines 670–672); the similarities between the three passages prove no more than that the poet admires vigorous horsemanship. Mabel Day's comment that "it would surely be unchivalrous to let a servant into the plot" scarcely proves that the guide must really be the Green Knight in disguise.[3] A man who had previously displayed such boisterous contempt for the knights of the Round Table as to call them "bot berdleȝ chylder" (280) could quite easily use a churl to test and even to ridicule Gawain.[4]

The evidence against the identification of the guide with the Green Knight, though admittedly not conclusive, is strong

---

[3] Gollancz, p. xxxvi.

[4] When Gawain arrives at Bercilak's castle and asks for lodging, the porter's reply suggests that he is "in the plot": " 'ȝe, Peter,' quoþ þe porter,' & purely I trow[e]e/ þat ȝe be, wyȝe, welcum to won quyle yow lykeȝ' " (813–814).

enough to cause me to reject Gollancz's theory. Firstly, the known sources and analogues of *GGK* do not give any authority for the identification of the guide with the Green Knight; whereas the churlish guide who is more wise than he seems, and who leads the hero to his next antagonist or adventure, is a recurrent figure in myth and legend.[5] The Green Knight's silence about the guide at the conclusion of the poem seems harder to explain if the Green Knight himself was the guide, than if he was not. Finally, we have the evidence of lines 1971–72—Gawain, Bercilak and the guide apparently all meet together in the hall of the castle the night before Gawain sets out:

> Þer asyngnes he a seruaunt to sett hym in þe waye
> & coundue hym by þe downeȝ, þat he no drechch had.

It is true that Bercilak might have pointed out the guide and then, on the following morning, assumed the guide's shape; but this seems to be rather a roundabout way to proceed, especially

[5] The following quotation documents this point and throws some interesting sidelights on the guide in *Sir Gawain and the Green Knight:*
> Not infrequently, the supernatural helper is masculine in form. In fairy lore it may be some little fellow of the wood, some wizard, hermit, shepherd, or smith, who appears, to supply the amulets and advice that the hero will require. The higher mythologies develop the role in the gerat figure of the guide, the teacher, the ferryman, the conductor of souls to the afterworld. . . . Goethe presents the masculine guide in *Faust* as Mephistopheles—and not infrequently the dangerous aspect of the "mercurial" figure is stressed; for he is the lurer of the innocent soul into realms of trial. . . . Protective and dangerous, motherly and fatherly at the same time, this supernatural principle of guardianship and direction unites in itself all the ambiguities of the unconscious—thus signifying the support of our conscious personality by that other, larger system, but also the inscrutability of the guide that we are following, to the peril of all our rational ends."

Joseph Campbell, *The Hero with a Thousand Faces,* Bollingen Foundation (New York, 1949), pp. 72–73.

when the power of shape-shifting is, as far as we can tell, under the control of Morgan le Fay rather than Bercilak.[6]

If the guide is not the Green Knight, what kind of person is he and why has the poet included him? The best hope of answering this question lies in a close textual analysis of the passages in which the guide appears or is mentioned; though in one or two places, where the meaning would depend on the tone adopted in oral delivery, interpretation must remain doubtful. We should note first that Bercilak spontaneously offers to provide Gawain with a guide to the Green Chapel, even though Gawain doesn't really need this help. In Bercilak's words: "Mon schal yow sette in waye, / Hit is not two myle henne" (1077–78). Gawain has won his way to the castle by his own efforts, overcoming great hardships in the course of his journey, and he could easily go the mere two miles to the Green Chapel alone. Nonetheless, he accepts the offer of a guide as a token of courtesy: "Þe lorde Gawayn con þonk, / Such worchip he wolde hym weue" (1975–76). As usual his courtesy and eagerness to do the right thing will bring him into danger. In his first journey Gawain was tested physically— by cold, rain, wild beasts, and so forth. Now, on the seemingly unchallenging final section of his quest, he is to be tested morally by his blustering and enigmatic guide.

The guide is supposed to be a mere servant and thus immeasurably below Sir Gawain on the social scale. But the first words he speaks to Gawain, after their departure from the castle, are familiar and crudely patronizing:

> "For I haf wonnen yow hider, wyȝe, at þis tyme,
> & now nar ȝe not fer fro þat note place
> Þat ȝe han spied & spuryed so specially after;

---

[6] Bercilak seems to be responsible for temptations which do not require magic powers—the temptations by his wife (see 2360–63) and by the guide—while Morgan le Fay controls Bercilak's shape-shifting (see 2445–66). It is, of course, possible (though, I think, unlikely) that Morgan could have transformed Bercilak into the guide.

> Bot I schal say yow forsoþe, syþen I yow knowe,
> & ȝe ar a lede vpon lyue þat I wel louy,
> Wolde ȝe worch bi my wytte, [yow] worþed þe better."
>
> (2091–96)

The guide also seems unusually well-informed about Gawain's long quest. In fact, he is taking advantage of his superior knowledge to play a cruel joke on Gawain. The lines just quoted are merely playful; but now the guide begins a vivid and terrifying account of the Green Knight's bloodthirstiness:

> Þer passes non bi þat place so proude in his armes
> Þat he ne dyn[g]eȝ hym to deþe with dynt of his honde;
> For he is a mon methles, & mercy non vses,
> For be hit chorle oþer chaplayn þat bi þe chapel rydes,
> Monk oþer masse-prest oþer any mon elles,
> Hym þynk as queme hym to quelle as quyk go hym-seluen.
>
> (2104–09)

The Green Knight does not really behave in this merciless way, of course, for he exists only to test Gawain's virtue and to terrify Guenevere.[7]

The guide now tempts Gawain to flee from the Green Knight's domain and offers to perjure himself in Gawain's defense. Like the Lady of the castle, the guide is offering Gawain a chance to escape; both tempters, to underline the similarity of their offers, use the same phrase:

> "Þat I schal lelly yow layne & lauce neuer tale
> Þat euer ȝe fondet to fle for freke þat I wyst."
>
> (2124–25)

Thus the guide; the Lady, asking Gawain to conceal the magic girdle, used the same expression:

> & bisoȝt hym, for hir sake, disceuer hit neuer,
> Bot to lelly layne f[ro] hir lorde;
>
> (1862–63)

7 See Gollancz, p. xxxvi, and lines 703–708.

231

Compared with the Lady's serious effort to seduce Gawain, however, the guide's temptation is insensitive and crassly humorous:

> "For-þy, goude sir Gawayn, let þe gome one,
> & gotȝ a-way sum oþer gate, vpon Goddeȝ halue;"
> (2118–19)

Up to this point Gawain's fourth temptation has been a rather lighthearted affair. The guide has been acting as a foil to Gawain's high seriousness by reversing the normal relationship of a commoner to a knight, by teasing Gawain with stories of the Green Knight's devastations, and by his clownish incomprehension of chivalric duties. But Gawain spoils the guide's joke by replying to his offer in a tone both indignant and patronizing:

> "Grant merci," quoþ Gawayn, & gruchyng he sayde,
> "Wel worth þe, wyȝe, þat woldeȝ my gode,
> & þat lelly me layne, I leue wel þou woldeȝ."
> (2126–28)

Given the unpleasant meeting which awaits him, we can excuse Gawain for being upset by his guide's strangely insolent behavior. He tries to regain the initiative by a boastful and at least partially dishonest explanation of his chivalric obligation to keep his word, and ends by invoking God's aid against the Green Knight:

> "Þaȝe he be a sturn knape
> To stiȝtel, & stad with staue,
> Ful wel con dryȝtyn schape
> His seruaunteȝ forto saue."
> (2136–39)

The guide's reaction to Gawain's pious invocation is extraordinarily contemptuous: " 'Mary!' quoþ þat oþer mon, 'now þou so much spelleȝ' " (2140). Ostensibly, the guide is angered by Gawain's foolhardiness—but the poet could hardly condone the sacrilegiousness of the guide's retort, strengthened as it is by his switch to the familiar *þou*. The real reason why he shows such open scorn for Gawain, I prefer to assume, is that he knows about the hidden girdle and therefore objects to Gawain's self-righteous invocation of Divine Providence.[8] The episode ends quickly after this, for the guide has had enough of Gawain's company. He directs Gawain to the Green Chapel, bids him a probably sardonic farewell as "Gawayn þe noble" (2149), and gallops off.

It may be objected that this reading of the fourth temptation takes too harsh a view of Gawain's sincerity. Does he not commend himself to God again after the guide has left?

> "Bi Goddeʒ self," quoþ Gawayn,
> "I wyl nauþer grete ne grone,
> To Goddeʒ wylle I am ful bayn,
> & to hym I haf me tone."
>
> (2156–59)

Has he somehow forgotten about the girdle and is he really putting all his trust in God? I think the answer is that the courtly code and the Christian code somehow occupy separate compartments in Gawain's mind. Immediately after accepting the girdle he went to confession and received absolution (1870–84). He apparently did not consider accepting the girdle to be sinful and therefore did not confess it to the priest. If he had confessed it, the priest would probably have ordered him to return it before giving him absolution.[9] The fact that Gawain

---

[8] There is no reason why Bercilak should not have told him about the hidden girdle the night before, when he gave him instructions for tempting Gawain on the morrow.

[9] The three prerequisites for absolution are confession, repentance (with restitution where possible) and a firm purpose of amendment; cf. Claudius' prayer, *Hamlet* III. iii. 50–56.

John Burrow, in "The Two Confession Scenes in *Sir Gawain and the Green Knight*," *MP*, LVII (1959), 73–79, suggests that Gawain did confess to accepting the girdle, but invalidated his confession by failing to return the girdle to his host. I prefer to consider Gawain's pact to exchange winnings with his host as a purely courtly obligation. To ex-has been disloyal to the agreement with Bercilak by concealing the girdle does not make it wrong to invoke God's protection later on, when he is alone and afraid. But Gawain is at fault when he flaunts his piety before the guide, who knows that Gawain has a second line of defense to fall back on if God should fail.

The conclusion of *Sir Gawain and the Green Knight* fails to explain all the problems connected with the role of the guide, but it does supply a few hints toward their solution. The sin of pride is a danger to Gawain throughout the poem because of his sense of his own worth and because of the flattery to which he is subjected by the Lady.[10] When the Green Knight reveals his true identity, Gawain is bitterly ashamed and full of self-reproach because he has been false to the ideals of knighthood (2370–88); but he must also realize that his show of virtue before the guide was at best self-deception and at worst pious hypocrisy. In future, he will wear the girdle to remind himself that pride is the camp follower of renown:

> Bot in syngne of my surfet I schal se hit ofte
> When I ride in renoun, ...
> & þus quen pryde schal me pryk for prowes of armes,
> Þe loke to þis luf-lace schal leþe my hert.
>
> (2433–34 and 2437–38)

It is not clear why the Green Knight says nothing about Gawain's temptation by the guide, but four reasons for this silence are worth considering: 1. Gawain did, after all, reject the temptation outright; 2. the Green Knight may prefer not to

piate his sin against the courtly code Gawain, after the confrontation at the Green Chapel, goes through a parody of confession and absolution administered by the Green Knight (2385–94). Burrow suggests that the two confessions are partial and complementary, each having what the other lacks; but I think it more likely that the poet intended each confession to be a good one within its own terms of reference.

[10] The knights of Arthur's court refer to this tendency in Gawain when they deplore that he must be "Hadet wyth an aluisch mon, for angardez pryde" (681).

embarrass Gawain by revealing that the churl was also "in the plot"; 3. alternatively, Gawain may have taken it for granted that he has been beguiled with magic ever since his arrival at the Castle, so that an elaborate explanation of all the details of his enchantment is not necessary; 4. the guide galloped off in the direction of the Castle and perhaps has not yet given his report to the Green Knight.

To summarize: during his journey from the Castle to the valley of the Green Chapel Gawain is faced by a temptation which contrasts with the merely physical tests of his journey from Arthur's Court to the Castle, and with the more refined subtleties of the Lady's temptations. The guide, as the agent of the fourth temptation, has three functions: to harass Gawain by frightening him and making fun of his mission; to observe his reaction when he is urged to flee; and finally, to maintain dramatic tension by showing the perceptive reader that from his arrival at the Castle Gawain can never escape surveillance by the powers that rule the magic world. This third role, integrating as it does the brief incident of Gawain's second journey into the theme of the poem as a whole, is the most vital: no interlude of security from the rigorous scrutiny of his judges can be granted Gawain in his time of trial.

15

GAWAIN AND THE GREEN GIRDLE

Stoddard Malarkey and J. Barre Toelken

IN *Gawain and the Green Knight,* AS GAWAIN approaches his destiny at the Green Chapel, the poet stresses the external influences on his "chere." He describes the wild valley in general, the "chapel of meschaunce" in particular, the sudden noise of monstrous whetting. These inspire in the hero a sense of foreboding, but he retains his courage, not to be daunted by the mere appearance of evil. Nonetheless, in lines 2214–16 we see that the atmosphere has begun to take its toll: Gawain does not plan to tarry long in the desolate spot if his adversary is not punctual. Suddenly the scene comes alive as the Green Knight leaps down from the cliff, ready for action. Presumably this exciting and frightening advance would at the least have startled Gawain, but if lines 2212–38 are to be taken as they are traditionally rendered, the poet does nothing more than catalogue the Green Knight's equipment, having Gawain greet him casually without so much as a nod.

In short, the poet appears to drop his consideration of Gawain's mental state at the very point at which it becomes most germane to the story. It is entirely likely, however, that the lapse is attributable not so much to the poet as to modern readings of the text. In view of the particular difficulty that

Reprinted, by permission, from the *Journal of English and Germanic Philology,* LXIII (1964), 14–20.

scholars and translators have encountered in line 2226, we propose that the line describing the Green Knight's axe,

Hit watȝ no lasse, bi þat lace þat lemed ful bryȝt[1]

constitutes an important crux in the poem, and that its solution will show the poet's continued concern with the reactions of Gawain, will offer a clearer reading of the entire stanza, and will suggest some valuable considerations of irony and imagery for the whole poem.

Editors and translators are generally agreed that the "lace" refers to something on the Green Knight's axe. A. C. Cawley, in his recent edition for Everyman's Library, reads for line 2226:

It was no less, measured by that brightly shining thong

and refers to the axe which Gawain had earlier used in beheading the Green Knight at Arthur's court, though his notes for lines 218–220 suggest that he reads "lace" in that context not as "thong" but as "lacework."[2] Brian Stone reads:

. . . and by the gleaming lace
It measured fully four feet in breadth.[3]

James Rosenberg has:

. . . four feet long—
It was no less in length—all wrapped in brightest lace.[4]

Gerould, in his prose rendering, preferred:

It was no smaller than the one used before, if measured by the gleaming thong. . . .[5]

---

[1] Sir Israel Gollancz, ed., *Sir Gawain and the Green Knight*, EETS, O.S. 210 (London, 1940). All references, unless otherwise noted, are to this edition.

[2] A. C. Cawley, ed., *Pearl and Sir Gawain and the Green Knight* (London, 1962), pp. 134 n., 59 n.

[3] Brian Stone, trans., *Sir Gawain and the Green Knight*, The Penguin Classics L 92 (London, 1959), p. 113.

[4] James L. Rosenberg, trans., *Sir Gawain and the Green Knight*, ed. and intro. by James R. Kreuzer (New York, 1959), p. 75.

[5] Gordon Hall Gerould, trans., *Beowulf and Sir Gawain and the Green Knight* (New York, 1935), p. 191.

Tolkien and Gordon read "(measured) by that lace," and refer to the scene in Arthur's court.[6] Berry is another who prefers "thong."[7] Many more notes and renderings might be cited which see "lace" as connected somehow to the axe and which differ chiefly as to whether the lace is a utilitarian thong which binds blade to handle or a graceful or festive decoration.

None of the above interpretations suggests clearly just what sort of comparison is being made, i.e., specifically what, if any, meaning exists in a statement like "The axe was no less (or smaller) by (measured by, in comparison with) that lace (thong)." The reading suggests, somewhat incautiously, that the medieval audience had some common knowledge of standard thong lengths; or it implies that Gawain in his agitation could not see without the aid of incidental trappings that this axe head "fowre fote large" was *twice* the size of the one ("þe hede of an elnȝerde," 210) which he himself had previously used.

Clearly, the confusion in comparison derives from the rendering of "bi," and the problem of meaning devolves on the rendering of "lace." If the sense here were really comparative between axe and thong, one might expect "no lasse þan þat lace," though certainly such an expectation would not of itself form a satisfactory objection to the line as it stands. Gollancz notes, however, that if lacing on the handle of the axe is meant, ". . . the first 'þat' is at least odd," since there has been no mention of lace in the passage, and, further, we do not expect the present axe to be ornamental. He thus suspects scribal error: either "þat" or "þe" or "lace" for "Lade."[8] Unfortunately, neither the forced subjunctive reconstruction of the former

[6] J. R. R. Tolkien and E.V. Gordon, eds., *Sir Gawain and the Green Knight* (Oxford, 1930), p. 113.

[7] Francis Berry, ed., "Sir Gawain and the Green Knight," in *The Age of Chaucer,* ed. Boris Ford, Pelican Books A 290 (London, 1954), p. 421 n.

[8] Gollancz, p. 127.

("if it were measured by the lace that gleamed full brightly"), nor the lengthy and awkward asseveration of the latter ("by the Lady [i.e., the Virgin] who gleams full brightly"), seems as fitting as the reading Gollancz implies in passing but apparently rejects, namely that "lace" refers to the lady's sash or girdle which Gawain is wearing, as he supposes, for his protection.

If we take "lace" as referring to the lady's girdle, a far better reading of the line results. The line would then read "It was no smaller by reason of that girdle that gleamed so brightly."[9] In other words, the gleaming girdle that Gawain wore had no effect in making that horrible four-foot blade seem any smaller. The poet, adopting an objective point of view, describes the Green Knight's equipment and, in line 2226, describes Gawain's mental reaction. This interpretation eliminates several difficulties, including those mentioned by Gollancz, and gives a far richer reading to the line.

That "lace" can refer to the lady's girdle is abundantly clear. It is called this in four previous and four subsequent instances.[10] Nor is there any question but that it is gleaming. Indeed the poet seems to make a point of this:

> Bot wered not þis ilk wyȝe for wele þis gordel,
> For pryde of þe pendaunteȝ, þaȝ polyst þay were,
> & þaȝ þe glyterande golde glent vpon endeȝ.
>
> (2037–39)

Further, when Gawain meets the Green Knight, and sees the axe "fowre fote large," the belt is shining in plain sight around his waist. In no commentary on the poem that we have seen has it been remarked that at the time of his meeting with the

---

[9] "Bi" is taken here in an instrumental sense: "by means of," "through the agency of." See *MED*, "bi," sense 7. "Þat" is taken, therefore, as a demonstrative adjective stressing the "lace" most recently referred to in the text, and certainly that lace most central to the story and hence uppermost in the minds of the audience.

[10] Ll. 1830, 1851, 1874, 2030, 2438, 2487, 2497, 2505.

Green Knight, the lady's girdle is the most conspicuous piece of Gawain's apparel, and hence would be gleaming brightly in the morning air.[11] Our own experience in reading and teaching the poem, one confirmed by an informal poll of others who have taught it, has been that there is an unconscious assumption that because the lady makes Gawain promise to conceal the gift from Sir Bercilak (1862–65), and because he conceals it before going to the chapel to confession (1874), and because he is so careful not to mention it to Bercilak that night, he continues to conceal it the next day when he goes to the Green Chapel.[12] But such is not the case.

When Gawain arises early in the morning of the appointed day, he gets dressed, goes to the stable, mounts Gringolet, and rides off. He never sees Sir Bercilak, who presumably is "sleeping in" after his hard hunt of the previous day.[13] Hence, in his mind, there is no need to conceal the girdle; nor does he. Our poet, with his usual attention to detail, takes us step by step through Gawain's toilette. The chamberlain helps him into his

[11] In fact, some commentators strenuously insist on the opposite. See, for example, Kreuzer's introduction, in which he says, "Stanza 81 serves to emphasize the fact that Gawain is careful to bind around himself the girdle . . . but also to keep it concealed" (Rosenberg and Kreuzer, p. xxx); and Joseph F. Eagan, S.J., "The Import of Color Symbolism in *Gawain and the Green Knight,*" *Saint Louis Univ. Studies,* Ser. A, Hum. I, 2 (1949), 79: "Gawain wraps the green silk girdle about his waist . . . upon the rich red cloth . . . the red coat worn under his armor symbolizes primarily the courageous nature of the knight. . . ."

[12] Such an assumption is undoubtedly due to the fact that the modern reader, who knows that Sir Bercilak and the Green Knight are the same, tends to forget that Gawain has no idea of their identity. A contributing factor to a widespread delusion is probably the fact that the word "girdle" has in our culture, as it did not in Gawain's, another meaning.

[13] This is what Gawain thinks. Actually, Bercilak is probably on his way to the Green Chapel already. There is no mention anywhere that Morgan le Fay was able to transport him instantaneously, and since Gawain takes the shortest way the Green Knight/Bercilak must have left ahead of him.

"cloþeʒ" (i.e., his undergarments) to ward off the cold (2015).
Then he dons his armor:

> & syþen his oþer harnays, þat holdely watʒ keped,
> Boþe his paunce & his plateʒ, piked ful clene,
> Þe ryngeʒ rokked of þe roust of his riche bruny. . . .
> (2016–18)

The chamberlain then goes to ready Gawain's horse (2024),
while Gawain completes his dressing:

> Whyle þe wlonkest wedes he warp on hymseluen,
> His cote wyth þe conysaunce of þe clere werkeʒ,
> Enuirened vpon veluet vertuus stoneʒ,
> Aboute beten & bounden, enbrauded semeʒ,
> & ferly furred with-inne wyth fayre pelures.
> (2025–29)

This is his surcoat, the overgarment on which is embroidered
the pentangle, symbolic of his pure deeds, his "clere werkeʒ."
It goes on over his armor.

Then the poet tells us that Gawain did not forget the "lace,
þe ladieʒ gifte" (2030). It is the last thing he puts on, even
after he buckles on his sword:

> Bi he hade belted þe bronde vpon his balʒe hauncheʒ,
> Þenn dressed he his drurye double hym aboute,
> Swyþe sweþled vmbe his swange swetely þat knyʒt.
> (2032–34)

We are told in considerable detail how well the girdle becomes
him, shining as it does against the rich red velvet of the surcoat:

> Þe gordel of þe grene silke þat gay wel bisemed
> Vpon þat ryol red cloþe þat ryche watʒ to schewe.
> (2035–36)

So Gawain leaves the castle, with the girdle wrapped around
his waist over his surcoat. If further evidence is needed, it is to
be found in a later incident. After the Green Knight has iden-
tified himself and explained the situation, Gawain in a mood of

remorse and shame "kaȝt to þe knot & þe kest lawseȝ, / Brayde broþely þe belt to þe burne seluen" (2376–77). Surely this would be difficult to do if the lace were concealed under his armor.[14]

Thus there appears to be ample justification for reading the "lace þat lemed ful bryȝt" as the lady's girdle which, wound around Gawain's waist on the outside, is gleaming in full view as he awaits the Green Knight. As a line of poetry, and in the context, it makes a far better reading than if it is taken as an ornament on the Green Knight's axe. If it refers to the lady's girdle, the poet has written a line rich in irony, and glancing with the humor that shows itself elsewhere in the poem.[15]

The whole trip from the castle to the Green Chapel has been carefully calculated to inspire Gawain with fear. The way to the place is rough and wild. The guide does everything in his power to make Gawain afraid and to tempt him to flight. When Gawain arrives at the place, there is no one there. In the foreboding silence, he becomes a little nervous, and remarks that this is the "corsedest kyrk" he ever saw. The first sound he hears is the horrid whetting of the Green Knight's axe. When he calls, the Green Knight answers, and comes "whyrlande out of a wro" carrying a "felle weppen." The scene, especially after the journey and the guide's warning, is enough to make any man think twice about the efficacy of his talisman. The horrible

---

[14] Also, it is more in keeping with courtly custom for a knight to wear his lady's favor somewhere in plain sight. Not much honor would accrue to a lady whose girdle was being worn like a truss.

[15] Ironic understatements and litotes are not rare in *Gawain*. A few examples will suffice to show that the poet utilizes these subtle stylistic devices to good advantage throughout the poem: Line 475 (Arthur), "For I haf sen a selly, I may not for-sake." Ll. 729–730, "he sleped in his yrnes / Mo nyȝtȝ þen in-noghe in naked rokkeȝ." Ll. 1288–89, "þe lady þenn spek of leue, / He granted hir ful sone." Ll. 2282–83, "Bot þaȝ my hede falls on þe stoneȝ, / I con not hit restore." Ll. 968–969 (of Morgan le Fay), "More lykker-wys on to lyk / Watȝ þat scho hade on lode." Ll. 2320-21, "Neuer syn þat he watȝ burne borne of his moder, / Watȝ he neuer in þis worlde wyȝe half so blyþe."

reality of that shining four-foot blade is not made any smaller "bi þat lace þat lemed ful bryȝt."

This helps to throw light on an incident that otherwise seems, on reflection, a bit uncharacteristic. If Gawain were fully confident of the power of the girdle, he would have no reason to shrink "a lytel wyth þe schulderes for þe scharp yrne" when the Green Knight gives the first blow. Indeed, this action can best be explained by Gawain's lack of confidence in the lace, a feeling that had begun before the blow was started. The requirements of the story necessitate the flinch, but unless Gawain has a reason for flinching, it is quite out of character. Here, if ever, he would want to appear in the best light: if he had had full faith in the girdle, he would have stood still under the blow. Our poet is too good a craftsman to have followed the requirements of the story without having provided Gawain with sufficient motivation. This reading of the line in question helps supply that motivation.

Besides making possible a more attractive reading of line 2226, the fact that Gawain wears the girdle in plain sight over his surcoat helps objectify the theme of the poem and externalize the symbolism inherent in the two garments. As has been noted, "treatises on knighthood . . . dwell on the moral significance of each piece of a knight's armor and other gear, including his coat of arms."[16] Gawain's surcoat is embroidered with the pentangle, the symbol of his knightly virtues, his "trawþe." When Gawain dresses that morning, the poet emphasizes the fact that the surcoat was emblazoned with this sign (2025–29, quoted above).[17] Over this surcoat he wraps the girdle, which is the symbol of his defection from the virtues of the pentangle.

---

[16] Robert W. Ackerman, "Gawain's Shield: Penitential Doctrine in *Gawain and the Green Knight*," *Anglia*, LXXVI (1958), 254–265.

[17] When Gawain dresses in Arthur's court (566–667), the pentangle is described as being on the shield, and no mention is made of the surcoat. Thus that the emblem is on the surcoat in 2025–29 must have some significance, or else be a lapse by the poet, which is doubtful in light of his passion for accuracy.

Hence, physically as well as spiritually, the girdle supersedes the pentangle, and Gawain rides to his "moment of truth" unaware (although we can be sure the poet's audience was not) that he has externalized his moral condition in such a blatant manner. This objectification of his internal condition serves to fix in visual form for the audience the irony of his situation.

All readers of the poem are struck by the poet's passion for order and balance. Indeed, one of the major elements in the beauty of the poem is its ordered structure, and the balancing of one theme against another, or one incident against another. The high degree of organization involved in balancing the hunting scenes with the temptation scenes, and in keeping both stories moving at the same time, is frequently remarked. A similar balance is achieved here. There is a balance between Gawain's spiritual condition and his dress. There is a further balance achieved between his appearance before and after the meeting at the Green Chapel. Several recent studies have dealt with the penitential doctrine to be found in the poem. "For Gawain, the girdle became the symbol of his falling away, however momentarily, from the pentangle, the symbol of his 'trawþe,' and for this he must do penance."[18] The girdle is worn by Gawain as an emblem of his guilt, as part of a formal penance for his sin.[19]

Thus we have a visualized balance in which the theme of the poem is made specific and external. Gawain after the encounter wears openly and consciously, as a symbol of guilt and a sign of penance, what he wore before the encounter openly and *un*consciously as an external manifestation of the fact that, indeed, the green girdle had momentarily superseded the pentangle.

---

[18] Ackerman, p. 254.

[19] John Burrow, "The Two Confession Scenes in *Sir Gawain and the Green Knight,*" *MP,* LVII (1959), 73–79. See also George J. Engelhardt, "The Predicament of Gawain," *MLQ,* XVI (1955), 218–225.

16

THE GREEN CHAPEL:
ITS MEANING AND ITS FUNCTION

Mother Angela Carson, O.S.U.

IN SO FINELY structured a poem as *Gawain and the Green Knight* it is surprising to find an apparent incongruity between what the term "Green Chapel" leads one to expect and what Gawain actually finds at the end of his journey. After the first part of the beheading test, the knight both designates the Green Chapel as the place where Gawain is to meet him and uses it as a means of identifying himself: "þe knyȝt of þe grene chapel men knowen me mony."[1] Upon his journey north toward Wyrale, Gawain's manner of inquiry about the Green Chapel reflects the emphasis which the Green Knight himself has put upon it:

> And ay he frayned, as he ferde, at frekeȝ þat he met,
> If þay hade herde any karp of a knyȝt grene,
> In any grounde þeraboute, of þe grene chapel.
>
> (703–705)

At Bercilak's castle he asks as a boon that his host tell him if he has heard

> "Of þe grene chapel, quere hit on grounde stondeȝ,
> And of þe knyȝt þat hit kepes, of colour of grene."
>
> (1058–59)

Reprinted, by permission of author and editor, from *Studies in Philology*, LX (1963), 598–605.
[1] *Sir Gawain and the Green Knight*, eds. J. R. R. Tolkien and E. V. Gordon; (1st ed. rev., Oxford, 1936). All following quotations from the text will be taken from this edition.

And the host twice reassures Gawain that he will be there on time:

> "For I schal teche yow to þat terme bi þe tymeȝ ende,
> Þe grene chapayle vpon grounde greue yow no more"
> (1069–70)

and

> . . . "As I am trwe segge, I siker my trawþe
> Þou schal cheue to þe grene chapel þy charres to make"
> (1673–74).

When he arrives at the place appointed for the completion of the beheading test, however, Gawain finds not a chapel but a burial mound.[2] After the final encounter the Green Knight is generous in his explanations of the puzzling elements of the action: he reveals himself as the host of the castle and the husband of the lady who tempted Gawain (2358–63); he explains that Morgan le Fay instigated the plot with the intention of frightening Guenevere (2456–60); and he acknowledges that he owes his name "Bercilak" to the power of Morgan who lives in his house (2445–47). But in this profusion of explanation we look in vain for an answer to the questions of why the Green Knight designated the meeting place as the "Green Chapel" when no chapel is there; and why—in view of the stress that has been put upon the chapel—he fails to explain the discrepancy.

I would like to suggest that the fact that Gawain looked for a chapel and found a burial mound is not the inconsistency that it seems to be; that the fact that it is left unexplained is in keeping with the poem as a whole; and finally, that the images evoked

---

[2] A. H. Krappe, "Who *Was* the Green Knight?" *Spec.*, XIII (1938), 213, sees the Green Chapel as "simply a modified form of the fairy hill or elfin knoll, the abode of the dead ancestors." Bertram Colgrave, "Sir Gawayne's Green Chapel," *Antiquity,* XII (1938), 352, attempts a more specific identification of the Green Chapel with one of the burial mounds of the Northwest Midlands.

by the term "chapel" function together to constitute an artistically sustained theme of irony.

In *Gawain and the Green Knight* mention is made of a chapel in three different circumstances: there is a chapel at Arthur's castle (63); there is one at Bercilak's (930, 1876); there is also the "chapel" which is the meeting place of Gawain and his antagonist. In each case Tolkien and Gordon gloss *chapel:* "chapel(le), chapayle, n. (private) chapel; [OFr. chapelle]."[3] In the fourteenth century *chapel* meant substantially what it means today,[4] and it is evidently this sense that is to be understood when it is applied to the chapel in either of the castles. However, when it is applied to the meeting place of Gawain and the Green Knight *chapel* is, I believe, a word that was archaic even in the fourteenth century: a twelfth-century word *chapel* derived from *chapler,* "to cut down."[5] *Chapel* is an old military term for "combat entre deux ou plusiers chevaliers, par couple ou par quadrille" [combat between two or more knights, by twos or by quadrille].[6] Further, ". . .—Il designe plus ordinairment les coups violents que les anciens chevaliers se donnaient avec leurs armes pesants, et aussi le combat, là bataille, et par

[3] *Sir Gawain and the Green Knight,* p. 145; the gloss by Gollancz is substantially the same: *Sir Gawain and the Green Knight,* EETS, O.S. 210 (London, 1940), p. 140.

[4] *Middle English Dictionary,* eds. Hans Kurath and Sherman M. Kuhn (Ann Arbor, Michigan, 1949), *chapele; NED,* eds. James A. H. Murray, et al. (Oxford, 1888–1928), *chapel* (3).

[5] *Dictionnaire d'Ancien Français: moyen âge et renaissance,* ed. R. Grandsaignes d'Hauterive (Paris, 1947): "*Chapler*: v. (XIe–XVIe s.). 1. Abattre: tailler en pièces, hacher. 2. Combattre; massacrer." [1. To strike: to cut into pieces, to hack. 2. To fight; to massacre.]; *Dictionnaire alphabétique et analogique de la langue Française* ed. Paul Robert (Paris, 1953): "*Chapler* au XIIe; du bas lat. *Capulare,* couper. Couper, taillader en elevant le dessus d'une chose. Il n'est usité aujourd'hui que dans le sens Chapler du pain" [. . . from Low Latin *Capulare* (to cut with a sword), to cut. To cut, to slash by raising up the top of something. It is only used nowadays in the sense of "to cut bread."].

[6] *Nouveau Dictionnaire National ou Dictionnaire Universel de la Langue Française,* ed. Bescherelle, Troisième édition (Paris, N.D.).

extens., le carnage, le massacre" [. . . —It designates most often the violent blows that the ancient horsemen gave each other with their heavy weapons, and also the combat, the battle, and by extension the carnage, the massacre].[7] Most significant for the purpose of this paper, however, is that one of the synonyms given for *chapel* is *abattis*;[8] ". . . Ce mot avait anciennement l'acception d'*abattoir,* et significait le lieu où bouchers tuaient les bestiaux" [. . . This word formerly had the sense of *abattoir* (slaughterhouse), and signified the place where the butchers slaughtered the beasts].[9] The twelfth century *chapel* has, then, not only the meanings of heavy blows and carnage, but more significantly, that of the place where they are given and where the slaying is accomplished.

Bercilak's explanation of the motive of the beheading test and the devices by which it was carried out includes no enlightenment as to the ambiguity of the Green Chapel, and Gawain does not inquire about it. Their mutual silence appears to be in perfect accord with the poem's subtlety and restraint.

Throughout the poem the reader sees the action mainly from Gawain's point of view. When the Green Knight sets the terms of the challenge and specifies the meeting place of the second encounter, Gawain appears to take all at face value. As he rides northward Gawain asks from time to time about the Green Knight or the Green Chapel; yet, it is only when he has come to Bercilak's castle that he receives his first assurance that the Chapel is near at hand. There is no indication in the text that until he arrived at the meeting place and found a burial mound instead of a chapel that Gawain thought of the "chapel" in

---

[7] *Dictionnaire de l'Ancienne Langue Française et tous ses Dialectes du IXe au XVe Siècle,* ed. Frédéric Godefroy (Paris, 1937).

[8] *Dictionnaire d'Ancien Français,* ed. Grandsaignes d'Hauterive: "*Chapel*: I n.m. (XIIe), Abattis; hachis; miettes [slaughtered animals; hash; bits]. Etym. *Chapler*."

[9] *Nouveau Dictionnaire National,* ed. Bescherelle, *Abattis.*

any but the current sense of the word. Having come to his destination, he

> . . . ofte chaunged his cher þe chapel to seche:
> He seȝ non suche in no syde, and selly hym þoȝt
> Sone, a lyttel on a launde, a lawe as hit were.
> (2169–71)

At the sight of the burial mound—green though it is—Gawain is disconcerted. He dismounts and walks around it

> Debatande with hymself quat hit be myȝt.
> Hit hade a hole on þe ende and on ayþer syde,
> And ouergrowen with gresse in glodes aywhere,
> And al watȝ holȝ inwith, nobot an olde caue,
> Or a creuisse of an olde cragge, he couþe hit noȝt deme
> with spelle.
> (2179–84)

That he still understands "chapel" in the usual sense is suggested by the fact that he observes: "Þis oritore is vgly, with erbeȝ ouergrowen" (2190); which might stand as confirmation of an ominous possibility:

> "We! Lorde," quoþ þe gentyle knyȝt,
> "Wheþer þis be þe grene chapelle?
> Here myȝt aboute mydnyȝt
> Þe dele his matynnes telle!"
> (2185–88)

In the next few lines we see fear rise rapidly in Gawain; he has already associated the spot with the devil (2187–89, 2191–92); and finally he says:

> "Now I fele hit is þe fende, in my fyue wytteȝ,
> Þat hatȝ stoken me þis steuen to strye me here.
> Þis is a chapel of meschaunce, þat chekke hit bytyde!
> Hit is þe corsedest kyrk þat euer I com inne!"
> (2193–96)

When the reader sees Gawain on the site of the final combat, his image of the conventional chapel dissolves and is replaced by that of the burial mound which—through the association of ideas—should lead him to the more sinister meaning of "chapel." This is the intermediary step which makes the gradual revelation artistically and psychologically convincing. In the last analysis, the mound is not the Green Chapel; it is only a part of it inasmuch as it stands in the dale and provides a grim background for the final scene of combat. We may assume, I believe, that the author wanted the reader to make these associations; and having done so, he would see them as having already been made by Gawain. The strongest reason for attributing Gawain's fear to his awareness that the "chapel" is in reality a "place of slaughter" is that after the combat he does not question the fact that there is no chapel on the scene. There would be no reason for him to do so; to one aware of the earlier meaning of the word, the "Green Chapel" is the exquisitely appropriate term for the place where he expected to meet his death in the manner specified.

The parallel elements of *Gawain and the Green Knight* serve mainly to unify the poem and to give it the rhythmic beauty of repeated action; such is the case of the feasts which are repeated in each fit, the detailed descriptions of clothing and armor, and the settings of Christmas festivity; but the parallels concerning the challenge and the test serve the further purpose of reflecting the past and foreshadowing the future. This is seen where between the first fit in which the challenge is initiated and the fourth in which it is completed, Gawain undergoes at Bercilak's castle another test which will determine the outcome of the encounter at the Green Chapel; its exchange of gifts parallels the exchange of blows, and the wiles of the lady and the evasiveness of Gawain parallel the struggles of the day's hunt.

Unlike these parallels which one can appreciate in the course of reading the poem, the chapel scenes show as a thread of irony only after the poem has been completed, for they fit so naturally and unobtrusively into the action that only with the reader's awareness of the ambiguity of the word "chapel" does he become conscious of their implication.

The poem begins and ends with the mention of a chapel; the first is perfectly unequivocal; just before the Christmas feast which was interrupted by the arrival of the Green Knight

> . . . þe kyng watʒ cummen with knyʒtes into þe halle,
> Þe chauntré of þe chapel cheued to an ende.
>
> (62–63)

A note of irony first appears in Gawain's search for the Green Chapel. His journey northward contains a quest for a chapel within a quest for a chapel, for on Christmas Eve Gawain prayed:

> . . . "I beseche þe, lorde,
> And Mary, þat is myldest moder so dere,
> Of sum herber þer heʒly I myʒt here masse,
> Ande þy matyneʒ to-morne, mekely I ask."
>
> (753–756)

And almost immediately Bercilak's castle appeared before him (763–775).

Cordially welcomed by the knights and ladies, Gawain enjoyed a festive dinner after which the chaplains rang the bells to call the court to chapel for evensong.

> Þe lorde loutes þerto, and þe lady als,
> Into a cumly closet coyntly ho entreʒ.
> Gawan glydeʒ ful gay and gos þeder sone;
> Þe lorde laches hym by þe lappe and ledeʒ hym to sytte,
> And couþly hym knoweʒ and calleʒ hym his nome,
> And sayde he watʒ þe welcomest wyʒe of þe worlde;
> And he hym þonkked þroly, and ayþer halched oþer,
> And seten soberly samen þe seruise quyle.
>
> (933–940)

And in this chapel of him who is the Green Knight, Gawain joined his antagonist and his temptress in evensong—a prayer which is as appropriate to the close of a life as to the close of a day.

The elements of this chapel scene constitute an ironic foreshadowing of the final meeting between Gawain and the Green Knight. Later they will meet in a place that Gawain has understood to be a "chapel" in the unequivocal sense of the word—

until at the last moment he realizes its sinister implication. He has been welcomed by the host and taken to the chapel much as on New Year's Day he will be welcomed to the chapel where his host appears as the Green Knight (2240). The lady of the castle is not physically present at the Green Chapel, but her presence is strongly felt since her lace which Gawain is wearing for protection is the reason for his receiving the blow from the challenger.[10]

When Gawain asks his host if he has heard of the Green Chapel, it is clear from the way his question is phrased that he envisions the chapel as a building. He begs of Bercilak

"Þat ȝe me telle with trawþe if euer ȝe tale herde
Of þe grene chapel, quere hit on grounde stondeȝ."
(1057–58)

Using the same words, the host replies in such a way that there is a slight but meaningful shift in relationship between "chapel" and "ground."

"For I schal teche yow to þat terme bi þe tymeȝ ende,
Þe grene chapayle vpon grounde greue yow no more."
(1069–70)

He does not mention the chapel standing on the ground; he speaks of the chapel on the ground in the sense of striking or slaying on the ground of a contest.[11]

Throughout the account of Gawain's visit at Bercilak's castle the chapel image is sustained if only by a brief and occasional phrase. After both his first and his second encounter with the lady, Gawain goes to Mass in the chapel (1311, 1558); and he receives his second assurance from the host that he will be at the Chapel on New Year's Day (1673–75). On the third day just before he accepts the girdle, Gawain dreams of having to abide the blow of the challenger. On this day Gawain goes to the chapel, approaches the priest in private to confess his faults

[10] Since the two ladies appear to be doublets of Morgan le Fay, Bercilak's wife is present too, in a sense, in the successful accomplishment of her plot.

[11] *NED, ground* (14).

and receive absolution (1876–84).[12] Within the confines of Bercilak's castle, the term "chapel" functions ambivalently; for Gawain the chapel which he has yet to find is a chapel in the sense of "oratory"; he is still thinking of chapel in this way as he rides toward the place of combat. His guide tells him that the Green Knight ". . . is stiffe and sturne, and to strike louies" (2099). Having elaborated on his size, the guide adds:

> He cheueȝ þat chaunce at þe chapel grene,
> Þer passes non bi þat place so proude in his armes
> Þat he ne dyngeȝ hym to deþe with dynt of his honde;
> For he is a mon methles, and mercy non vses,
> For be hit chorle oþer chaplayn þat bi þe chapel rydes,
> Monk oþer masseprest, oþer any mon elles,
> Hym þynk as queme hym to quelle as quyk go hymseluen.
>
> (2103–09)

Gawain could hardly have been told more specifically that the Green Chapel is a place of slaughter. The irony is complete, however, when Gawain stands on the site of the Green Chapel; only from this vantage point of time and of awareness does the pattern of chapel imagery come clear.

The most brilliant thread of irony in *Gawain and the Green Knight* can be traced only after the final knot of equivocation is loosened by an understanding of the dual meaning of "chapel." On this ambiguity rests the contrast between what Gawain expects and what he encounters. The fact that he does not question the Green Knight about the chapel suggests Gawain's awareness that he has been the victim of a deception which now needs no explanation. From this point of view one can see the ambiguous nature of the entire quest and challenge. In Bercilak's castle where he attended Mass and evensong, Gawain had found the chapel of the Green Knight—if not the Green Chapel; and after each of his conversations with the lady, he returned to this

---

[12] John Burrow, in "The Two Confession Scenes in *Sir Gawain and the Green Knight*," *MP*, LVII (1959), 73–79, points out specific connections between the confession Gawain made to the priest and the admission he made to the Green Knight.

chapel—twice to attend Mass and once to confess his sins. In questioning the host about the Green Chapel, Gawain is unaware of the implications of the latter's subtle shifts of language; he is unaware, too, that in inquiring about the direction of the chapel he unwittingly phrased his question in such a way that it was true to the actual situation (705). Finally, from the guide's description of the Green Chapel, Gawain might have conceivably understood that he was coming to a place of slaughter; but he did not.

At the end of the poem Gawain curses the covetousness which led him to break faith with his host (2374–78); for this he clearly blames himself. Later in the poem he enumerates others who were led to sorrow "þurȝ wyles of wymmen" (2415–19). This follows immediately upon his telling Bercilak that he wishes to be commended to the lady of the castle,

> "Boþe þat on and þat oþer, myn honoured ladyeȝ,
> Þat þus hor knyȝt wyth hor kest han koyntly bigyled."
>
> (2412–13)

It appears that Gawain realizes that the elderly woman was involved in the strategy of the challenge before Bercilak confirms it by naming Morgan the instigator of the plot. This perception on Gawain's part is an attractive contrast to his apparent predisposition to being deceived. He was led by covetousness into taking the lace, but he was deceived by Morgan's test which from start to finish was not what it seemed. In good faith and innocence Gawain was deceived by the host, the lady, and the Green Chapel itself. Finally, Gawain does not see himself as he is; he sees himself as a faith-breaker who must wear the lace as a badge of infidelity (2433–38). His shame is not lessened when the Green Knight praises him:

> As perle bi þe quite pese is of prys more,
> So is Gawayn, in god fayth, bi oþer gay knyȝteȝ . . .
>
> (2364–65)

nor when he hears the welcoming laughter of Arthur's court. This is the final irony implicit in Gawain's quest for the Green Chapel.

PART FIVE:

INTERPRETATIONS

17

ROMANCE AND ANTI-ROMANCE IN
SIR GAWAIN AND THE GREEN KNIGHT

Sacvan Bercovitch

Sir Gawain and the Green Knight IS WITHOUT QUESTION a "profound celebration of the romance values . . . [of] Christian chivalry and courtesy," and in this sense we undoubtedly have an "obligation to read[it] . . . constantly as a romance."[1] Unfortunately, however, the obligation seems to have misled modern readers into a disproportionate emphasis on its sombre and sacral qualities. The *Gawain*-poet, writes an influential critic, "is as civilized as Chaucer, but sterner, much more of a moralist, a great deal less of a humorist."[2] Such highly serious interpretations neglect the function, if not the presence, of the poem's humor and realism, though in fact these are among its chief characteristics, deliberately counterbalancing the romance properties and ameliorating the "stern morality." This paper attempts to show that an essential part of the poem's structure and meaning lies in its anti-romance elements: in the overriding comic-realistic spirit which good-naturedly laughs at certain artificial romance conventions—and thereby vitalizes and enlarges its affirmation of romance values.

Reprinted, by permission of author and editors, from *Philological Quarterly*, XLIV (1965), 30–37.
[1] Alan M. Markman, "The Meaning of *Sir Gawain and the Green Knight*," *PMLA*, LXXII (1957), 586.
[2] Dorothy Everett, "The Alliterative Revival," in *Essays on Middle English Literature* (Oxford, 1955), p. 85.

Sir Gawain and the Green Knight builds upon a series of dualisms. The first stanza tells us that since its founding "blysse and blunder / Ful skete haþ skyfted" in Britain;[3] and correspondingly, the scenes alternate between festivity and trial in a regular A, B, A, B pattern, each stage of which alternates a traditional romance episode with a humorous and realistic scene that implicitly undercuts its predecessor.[4] After the "aghlich mayster" (line 136) leaves, "þe kyng and Gawen þare / At þat grene þay laȝe and grenne" (463–464), and—comforting the distraught ladies—Arthur summarizes the whole experience as a bit of clever Christmas entertainment:

> "Wel bycommes such craft vpon Cristmasse,
> Laykyng of enterludeȝ, to laȝe and to syng."
>
> (471–472)

At Bercilak's castle, Gawain undergoes what he considers three tests of courtesy and honor, but the aftermath of each test passes in a spirit of merriment that seems to belie the serious import of the morning exchange. Directly following the first temptation "ho gef hym god day, and wyth a glent laȝed" (1290); after the lady's second, stronger attempt "þay laȝed and layked longe" (1554); and on the third afternoon Gawain

> mace hym as mery among þe fre ladyes,
> With comlych caroles and alle kynnes ioye,
> As neuer he did bot þat daye, to þe derk nyȝt,
> with blys.
>
> (1885–88)

In every case, the relaxation of tension reduces the temptation, in retrospect, to a game—as in fact, from the lady's viewpoint, it is. Similarly, the climactic second part of the Beheading Game

---

[3] *Sir Gawayne and the Grene Knight,* ed. J.R.R. Tolkien and E.V. Gordon (Oxford: Clarendon Press, 1960), lines 18-19. All quotations from the poem are taken from this edition.

[4] If A represents a realistic scene and B one of romance, the poem follows the pattern A, B, A (first fit); A, B, A (second fit); B, A-B, A-B, A (third fit); B, B-A, A (fourth fit). The shift of alternation in the last fit helps, first, to heighten the tension, and second, to reinforce the humorous and realistic conclusion.

leads into a general unmasking where we learn that the challenge, the blows, and the Green Knight himself were one huge hoax, and that the enchantress herself has only the friendliest feelings towards her nephew (2452–68).[5] Far from uniting the various elements of romance, the dénouement brings to the fore the comic-realistic countercurrent of human warmth and Christian forgiveness.

The same dualism characterizes each scene in itself. At Camelot the realistic setting stands in deliberate contrast to the Green Knight's antics. Only after the Christmas festivities have sprung vividly to life, and Arthur—"so joly of his joyfnes, and sumquat childgered" (86)—has called for some diversion from the usual, does the Green Knight enter. Strutting back and forth, he twists his beard, rolls his eyes, brags and taunts (304–322)—and yet for all this "Wel gay watȝ þis gome" (179), "þe myriest in his muckel þat myȝt ride" (142). At first sight he appears "On þe most on þe molde on mesure hyghe" (137); upon closer inspection he turns out to be only "Herre þen ani in þe hous by þe hede and more" (333). And, *post facto,* his terrible challenge hardly terrifies the king. " 'If þou redeȝ hym ryȝt,' " Arthur promises Gawain,

> "redly I trowe
> Þat þou schal byden þe bur þat he schal bede after."
> (373–374)

---

[5] It should be noted, too, that Morgan's motive for the enchantment by no means clashes with her friendly gesture at the end. Bercilak tells Gawain:

> "Ho wayned me vpon þis wyse to your wynne halle,
> For to assay þe surquidré, ȝif hit soth were,
> Þat rennes of þe grete renoun of þe Rounde Table."
> (2456–58)

According to some readings of the poem, Morgan's motive is *implicitly* vicious and sinister (e.g., Denver E. Baughan, "The Role of Morgan le Fay in *Sir Gawain and the Green Knight,*" *ELH,* xvii [1950], 241–251). But see Albert B. Friedman's thorough refutation of this position in "Morgan le Fay in *Sir Gawain and the Green Knight,*" *Spec.,* xxxv (1960), 260–274.

One by one the supernatural implications dissolve until it all seems, finally, just what the Green Knight promised at the outset, "a Crystemas gomen" (283). But the onlookers tremble credulously while it lasts—and for that very reason they are slyly poked fun at. A satirical note underlies the description of the court's awe at the exaggerated buffoonery of the Green Knight (237–249), and of its imagining the tall knight (333) to be "Half etayn" (140). This note of levity continues to the end of the first fit, through the mock-serious tone of Arthur's warning to his knight (487–490) to Gawain's too solemn farewell—"He wende for euer more" (669)—as he sets out on his journey.

The artificial romance atmosphere is further opposed by the vivid realism of Gawain's journey. The wasteland through which the romance hero travels invariably involves supernatural peril and incidental combat; but the "wormeʒ" (720) and "wodwos" (721) which Gawain encounters receive the most cursory treatment, and present ineffectual if not absurd obstacles in the striking naturalism of the landscape:

> Þe hasel and þe haʒþorne were harled al samen,
> With roʒe raged mosse rayled aywhere,
> With mony bryddeʒ vnblyþe vpon bare twyges,
> Þat pitosly þer piped for pyne of þe colde.
>
> (744–747)

Even his battles with the inevitable "etayneʒ" (723) dim beside the harshness of the weather:

> For werre wrathed hym not so much, þat wynter was wors.
>
> (726)

Consistent with the tone and meaning of the poem, the juxtaposition of actuality with the marvelous becomes largely a means of stressing the former. By their very ineffectuality, the fanciful "werreʒ" direct the reader's attention to the natural hardships of the journey—an insistence upon reality which serves for a sophisticated audience to enhance the knight's heroic perseverence.

With a similar counter-romance effect, piety, elegance, and courtesy set the tone at Bercilak's halls; the magic antagonist and his retinue offer the stranger warm hospitality and display exemplary courtly behavior. The Christmas celebrations have all the realism of the Camelot setting; the solemn religious observances perhaps suggest a reprimand to Arthur's court;[6] and the glowing detail of castle life continues in the character portrayals, which create in Bercilak and the ladies (disguises and enchantments notwithstanding) impressively *real* people. Similarly, the deer, the boar, and the fox, whatever their emblematic meanings,[7] are *real* animals. The hunts form an accurate picture of actual practice,[8] and moreover add a second foil to the romance-conventions aspect of Gawain's journey. Nature may produce satyrs, serpents, and giants, but here it reveals itself to be primarily the home of the wild game that provides civilized man with pleasant sport and with "dayntés" (1401) for his festivities. Nowhere at the castle of the Green Knight and of "Morgne þe goddes" (2452) is there a hint of magic or enchantment. Where supernaturalism should most abound, the poem's realism most attractively affirms knightly life and values.

Finally, magic and the natural contend in the dual nature of

[6] Contrast lines 929–934 with lines 60–70 describing Arthur's court, where the lords and ladies hurry the services in their eagerness to uncover the gifts.

[7] See Henry L. Savage, "The Significance of the Hunting Scenes in *Sir Gawain and the Green Knight*," *JEGP*, xxvii (1928), 1–15.

[8] See, for example, Dorothy Everett, "English Medieval Romances," in *Essays*, p. 8. Miss Everett continues: "He who looked to them [English medieval romances] for realistic pictures of medieval manners and practices would be disappointed, except in . . . *Havelok* and *Sir Gawain and the Green Knight*." Significantly, *Havelok*'s realism also tends to work against certain of its romance elements, though not of course consciously; in this case, realistic scenes of folk interest, inserted into a romance framework by a folk minstrel, place *Havelok* midway between the epic form and the romance.

the Green Chapel. On one hand the place corresponds, in appearance and in name, to the entrance to the fairy Other-World.[9] But on the other hand Gawain's surprise at finding "nobot an olde caue" (2182) expresses the true state of things. The "vgly oritore" (2190) *may* prove to be witches' heath, as Gawain fears (2195); in fact, it is simply what it seems to be, an earthen mound. This second, accurate view of the Green Chapel coincides with the use of green imagery throughout the poem as at once fairy color and color of nature (e.g., 166–167, 525–527). It is in keeping, too, with the Green Chapel as background for the disenchanting—and humanizing—realism of the Beheading Game *finale*.

The characters, like the scenes of the poem, develop through reversals, contrasts, and parallels. Crabbed age highlights Bercilak's wife's youthful beauty, and Gawain's greeting to the two ladies perhaps smiles at his chivalry:

> When Gawayn gly3t on þat gay, þat graciously loked,
> Wyth leue la3t of þe lorde he went hem a3aynes;
> Þe alder he haylses, heldande ful lowe,
> Þe loueloker he lappe3 a littel in arme3,
> He kysses hir comlyly, and kny3tly he mele3.
>
> (970–974)

In any case, the more interesting counterplay lies between the real and the pretended self in each of them. The young lady is both temptress and faithful wife; her temptations, accordingly, complement the Beheading Game in that the disguised antagonist is at once testing and jesting with Gawain's courtesy. As C. S. Lewis has pointed out, a prominent convention of romance compels the courteous knight to adultery,[10] and Gawain's discomfort in the bedchamber conversations stems largely from his hostess's harping on his renowned courteousness. "For I wene

---

[9] William A. Nitze, "Is the Green Knight Story A Vegetation Myth?," *MP*, XXXIII (1936), 352.

[10] *The Allegory of Love* (Oxford, 1958), p. 13. Regarding Gawain in particular, see *The Gest of Sir Gawain* and *The Wedding of Sir Gawain*.

wel, iwysse, Sir Wowen ȝe are," she tells him at the outset.
"Your honour, your hendelayk is hendely praysed" (1226,
1228). This note returns insistently on the following days.
Twice she asks him pointedly why he does not act according
to the customs of chivalry:

> "Sir, ȝif ȝe be Wawen, wonder me þynkkeȝ,
> Wyȝe þat is so wel wrast alway to god,
> And conneȝ not of compaynye þe costeȝ vndertake." (1481–83)

> "And ȝe, þat ar so cortays and coynt of your hetes,
> Oghe to a ȝonke þynk ȝern to schewe
> And teche sum tokeneȝ of trweluf craftes." (1525–27)

The tension and the sparkling wit of the temptations center in
this play on chivalric values: the lady's surprise that one "so
cortays" restrains himself in love and (on the other hand)
Gawain's overriding concern "for his cortaysye lest craþayn he
were" (1773). To round out the comic impasse of his predica-
ment, the lady pretends to rely on Gawain's courtesy to keep
secret the gift of the green lace. In all its forms her masquerade
laughs at the "trweluf craftes" of romance heroes; and the force
of the satire derives from the fact that she remains true to
her husband all along. Like Bercilak at Arthur's court, she is
making merry with romance conventions; and like Bercilak's,
her sport deepens the import of Gawain's sense of honor pre-
cisely by supplanting the atmosphere of rigid knightly heroes
with one of psychological realism.

The old woman is so peripheral and her unmasking as Mor-
gan le Fay so unintegral to Gawain's adventure, that her mean-
ing suggests itself only indirectly, as a reflection of larger themes
and attitudes. In the context, then, of the dualistic structure of
the poem, is it not possible that the very absurdity of the Mor-
gan disclosure affords still another caricature of the romance
mode? Frequently the romance adversary is the pawn of an
evil enchanter: if the hero fails the cause lies in some uncon-

trollable superhuman factor.[11] But Gawain takes no comfort, indeed reacts not at all, when Bercilak tells him about Morgan. He bears upon himself the blame of the green lace and when he returns to Camelot he makes no mention of the fay. Despite her unearthly powers, Gawain is seen, and sees himself, to be the sole shaper of his destiny. This *tour de force* not only increases the knight's stature but throws Morgan into a new and realistic perspective. She becomes an anti-romance device in precisely the way of Lady Bercilak; her real self contrasts with and ultimately serves to deflate her enchanted alter ego, to the enrichment of the narrative as a whole. Just as at the last the temptress stands revealed as the faithful wife, so the fearful fay seems, when all is said, a rather sentimental, kindly, and honored old lady.

A similar personality split offsets the romance qualities of the Green Knight. Bercilak shows himself a genial host whose great capacity for enjoyment and bounty of nature match those of the magic Challenger. If one is a figure of fun, the other is fun-loving; the "behooding" game which Bercilak proposes upon Gawain's arrival (983-984) parallels the Beheading Game at Camelot. But the Lord of Hautdesert is also a sophisticated gentleman, and as such he contrasts with the "gomen in grene." His histrionics in Arthur's court seem ludicrously overdone not only because of the realism of the setting but equally because the actor is a devout and urbane aristocrat. So, too, at the Green Chapel Gawain's "aghlich" antagonist becomes his own parody. His overelaborate gestures (2231-34, 2261-63) and

---

[11] Thus in Beaumont and Fletcher's satire on romance, *The Knight of the Burning Pestle* (*Works,* ed. A.R. Waller, 10 vols. [Cambridge Univ. Press, 1908], VI, 187-188), the husband and wife excuse their hero's defeat by enchantment:

Wife: Sure the devil (God bless us!) is in this springald! Why George, didst ever see such a firedrake? I am afraid my boy's miscarried. . . .

Cit: No, no; I have found out the matter, sweetheart, Jasper [the antagonist] is enchanted; He could no more have stood in Rafe's hands than I can stand in my lord mayor's.

his rude mockery of the hero (2269–73)—both characteristic
of romance—are twitted in the humaneness he displays a
moment later:

> "Bolde burne, on þis bent be not so gryndel.
> No mon here vnmanerly þe mysboden habbeʒ.
>
> * * *
>
> Þou art confessed so clene, beknowen of þy mysses,
> And hatʒ þe penaunce apert of þe poynt of myn egge,
> I halde þe polysed of þat plyʒt, and pured as clene
> As þou hadeʒ neuer forfeted syþen þou watʒ fyrst borne;
> And I gif þe, sir, þe gurdel. . . ."
>
> (2338–95)

Most clearly, Bercilak's anti-romance qualities stand out in op-
position to Gawain. Gawain undergoes two tests, the challenge
and the temptation. His courage in the former complements
his loyalty in the latter and if finally he falls short of perfection
in both situations he remains eminently correct throughout.
This knightly correctness becomes the butt of the character con-
trast between his host and himself. His self-conscious sense of
propriety turns into a source of Gawain's embarrassment; Ber-
cilak, on the contrary, grows in personal force by virtue of his
exuberant human warmth and flexibility. When he learns that
Gawain has arrived at his castle, "Loude laʒed he þerat" (909)
—a generous and delighted, not a threatening laughter. The
gift-exchange pact which Gawain treats so earnestly is for him
a form of Christmas sport (1086–93, 1122–25). He does ques-
tion his guest about his gifts, but when he is rather stiffly
refused an answer he "laʒed, and made hem blyþe" (1398).
Similarly, after the exchange on the third evening,

> Þay maden as mery as any men moʒten—
> With laʒyng of ladies, with loteʒ of bordes
> Gawayn and þe gode mon so glad were þay boþe,
> (1953–55)

though presumably Bercilak knows of Gawain's foxiness. With
laughter, too, at the Green Chapel, he minimizes the impor-

tance of the hidden lace (2389) and reassures the knight that he remains "þe fautlest freke þat euer on fote ȝede" (2363). Again and again his tolerance and mirth contrast with Gawain's concern for perfection until, at the end, Gawain's penance seems *un peu de trop,* he takes himself too seriously. Three times he curses his "cowarddyse and couetyse" (2374) though both Bercilak and Arthur bring out the comic aspect of his "meschaunce." True, he sheds blood for his failure, but the "snyrt" on his neck (2312) signifies neither malice nor danger, and the total effect of the scene—the blood spurts upon the snow, Gawain leaps free (2314–16)—indicates that his imperfection figures in his deliverance. In precisely this spirit Arthur later "comforteȝ þe knyȝt, and alle þe court als"—adopting the green lace as a token of their "broþerhede" in a sort of symbolic repudiation of the "romance maxim . . . [that] the hero is a superman"[12]—"Laȝen loude þerat" (2513–14).

In one sense, such anti-romance laughter almost turns Gawain into the jest of *Sir Gawain and the Green Knight.* It makes light of his ordeals, it contrasts a buoyant natural vitality to his chivalric pride, it even seems subtly to belittle the enchantments that leave the hero a sadder and a wiser man. But this is to confuse means with ends. Though the laughter of Bercilak and his lady, of Arthur and his court, tempers Gawain's anguish, this laughter, far from decrying the knight's morality, in effect adds another dimension to it. Though Gawain is sometimes ridiculed, his courtesy, because thus humanized, provides the pattern of civilization, of good breeding and proper conduct. As the "literary" romance elements are subverted, the poem becomes a "profound celebration" of courtly life and ideals, through the triumphant balance of humor and realism.

[12] "English Medieval Romances," in *Essays,* pp. 8–9. More generally the poem counters the "romance device" of having "every man . . . a hero . . . or a villain."

18

THE LESSON OF SIR GAWAIN

Jan Solomon

AS *Sir Gawain and the Green Knight* IS CREATED out of two older stories, the beheading game and the chastity test with its concomitant bargain to exchange the day's gains, so the interpretations of the poem have tended to concentrate on one or another of these elements and to distort the balance and unity of the romance. Since the elevation of the green girdle to a badge of honor clearly implies the seriousness of the lesson learned by the knight, Gawain has been seen as undergoing tests in chastity, courage, or loyalty, depending on which aspect of the poem is considered focal. This study takes into consideration the carefully developed structure and unity of the poem, as well as the highly artistic balance between divergent moods and tones. It posits for *Sir Gawain and the Green Knight* a lesson in humility and in moderation regarding Gawain's own self-esteem and pride in his knightly virtues. Thus the situations which try the loyalty, courage, and chastity of Gawain are comprehended as separate elements which by jeopardizing specific aspects of Gawain's excellence undermine the knight's pride in himself.

Reprinted, by permission of author and editor, from *Papers of the Michigan Academy,* XLVIII (1963), 599–608. [The editors are grateful to Prof. Sam J. Borg for his aid in translating passages of Old French in this article.]

Gawain's pride is certainly well-founded, and the poet is careful to show us just how well his hero can handle not only those trials which a knight might be expected to encounter but, more especially, difficult and even embarrassing situations which call for discretion and tact. At the opening of the story the tact of Gawain is sufficient to convince King Arthur that he, Gawain, should accept the beheading challenge. So graciously is this done that never a note of false humility nor of bravado is struck. Similar finesse is demonstrated when, later in the romance, Gawain parries his host's question as to the source of the kisses Gawain has received. Caught between the rudeness of refusing bluntly to reply and the baseness of betraying his hostess, Gawain assumes the blunt comical manner of his host and replies, "þat watȝ not forward . . . frayst me no more"[1] (1395), and escapes by the terms of the bargain itself. The bedroom scenes are, of course, created around the necessity for care and discretion: how to fend off the lady's advances while remaining a perfect gentleman.

Just as the poet carefully illustrates the many excellences of Gawain which might indeed have induced in him this immoderate pride, so does he establish the existence of pride early in the poem. At the time of Gawain's departure from King Arthur's court, the other knights, while admiring the courage exhibited here, feel that such courage might well have been tempered with caution.

> A lowande leder of ledeȝ in londe hym wel semeȝ,
> & so had better haf ben þen britned to noȝt,
> Hadet wyth an aluisch mon, for angardeȝ pryde.
>
> (679–681)

It is, after all, a waste of a very bright future to stake everything at such a game, and a Christmas game it is several times called by the poet (272, 283, 689).

---

[1] All excerpts from *Sir Gawain and the Green Knight* are from the edition of Sir Israel Gollancz, EETS, O.S. 210 (London, 1940). Throughout the paper the line references will immediately follow the quotations.

Gawain, the excellent knight who suffers a bit from pride, moves through a series of tests in *Sir Gawain and the Green Knight* which try his several virtues. The courage of Gawain is put to the test of the beheading game and for the most part comes out very well; Gawain accepts the challenge, journeys toward the meeting at the Green Chapel, and even stretches out his neck to receive the blow of the enormous axe. Nevertheless there are slight shadows cast on the vaunted courage of Gawain, not sufficient for us to consider him craven, but sufficient to give Gawain himself pause. For one thing, the Green Knight sees Gawain flinch at the anticipated blow and takes the opportunity to prick Gawain's pride by professing to doubt that this knight could be Gawain "þat is so goud halden. . . . Such cowardise of þat knyȝt cowþe I neuer here"(2270–73). The comic intent is clear, but what better technique for pricking the bubble of self-esteem? In relation, further, to the green girdle, Gawain's courage falters, for Gawain is led to accept the lace partly because it is said to contain the power of protecting the wearer from death. The poet emphasizes this by portraying Gawain as suffering from insomnia due to his growing apprehension about the meeting at the Green Chapel. "Ȝif he ne slepe soundyly, say ne dar I, / For he hade muche on þe morn to mynne, ȝif he wolde, in þoȝt" (1991–93).

Similarly, the courtesy of Gawain is submitted to situations in which it is sorely tried. The Lady of the Castle is sent to test Gawain during his *fait-néant* [idle] mornings. Although he must avoid her advances, he would do so while still preserving his courtesy. This difficulty is increased by the reputation Gawain enjoys for success with the ladies, for "luf-talkyng" (927). Finding the behavior of the knight to accord so ill with repute, the Lady adopts the same approach as the Green Knight and affects to doubt Gawain's identity. "Bot þat ȝe be Gawan," she says, "hit gotȝ [not] in mynde" (1293). On the second day she adds an insinuating, "Ȝif ȝe be Wawen . . ." (1481). The comic possibilities are again fully realized, for we find Gawain reduced to such a ruse as feigning sleep rather than contending with his host's wife (1189–90); here no doubt discretion is the better part of valor.

That Gawain must parry the attacks of the Lady of the Castle is made more complicated by the bargain he has entered into with the host to exchange what each has acquired during the day. Again comedy works toward the diminution of Gawain's self-esteem, for when the host presents him with a deer, a boar, or even a fox, Gawain can respond only with the number of kisses he has received from the Lady. Even when Gawain demonstrates his loyalty and lives up to the terms of the bargain by kissing the Lord, this in itself must make him a comic figure. The days passed at the castle are for Gawain days when his virtues of courtesy, luf-talking, and loyalty are placed in opposition to each other, and none can be successfully realized without damage to another or to his dignity.

This opposition of separate virtues is stated clearly in the poet's explanation of Gawain's difficulty in avoiding the Lady's advances.

> Oþer lach þer hir luf oþer lodly re-fuse;
> He cared for his cortaysye, lest craþayn he were,
> & more for his meschef, ȝif he schulde make synne
> & be traytor to þat tolke þat þat telde aȝt.
> (1772–75)

Conflicting demands on Gawain's courtesy create a situation wherein it is impossible for this courtesy to be preserved on all counts. Similarly, his separate loyalties are placed in conflict. Here the dilemma centers about the green girdle. The terms of Gawain's bargain with his host make it a breach of loyalty for Gawain to keep the girdle. On the other hand, the Lady has demanded secrecy; to turn the girdle over to the Lord of the Castle would be an equally disloyal act. The cards are stacked against Gawain, and they are so stacked not to test any one virtue, but to teach that even so dazzling an array of virtues as those for which Gawain was so renowned are not proof in themselves against all temptations.

The interrelation of all the virtues in question, and the consequent unity of the poem, is demonstrated by the centrality of the green girdle; for in relation to the girdle each virtue suffers. Gawain's courage takes him to the Green Chapel, but the girdle is with him as a talisman. Gawain's success in avoiding the Lady is nearly complete, but she weakens him sufficiently to encourage him to take the lace. And finally, the loyalty of Gawain that has led him to fulfill the terms of the bargain also falters in the case of the green lace, which he does not turn over to the Lord of the Castle.

The focal nature of the green girdle is reinforced by the structure of the poem, which might best be described as a set of concentric circles. The story begins, typically, and ends, rather atypically, with an allusion to Brutus as ancestor of the Britons. This can be considered the most outward-lying of the circles. The second circle, or second and penultimate incidents, involves a festive gathering at the court of King Arthur. Working progressively inward the circles move thus: an explanation either of the rules of the beheading game or of the fabric of the plot, the blow with the green axe, the arming and journey of Gawain, parties at the Castle of Bercilak de Hautdesert, the hunt, and finally the bedroom scenes. The hunt and bedroom scenes are tripled, but the structure remains intact as each bedroom scene is surrounded by the two parts of the corresponding hunting scene with a party separating each group. The circles serve as a series of frames surrounding the moment when Gawain accepts the lace, for this is the climactic third of these interior scenes.

Just as the structure of the poem underlines the plot and thematic elements, so do the mood and tone, which are carefully balanced between suspense and humor. Although the reader is never allowed to forget the perilous nature of all that Gawain has undertaken, as the descriptions of a bleak and hostile nature through which Gawain travels remind us (713–739,

1988–05), nevertheless the comic elements continue the slight diminution of Gawain's heroic stature which is thematically necessary. This balance permits us to see the knight both as hero and as human, and we watch him learn humility without ever losing our admiration for him.

One method which the poet employs here is the contrast between Gawain's attitude toward his adventure and that of the other people involved. The Green Knight considers it all a subject for his somewhat brash and overbearing sense of humor. The knights at Arthur's court cannot help but see the funny side of the tale. But not so Gawain, who can see only that he is guilty of cowardice, covetousness, treachery, and untruth or disloyalty (2379–84). It is in the midst of Gawain's self-recriminations that the Green Knight takes the opportunity to lecture him on the ills that flesh is necessarily heir to, by citing examples of Biblical heroes who like Gawain were ensnared by women and thus exposed to treachery (2414–19). The point of these remarks is no exhortation to chastity nor for that matter to any virtue at all, but the suggestion that better men than Gawain have fallen prey to women, coupled with the hearty man-to-man advice, "To luf hom wel & leue hem not" (2421). Thus the serious and comic tones remain in equilibrium even at so crucial a moment as that of Gawain's first taste of humility and the consequent lessening of his pride.

The attitude of the *Gawain*-poet, the play of comedy with which he colors the romance and diminishes the heroic nature of Gawain, is demonstrated by the overall movement of the poem. For this adventure viewed as a whole is extremely atypical. Gawain fights no knights or dragons and neither rescues nor woos any fair ladies, and in short is permitted none of the normal chivalric heroisms.[2] On the contrary, he is forced to fend off the Lady and to submit meekly to the axe of the Green Knight. When, having received the axe-blow which only

---

[2] That the *Gawain*-poet intended to dismiss as insignificant any typical adventures is evidenced in his handling of Gawain's journey. Here, in

nicks him, Gawain leaps up and dramatically seizes his sword
and shield to do battle with his outsized and enchanted enemy,
he is confronted not with an equally belligerent opponent, but
rather with an insolent figure leaning on the handle of his axe
and saying with devastating condescension, "Bolde burne, on
þis bent be not so gryndel" (2338).[3]

The diminishing of the pride of Gawain towards which the
overall progress of the romance operates is enforced by the
poet's use of irony in specific circumstances. For example, he
thrice juxtaposes the athletic hunting days of the Lord of the
Castle, filled with movement and excitement, with the som-
nolent mornings of Gawain.

> Þus laykeȝ þis lorde by lynde-wodeȝ eueȝ,
> & Gawayn þe god mon in gay bed lygeȝ.   (1178–79)
>
> Þis day wyth this ilk dede þay dryuen on þis wyse,
> Whyle oure luflych lede lys in his bedde.   (1468–69)

less than ten lines, he passes quickly and with the greatest economy
over the perils to which Gawain was exposed.

> At vche warþe oþer water þer þe wyȝe passed
> He fonde a foo hym byfore, bot ferly hit were,
> & þat so foule & so felle þat feȝt hym byhode.
> So mony meruayl bi mount þer þe mon fyndeȝ,
> Hit were to tore for to telle of þe tenþe dole.
> Sumwhyle wyth wormeȝ he werre, & wyth wolues als,
> Sumwhyle wyth wodwos, þat woned in þe knarreȝ,
> Boþe wyth bulleȝ & bereȝ, & boreȝs oþerquyle,
> & etayneȝ, þat hym anelede of þe heȝe felle.
> (715–723)

[3] *Gryndel* would seem to be a favorite word of the Green Knight's;
in another form he uses it early in the poem when he is taunting the
Knights of the Round Table for not responding to his challenge. The
same overtones of mockery are implicit.

> "What, is þis Arþures hous," quoþ þe haþel þenne,
> "þat al þe rous rennes of þurȝ ryalmes so mony?
> Where is now your sourquydrye & your conquestes,
> Your *gryndellayk* & your greme, & your grete wordes?
> Now is þe reuel & þe renoun of þe Rounde Table
> Ouerwalt wyth a worde of on wyȝes speche,
> For al dares for drede withoute dynt schewed!"
> (309–315)

> On þis maner bi þe mountes, quyle myd-ouer-vnder,
> Whyle þe hende knyȝt at home holsumly slepeȝ.   (1730–31)

For all of this the serious side of the romance is never forgotten. The Lord of the Castle will one moment jest with Gawain over the kisses he pays according to their bargain.

> ". . . bi saynt Gile,
> ȝe ar þe best þat I knawe;
> ȝe ben ryche in a whyle,
> Such chaffer & ȝe drawe."
> (1644–47)

And at the next add with full seriousness, "I haf fraysted þe twys & faythful I fynde þe," with the warning for the future, "Now þrid tyme, þrowe best" (1679–80). Similarly, for all the farce inherent in the bedroom scenes, the poet can suddenly comment, "Gret perile bi-twene hem stod, / Nif Marye of hir knyȝt [con] mynne" (1768–69). And when the mechanism of the plot is explained by the Green Knight, he justifies the nick with the axe by the fact that Gawain "lakked a lyttel" (2366). It was "for no wylyde werke, ne wowyng nauþer" (2367), but that while on the first two days of the bargain "Trwe mon trwe restore," on the "þrid þou fayled þore, / & þer-for þat tappe ta þe" (2354–57). The green girdle, the symbolic and thematic nexus of the poem, was not restored to the host, and notwithstanding all the humor, this was truly a breach of conduct and of virtue.

While the breach is relatively a minor one in the eyes of the Green Knight, it is quite serious to Gawain. So great is his chagrin that he vows to wear the girdle always, "in syngne of my surfet" (2433).

> ". . . I schal se hit ofte
> When I ride in renoun, remorde to myselven
> Þe faut & þe fayntyse of þe flesche crabbed,
> How tender hit is to entyse teches of fylþe;
> & þus quen pryde schal me pryk for prowes of armes,
> Þe loke to þis luf-lace schal leþe my hert."
> (2433–38)

Thus, the pride of Gawain will in future be tempered by the knowledge of his humanness and consequent frailty.

While this theme is not common to the English romance, it appears with some frequency in French material, both chivalric and religious, as the sin of *desmesure*. *Desmesure* is an excess of any kind: *immoderatus* as a thirteenth-century French-Latin vocabulary translates it.[4] Generally, however, it is an excess in pride or self-esteem, used in contexts which associate it with and yet slightly differentiate it from such variations of pride as *orgueil, arrogance,* and *bobance*. In short it is a breach of *mesure*, moderation, or balance.[5] This term became obsolete

[4] Guillaume le Breton, historian to Philippe-Auguste, so translates *desmesurables* in his French-Latin vocabulary; cited in Adolf Tobler and Erh. Lömmatzsch, *Altfranzösisches Wörtenbuch* (Wiesbaden, 1956).

[5] R. E. Godefroy, *Dictionnaire de l'ancienne langue française du IXe au XVe siècles* (Paris, 1892), defines a person who is *desmesuré* as one "qui porte un vice quelconque à un excès . . . et en particular orgueilleux à l'excès, arrogant" [who carries any vice to excess . . . and, in particular, (is) excessively proud, arrogant]. Among the citations in Godefroy are those which group *desmesure* with other forms of pride: "Orguel, fierte, et *desmisure*" [Pride, haughtiness, and *desmesure*] (Gerv. *Best*), "N'ai covoitise ne orguil, / Ne *desmesure* ne bobance" [I have neither covetousness nor pride, / Neither *desmesure* nor boastfulness] (MS Ars); and those which contrast it with chivalric virtues: "Quar *desmesure* ne outrage / N'est pas honor ne vasselage" [For *desmesure* and foolhardiness / Are not honor or valour] (*Perceval*, MS. Mont.). Tobler-Lömmatzsch has citations which show *desmesure* as a vice which the code of chivalry must guard against:

> Je sui rois, de doi pas mantir
> Ne vilenie consantir
> Ne fausseté ne *desmesure*
> Reison doi garder et droiture.

[I am king: I should not lie or give in to baseness, falsehood or *desmesure*. I must be reasonable and righteous.]
(Ch. de Troyes, *Erec et Enide*)
Other excerpts cited here set up the contrast between *desmesure* and *mesure,* reason or balance.

> Nus preudom ne se doit si tost *desmesurer,*
> Mais quant il voit celui ki trop se *desmesure,*
> Si le doit sagement ramener a mesure.
> N'est nus si grans savoirs com'est amesurance,

275

in French and never entered English at all, but a similar word, *sourfaite,* did. *Sourfaite* carries much the same connotation as does *desmesure;* it too is often used in conjunction with the various synonyms for pride and contrasted with *mesure.* Immoderation, particularly in pride, is the meaning it carries; more specifically it implies presumptiveness or impertinence coming from an excess of self-assurance.[6] *Surfet,* as the word appears in *Sir Gawain and the Green Knight,*[7] is an excess that has led

---

> Ne si tresgrans folie com'est *desmesurance.*
> S'il croit ta crüalté, si se *desmesurra*
> Ke jamais a droit point nus ne l'amesurra.

[No honorable man should ever forgo moderation. On the contrary, he should, when he sees someone else overstep the bounds of moderation, prudently bring him back to moderation. There is no wisdom as great as moderation, nor folly as great as immoderation. If he is swayed by your cruelty, he will become so immoderate that no one will ever bring him fully back to moderation.]

(G. Coincy, *Crist.*)

> Trop fu outrequidiés et plains de *desmesure,*
> Mais cil ki a cascun sen gueredon mesure
> Selonc çou qu'il desert, si bien li mesura,
> Bien parciut que faus fu quant se *desmesura.*

[He was exceedingly wanton and immoderate. But He (God) who metes out to everyone his just dues, in keeping with one's deserts, repaid him (his iniquity) so fittingly that he realized how foolish he was when he gave way to immoderation.]

(G. Coincy, *Crist.*)

These passages have been expanded beyond the extent of their citation in Tobler-Lömmatzsch from their sources. For much of this information I am indebted to Hans E. Keller of the University of Michigan.

[6] In Godefroy *sourfaite* is included in the list of variations of pride: "L'orgoil, le pris e la bobance / E la tres *sorfaite* arrogance" [Pride, reputation and boastfulness / And excessive arrogance] (Ben, *D. de Norm.*); "Tant a Normanz tant a Bretons / *Sorfaiz,* orguillos e felons" [So many vain, proud, and villainous Normans and Bretons are there] (ID, *D. de Norm.*); and with general vices, "Ne tort ne volt soffrir, orgoil ne *surfeiture*" [He would brook no wrong, pride, or vanity] (Th. de Kent, *Geste d'Alis*). Here it is contrasted with *mesure,* "Mais ele hahoit tant *sorfait* / Et amoit raison et mesure" [But she hated *sorfait* so much / And loved reason and moderation] (*De Sainte Ysabel*).

[7] Similar uses of the word *surfet* in Middle English are found in several works. The *Oxford English Dictionary* handles *surfeit* as excess or superfluity, without specifying an excess of pride; or as a trespass or crime,

Gawain to exceed the limits of moderation; Gawain trusted too implicitly in his own virtues and found them, fine as they were, not enough to meet the situations created by the Green Knight. This trust in himself, this pride and self-esteem were excessive, and having learned his lesson, Gawain vows to wear the lace, "in syngne of my surfet."

Gawain then learns a lesson in *mesure,* in humility or moderation, and this lesson is enforced by the structure, the plot, and the tone of the romance. The special tests that try each of the virtues for which Gawain felt a pride and assurance amounting to *surfet,* the tests of his loyalty, courage, and courtesy are the occasions for the pricking of that pride. Thus the trials of specific virtues in *Sir Gawain and the Green Knight*

---

citing *Sir Gawain and the Green Knight* here; this is indeed the standard rendering of this word in the passage in question. Nevertheless a careful look at the context here and at the uses of the word in Old French would suggest the possibility of a more specific meaning in *Sir Gawain and the Green Knight* and in the passages from other Middle English works which follow. For these references I have used the files of the Middle English Dictionary with the kind permission of the editor, Sherman M. Kuhn. Concerning man's attempt to understand the ways of God: "Agh we þer-on to seke resun / Hu he does alkin thing to nait, / Certes þat war bot *surfait,*" (*Cursor Mundi,* 22884–22886). Concerning the care of the sick in a convent and the proper behavior of the sick themselves: "Bot tay sal recaiue þe onur / of god þe seruise þat man does tam; / þai ne sal noht þur þair *surfait* þaire sistirs þat seruis þam." (Here *surfait* translates the Latin *superfluitates; Rule St. Benet,* ed. Ernst A. Kock, EETS, O.S. 120 [London, 1902], p. 26, ll. 31–33.) Finally, concerning the vice of excess in relation to slander:

> I fond a lyknesse depict upon a wal,
> Armed in vertues, as I walk up and doun,
> The hed of thre ful solompne and roial,
> Intellectus, memorye, and resoun;
> With eyen and erys of cleer discrecioun,
> Mouth and tonge avoiden al outrage,
> Ageyn the vice of fals detraccioun,
> To do no *surfet* in woord nor in language.

(Lydgate, *Minor Poems,* Percy Society, 1840, p. 177)

For great help here and indeed throughout this paper I am indebted to John N. Reidy of the University of Michigan and the Middle English Dictionary.

are subordinated to the more pervasive theme of pride and humility, of *desmesure* and moderation, and the lesson Gawain learns of the evils of *surfet* is the central concept of a highly artistic and unified work of art.

19

A PSYCHOLOGICAL INTERPRETATION OF
SIR GAWAIN AND THE GREEN KNIGHT

Stephen Manning

D. W. ROBERTSON has recently challenged "psychological" inter-
pretations of medieval literary art, which, he contends, is "rigor-
ously nonpsychological." He strikes me as being annoyingly
perverse about the term *psychological,* but what he seems to insist
upon is that the implications of medieval art are not psychological
but moral, and that such art is exemplary (i.e., objective and
dealing with types) rather than expressive of subjective emo-
tions.[1] Robertson's point is a proper antidote to a nineteenth-
century view of literature, but this emphasis makes him guilty
of what C. G. Jung refers to as an *"only* psychological" atti-
tude. To Jung, political, social, philosophical, moral, and reli-
gious conditions all influence the unconscious, and to isolate the
"psychological" from these other factors is to reduce the neces-
sary effectiveness and accuracy of the analysis.[2] Further, Erich
Neumann insists that "The archetypes are varied by the media
through which they pass—that is, their form changes according
to the time, the place, and the psychological constellation of the

Reprinted from *Criticism,* VI, No. 2 (1964), 165–177, by Stephen Man-
ning by permission of the Wayne State University Press. © 1964 by the
Wayne State University Press.

[1] *A Preface to Chaucer* (Princeton, 1962), pp. 34, 36, 161.
[2] *Psychological Reflections,* ed. Jolande Jacobi (New York, 1961), pp.
18, 61, 139.

individual in whom they are manifested."[3] The relevance of these concepts for the literary critic is obvious enough: one who seeks to utilize the archetypal approach of depth psychology must use it in conjunction with the "historical" aspects of the individual work, much as Robertson himself argues for in his concept of "historical criticism." The resulting interpretation will be psychological *and* moral (or philosophical or religious or whatever), according as the individual work dictates. Such an emphasis upon the individuality of the particular work of art will also lead to a demonstration of its peculiar, perhaps unique, characteristics as art. But whether that work is exemplary or expresses subjective emotion remains to be determined; it is not predetermined by the archetypal approach. Such an approach, then, does not necessarily conflict with the values of medieval literature as Robertson has expressed them.

If, instead of Robertson's sense, the term *psychological* is taken to indicate some consideration of mental states, especially as they affect behavior, then *Sir Gawain and the Green Knight* has claims to being psychological. The most obvious of these claims is the emphasis the poet gives to Gawain's feelings of guilt and shame after he realizes Bercilak's deception. For example, when he returns to Arthur's court,

> He tened quen he schulde telle,
> He groned for gref and grame;
> The blod in his face con melle,
> When he hit schulde schewe, for schame.
>
> (2501–04)[4]

Moreover, we can interpret some of the later action of the poem in terms of unconscious and conscious behavior. For example, when Gawain glances at the descending axe, he flinches; when the Green Knight rebukes him, he answers: "I schunt

[3] "Art and Time," in *Man and Time: Papers from the Eranos Yearbooks* (New York, 1957), pp. 3–4.
[4] Quotations are from the slightly modernized ed. of A. C. Cawley (London, 1962).

ones, / And so wyl I no more" (2280–81), and he remains resolute. Thus, the possibilities of detecting unconscious and conscious behavior and of recognizing the poet's emphasis upon Gawain's sense of shame suggest that a psychological approach might indeed be fruitful. As a final suggestion of the value of the psychological approach, especially in the interrelation of religious and psychological values in the poem, let me quote three passages. These passages are religious, psychological, and literary expressions of the same basic principle. The religious statement appears in Genesis (viii. 21): "The imagination and thought of man's heart are prone to evil from his youth"; the psychological formulation is Jung's: "Unfortunately there is no doubt about the fact that man is, as a whole, less good than he imagines himself or wants to be. Everyone carries a shadow";[5] finally, Sir Gawain recognizes his specific inclination to evil (i.e.. his shadow) when he confesses to the Green Knight:

> "For care of thy knokke cowardyse me taght
> To acorde me with covetyse, my kynde to forsake,
> That is larges and lewté that longes to knyghtes.
> Now am I fawty and falce, and ferde haf ben ever;
> Of trecherye and untrawthe bothe bityde sorwe and care!"
> (2379–84)

Specifically, what I propose to do is to analyze the poem in archetypal terms as a story about the ego's encounter with the shadow. This archetype corresponds to a concept within the moral-religious framework of the poem itself and of its period, viz., the concept of the inclination to evil (the "evil imagination" of Genesis), which accompanies original sin. The psychological approach will also illumine five aspects of the poem; first, the ambiguous nature of Bercilak's character as both good and evil; second, a justification of Morgan le Fay, whose presence has been considered an artistic blemish; third, the nature of the temptations by Lady Bercilak, and of what is central to the

[5] *Psychological Reflections*, p. 214.

approach as a whole, the sense of guilt which Gawain experiences; fourth, an underscoring of certain aspects of the parallel structure, especially Gawain's dual role as ideal Arthurian knight and as individual; and fifth, a heightening of the theme as a "Christian declaration of man's imperfection."[6]

In the psychological interpretation as the ego's encounter with the shadow, Gawain is the ego, and Bercilak is the shadow, the dark or bad aspect of the psyche which has received its most popular formulation in Stevenson's Mr. Hyde. The shadow contains everything that the ego finds unacceptable, whether disagreeable, terrifying, detestable, or immoral; it thus conflicts with the ego's goals and dispositions, and personifies everything that the individual will not recognize in himself, especially inferior traits of character. To recognize this dark aspect as present and real is to take the first step towards any kind of self-knowledge, but the ego generally does not want to make this kind of admission about itself.[7] Paradoxically, the shadow is not only nefarious and evil but shares in the dual aspect of the unconscious in general. The unconscious is "not only dark but also light, not only bestial, semihuman, and demonic but superhuman, spiritual, and, in the classical sense of the word, 'divine.' " Similarly, the shadow is "on the one side regrettable and reprehensible weakness, on the other side healthy instinctivity and the prerequisite for higher consciousness." As a result of its encounter with the shadow, the ego looks hypercritically upon its helplessness and ineffectuality.[8] What the ego must do is, in Neumann's term, make friends with

[6] The quotation is Alan M. Markman's phrasing of an interpretation he rejects in "The Meaning of *Sir Gawain and the Green Knight*," *PMLA*, LXXII (1957), 586.

[7] Victor White, *Soul and Psyche* (London, 1960), pp. 144, 159; Jung, *Archetypes and the Collective Unconscious* (New York, 1959), pp. 284–285.

[8] Jung, *Aion* (New York, 1959), p. 8; *Psychological Reflections*, pp. 219–220; *Aion*, p. 255; Jolande Jacobi, *The Psychology of Jung* (New Haven, 1944), p. 104; Jung, *Archetypes*, p. 21.

the shadow, i.e., become conscious of its inferior traits and integrate them.[9] The shadow, then, is the personal unconscious; it personifies certain weaknesses in the personality which must be recognized if the ego is to advance in self-knowledge. Although a man's unconscious is generally conceived as feminine, the shadow appears as masculine, a reflection of the "young hero's growing masculinity."[10] Bercilak's role as shadow (i.e., as a projection of traits in Gawain's personality which, by his religious and chivalric standards, are undesirable) is supported by the values of certain images: first, the color green, recognized in the Middle Ages as suggesting the Other World,[11] is associated with the other world of the unconscious; second, the axe, a symbol of the destructive side of the shadow,[12] is specifically the instrument of beheading (i.e., loss of consciousness); and third, the hunt, associated in the Middle Ages with the foreboding Wild Huntsman and also with the devil himself, here also represents the destructive aspect of the unconscious.[13] As huntsman, Bercilak is moreover associated with the animal level of the personality. Jung, in fact, defines the shadow as "the inferior personality, the lowest levels of which are indistinguishable from the instinctuality of an animal."[14] Through his instinctual desire for self-preservation, Gawain yields to the unconscious; only by opposing himself to instinct can he create consciousness. When he flinches at the stroke of the axe, he yields instinctively to

[9] *The Origins and History of Consciousness* (New York, 1954), p. 353.
[10] Ibid., p. 179.
[11] Both the Other World of fairyland and of hell; for the former see, e.g., Mother Angela Carson, "Morgain La Fée as the Principle of Unity in *Gawain and the Green Knight*," *MLQ*, XXII (1962), 13; for the latter, see D. W. Robertson, "Why the Devil Wears Green," *MLN*, LXIX (1954), 470–472.
[12] Neumann, *Origins,* p. 179.
[13] For the Huntsman figure as consort of Morgan, see Mother Angela, p. 7; for the association of the hunt with the devil, see Robertson, p. 472; for the connection with the Terrible Mother, see Neumann, *Origins,* p. 83.
[14] *Aion,* pp. 233–234.

the unconscious; once he is made aware of his flinching, he remains firm, "stylle as the ston other a stubbe auther / That ratheled is in roché grounde with rotes a hundreth" (2293–94). The landscape of Gawain's journey to Bercilak's castle resembles the approach to the Other World, and his battles with serpents, wolves, satyrs, bulls, bears, boars, and giants (720–723) foreshadow his struggles with the animality of the temptations he encounters in the castle.[15] Gawain does not himself participate in the hunt, for he is not, as Bercilak, in the service of the unconscious. But paradoxically, Bercilak's conquering the animals he hunts is what Gawain must achieve by conquering the animal in himself. He must become not the prey, but the hunter. As the prey, he is the object of the love-hunt of Lady Bercilak. Interestingly enough, Bercilak's success in the chase on the first two days corresponds to Gawain's success in conquering his animal nature; his success on the last day is limited to only one fox, and Gawain's success is correspondingly limited. Gawain overcomes the temptation against chastity, but yields to his instinct, takes measures for his self-preservation, and fails to fulfill his bargain with his host.

The Green Chapel may well be an entrance to the Other World,[16] and Gawain's feeling that he has fallen into the clutches of the fiend (2191–95) seems to argue for his so viewing it. At any rate, his suspicion of the Green Knight's fiendish aspect links the Knight as personal shadow to the Christian embodiment of the transpersonal shadow, the devil himself. Bercilak's jumping across the stream at the Chapel indicates the transitional point of the shadow's coming into consciousness, preparatory to the discovery of self-knowledge. At this crucial transitional point, the danger of regression (i.e., yielding

[15] See Ingeborg Oppel, "The Endless Knot: An Interpretation of *Sir Gawain and the Green Knight* through Its Myth," unpubl. diss. (Univ. of Wash., 1960), p. 60.
[16] Mother Angela, pp. 7–8.

to the unconscious) is great and "makes itself felt as fear";[17] thus Gawain flinches, but when he is made to realize what he has just done, he does not flinch again. We thus see signs that Gawain will successfully integrate his shadow. Later, he rather grudgingly makes friends with Bercilak (2471–73)—as Neumann has characterized what the ego must do with the shadow. Furthermore, we probably have here a remnant of the folk belief that to know someone's name is to have power over him. The Green Knight learned Gawain's name at Arthur's court (381), but not until this point does Gawain learn the name of the lord of the castle (2445), and at this point Gawain begins to learn the significance of his encounter. That he will successfully integrate his shadow is also demonstrated by the symbolism of the beheading. The head symbolizes consciousness—the goal towards which the psychological process of individuation (i.e., self-realization) aspires. The stakes of the psychological challenge of the Green Knight are thus made amply clear at the beginning: this is a test of consciousness, and if Gawain is successful, he will not lose his head. That he is only nicked indicates that he has yielded only slightly to the unconscious.

As shadow, then, Bercilak represents something which is both good and evil. This ambivalence is seen immediately in the color green, which is the symbol of chthonic (i.e., earthly or material) life as opposed to the life of the spirit;[18] but it is also the color of hope and of rebirth. Thus, although the Green Knight represents the dark or evil side of the personality, he contains within himself the possibilities of self-knowledge. As the Knight, he is formidable; as the lord of the castle, he is affable. His wanting to become friends with Gawain fits his role as shadow eager to live with the ego. The characteristics that he displays which are similar to Arthur's, and the high degree of chivalry that exists in his castle not only provide a fitting con-

---

[17] Gerhard Adler, *The Living Symbol* (New York, 1961), p. 153.
[18] John Speirs's remarks on the Green Man are relevant here: *Medieval English Poetry, the Non-Chaucerian Tradition* (London, 1957), p. 220.

text for the emergence of Gawain's shadow qualities, but also suggest an inherent weakness in the chivalric system itself.

That the challenge issues from Morgan le Fay and that she controls the appearance of Bercilak (the shadow) reveals her role as the Terrible Mother, i.e., the dark side of the unconscious which seeks to destroy the conscious ego. Unlike the shadow, the Terrible Mother is a transpersonal figure; she personifies the negative aspect of the unconscious as a whole, in contrast to the shadow, which represents the personal unconscious. Morgan's temptation is therefore directed towards Arthur's court, which, because of its deliberate dedication to knightly ideals, represents consciousness as a whole.[19] The poet's emphasis upon the youth of the court suggests the adolescent, whose growing masculinity is challenged by the unconscious. Guenevere is probably an anima figure, but in a far more advanced state than we meet in Lady Bercilak. Guenevere, as Arthur's wife, represents here the so-called "feminine" traits in a man's character which have been recognized and brought under conscious control. Guenevere's marriage to Arthur is the necessary prerequisite for the courtesy practiced in the court. Morgan's attempt to frighten her is to challenge the Queen's role as anima and Arthur's subordination of the unconscious, and to keep reasserting the claims of the unconscious in general. She cannot now overthrow Guenevere, but she tries to upset the Arthurian balance. "If the ego presumes to wield power over the unconscious, the unconscious reacts with a subtle attack," says Jung.[20] Morgan's goal of attacking Arthur's pride—i.e., his consciousness—is achieved, if not in the apparent cowardice of the knights in their reluctance to accept the Green Knight's challenge (the poet's comment in lines 246–247 that some undoubtedly refrained from courtesy draws attention

[19] For Arthur the shadow would have been associated with the self rather than the ego; for the distinction, see Jung, *Memories, Dreams, Reflections*, ed. Aniela Jaffé (New York, 1961), p. 244.

[20] *Two Essays on Analytical Psychology* (New York, 1953), p. 232.

to the cowardice as well as to the courtesy)—if not at this point, then when Gawain leaves the castle, and the court complains of Arthur's behavior: "Who knew ever any kyng such counsel to take / As knyghtes in cavelaciouns on Crystmasse gomnes?" (682–683). In a small way this poses a questioning of Arthur's values, and Morgan achieves a minor victory. Her role in the plot is thus psychologically appropriate; it is she who instigates the action against Arthur and Guenevere by sending the Green Knight, but it is Bercilak who takes over the testing of Gawain in personal terms.

A third point which the archetypal approach makes concerns the nature of the temptations of Lady Bercilak and of the terrible sense of guilt which Gawain feels. Lady Bercilak is the anima, the feminine counterpart to the hero, with whom he must relate. This archetype represents those qualities which we generally characterize as more properly feminine than masculine. Jung tells us that the anima is "endowed with considerable powers of fascination and possession"; when she first appears, she often accompanies the shadow. In fact, the two are "contaminated with each other," a state often represented by marriage.[21] Although the anima in her highest form symbolizes wisdom, the "first encounter with her usually leads one to infer anything rather than wisdom."[22] The anima, then, as all archetypal figures, is ambivalent. In her negative aspect she is strikingly similar to the description of the feminine as the irrational, concupiscent aspect of man in St. Augustine and other writers. But the *Gawain*-poet is not concerned with developing the positive aspects of Lady Bercilak's role as anima; all that is important at this stage is her "contamination" with the shadow, and the fact that she is a personal source of temptation to Gawain (as opposed to the transpersonal Morgan). Gawain's

[21] *Archetypes*, p. 270; *Psychology and Alchemy* (New York, 1953), p. 169 n. When these two figures are separated, it is found that the shadow belongs to the ego, while the anima does not.
[22] *Archetypes*, p. 31.

relating to his anima is a later stage of self-realization; Lady Bercilak appears here to reinforce the "feminine" (and unconscious) nature of lust and cowardice as aspects of Gawain's shadow, for the shadow qualities are emotional (i.e., feminine) in nature.[23] The poet stresses the lady's powers of fascination, especially in the lines contrasting her with the old hag (950–969), and her negative character, especially the remarks about Mary's preserving the chastity of her knight (1768–69). That her temptation is initially sexual and on a biological plane is fitting, for lechery, as we see in Dante, is among the least rational of sins and therefore all the more seductive. But Gawain does not yield to her temptations for at least two specific reasons: first, because he has other things on his mind,

> lur that he soght
> boute hone,
> The dunte that schulde hym deve,
> And nedes hit most be done;
> (1284–87)

and second, when the temptation apparently becomes most acute on the third day, "Gret perile bitwene hem stod, / Nif Maré of hir knyght con mynne" (1768–69). Gawain does not sin, even though he comes perilously close to it; there is no reason to doubt his confession (1880–81), even if afterwards he ironically enjoys the ladies' company more than ever before (1885–88).[24] When Lady Bercilak gets nowhere by appealing to Gawain's sexuality, she shifts tactics and appeals to a deeper element in his unconscious—self-preservation. This the poet has carefully prepared for, not only by lines 1284–87 quoted above, but also by telling us something of Gawain's troubled thoughts on the third morning (1750–54). But accepting the girdle is not a sin in the theological sense (nor for that matter

---

[23] Jung, *Aion*, p. 8.
[24] As pointed out by J. Saperstein, "Some Observations on *Sir Gawain and the Green Knight*," *English Studies in Africa*, v (1962), 35.

is failing to keep one's bargain in a Christmas game). Any sin involved here is rather a sin against chivalry. Thus, instead of presenting Lady Bercilak in strictly psychological terms, the poet has translated these terms, as it were, into theological and chivalric values. On a psychological plane, both temptations (of lust and self-preservation) are appeals to Gawain's shadow qualities; what makes them shadow qualities and therefore undesirable is that they conflict respectively with Gawain's religious and chivalric values.

These observations help us understand the keen sense of guilt which Gawain manifests: such a sense accompanies the encounter with the shadow, but more important, Gawain's guilt is psychological, not theological. In accepting the girdle, Gawain acts involuntarily, and, as Father White points out, to act "without consciousness and responsibility is to act infra-humanly; and, according to St. Thomas Aquinas himself, so to act is rightly felt as particularly shameful." Aquinas' term, *verecundia,* "shame,"

> is a dread arising from having already done something disgusting . . . especially in so far as it is offensive to self-esteem. . . . Unlike contrition, it is not concerned with the sinfulness of sin, in the moral or theological sense, but with the disgusting and humiliating characteristics which accompany certain sins. . . . What is felt by human beings as more disgusting and humiliating is, all other things being equal, what is more remote from specifically human and rational behaviour, "for the splendour of being human arises from rationality."[25]

This, then, is psychological guilt; it is the guilt which Gawain feels; and it is very possible that the poet had some such concept in mind. Perhaps this is why the Green Knight assumes the role of confessor:

> Thou are confessed so clene, beknowen of thy mysses,
> And has the penaunce apert of the poynt of myn egge.

[25] "Guilt: Theological and Psychological," in *Christian Essays in Psychiatry,* ed. Philip Mairet (New York, 1956), pp. 165–166. The passages are from Aquinas, *Summa,* I. ii. 44, I. ii. 41, II. ii. 106.

> I halde the polysed of that plyght and pured as clene
> As thou hades never forfeted sythen thou was fyrst borne.
>
> (2391–94)

The reason the poet spends so many lines on this sense of guilt is to drive home the truism that man is imperfect. Gawain seems to recognize the implications of his act, the potentiality in himself which he had never suspected. He remains true to psychological form by becoming hyperconscious of his failing. Typically, he blames Lady Bercilak in a furious diatribe (2414–28), citing other instances of the woman's betrayal of the man, and thereby justifying himself at any rate momentarily to himself, betraying what Maud Bodkin has called "a sense of man's terror of that weakness in himself which he projects upon the type-figure of woman."[26] Gawain's pentangle should have reminded him of his physical and supernatural strength, and he should never have even considered any such magic talisman as the girdle. But the pentangle itself, curiously, marks Gawain's psychological condition, for the number of self-realization (individuation) is four, not five.[27] Gawain turns out not to be the perfect knight, and the poet's use of the pentangle thus becomes particularly ironic and contrasts with the use of the girdle. The girdle is the circle of the womb, of what Neumann calls the uroboros, of regression, of conquest by the unconscious, and it is worn hidden. It is, however, potentially the mandala, the circle of individuation, and it is worn externally. It thus symbolizes both Gawain's shame and his self-knowledge.

The roles which the three archetypal figures play in this poem heighten the parallel structure. Morgan is the Terrible Mother, the collective unconscious challenging the symbol of conscious-

---

[26] *Archetypal Patterns in Poetry* (New York, 1958), p. 167, commenting upon similar passages in *Paradise Lost* and *Hippolytus*.

[27] Jung, *Psychology and Religion: West and East* (New York, 1958), p. 167. The four aspects of psychological orientation are sensation, thinking, feeling, intuition.

ness, Arthur's court. Lady Bercilak is the personal unconscious, challenging Gawain's values through his shadow qualities. Bercilak is the shadow, moving in both worlds of the collective and the personal unconscious,[28] and in his dual nature as Green Knight and Bercilak, tying together the two plots of the Champion's Bargain and the Exchange of Winnings. Other parallels in the two plots invite us to extend the parallelism to the nature of the temptations in both instances, viz., losing one's head literally and figuratively, or, in other words, yielding to the unconscious. Both are also tests of chivalry; in fact, the parallel Christmas games at the two castles specifically reinforce this idea. Other parallels may be drawn and have been. Let me note here two further ones: first, that between the court's reaction to the Green Knight's challenge and Gawain's later behavior. The fear which some members of the court exhibit foreshadows Gawain's later flinching and also raises questions about the Arthurian ideal. Second, the two plots stress Gawain's dual role of ideal Arthurian knight and of individual. He is tested in both capacities, and the individual conflicts with the ideal. Although the ideal is shattered, the individual gains thereby. The self-knowledge which Gawain acquires makes him a better man, if not a better knight. His danger lies in the conflicting claims of courtesy and chastity. The chastity test might, of course, be seen only from a chivalric perspective as a dilemma between courtesy to the host and to the host's wife, but the poet deliberately brings in religious perspectives. He thus suggests an area in which the Arthurian ideal does not function, or at least is vulnerable. As Mary's knight, Gawain does not succumb; as Arthur's, he does. Just because he is Arthur's knight, he almost succumbs as Mary's. The double testing of Arthur's and Gawain's values thus ultimately assesses the chivalric code. Gawain can easily resist the first aspect of the temptation (not to accept the challenge), but he is a bit

---

[28] Neumann, *Origins*, p. 352.

slow about it. Similarly, he can resist the second aspect (not to show up) just because he is such a product of chivalry. But when the temptation assumes a personal guise, he falters. His diatribe against women should not surprise us; his sense of guilt causes him to blame anyone but himself. But the diatribe is heavily ironic, for his momentary loss of self-control demonstrates exactly the same yielding to the unconscious which his diatribe deplores. When Gawain cites his exempla to justify himself, we may suspect that even he half realizes that perhaps he has carried courtesy a bit far in his treatment of Lady Bercilak. Indeed, we might argue that Gawain's eager courtesy has gotten him into much of his predicament in the first place, and his sense of guilt may arise partially from realizing how weak he was and what all he might have done.

Such considerations suggest a weakness in the ideal which Gawain represents;[29] Arthurian courtesy is not perfect, probably not as perfect as Gawain. Although the poet presents his central character as a concrete verification of mankind's weakness, he seems simultaneously to extol him as the best that mankind has to offer. He does not lose sight of the spiritual dangers of the unconscious as represented by the anima, but restricts himself to something not so much in the realm of Christian morality as of social morality. No sin resides in self-preservation, but there is violation of an ideal. The Green Knight might well laugh, as might Arthur's court, but Gawain's knowledge transcends theirs because he sees more clearly than they the fine dividing line between "good" and "bad" behavior, the mixed motives and the harmful consequences, and finally, the blow to man's pride when he realizes the shamefulness of his behavior. He has learned through painful experience what being human means. It is this sense of guilt which contrasts sharply with the attitude of Arthur's court and which marks his experience as so painfully personal. We have in *Sir Gawain*,

---

[29] For similar views, see Saperstein, p. 32, and Oppel, pp. 84–88.

then, as we have in much medieval literature, a protagonist who encounters in personal terms a well-established truism, usually doctrinal or moral, and by his personal experience of this truism, he verifies the truism for the audience. In other words, the protagonist becomes typical of mankind, and while the story is personal, it is simultaneously exemplary. The principle behind this method of presentation has been well and simply expressed by Jung: "In religious matters it is a well-known fact that we cannot understand a thing until we have experienced it inwardly."[30] The point at issue is not that if Gawain had been a good Christian to begin with, he would have realized the imperfection of man; what Gawain discovers for the first time is how imperfect *he* is. The poem heightens the difference between knowledge taken for granted or accepted on authority, and knowledge acquired through personal experience. The laughter of the court at the end of the poem echoes their laughter at the beginning, and reverberates with all the occasions of laughter throughout the poem. The narrator shares this laughter, too, because he recognizes the admixture of good and evil which makes being human essentially comic.

A psychological approach to *Sir Gawain*, then, centers in Gawain's feelings of guilt, and sees the appropriate reasons for it through the archetypes of the shadow and the anima. The ambiguous nature of the archetype emerges clearly in Bercilak's dual role as Green Knight and host, an ambiguity reflected also in the color green and the symbol of the girdle, and, inversely, of the pentangle. The psychological approach also gives added depth to the parallel structure, seeing Gawain's double role as Arthurian knight and as individual, and the single nature of the double temptation. It explains Morgan's role as the Terrible Mother, the negative aspect of the collective unconscious, thus justifying psychologically the overlapping dual part she plays in

---

[30] *Psychological Reflections*, p. 300.

the parallel structure: first, she is tester of Arthur's court, as Bercilak is of Gawain, and second, her relationship to Bercilak parallels Bercilak's to his wife as instigator and instrument respectively. The psychological approach thus stresses the importance of the double aspects of the poem's structure, supplementing the more emphasized use of threes. And finally, although the poet seems consciously to employ definite psychological overtones, he translates the basic archetypal motif of the encounter with the shadow into social (chivalric) and ultimately religious terms: the poem becomes a "Christian declaration of man's imperfection." The psychological approach thus actually supports the exemplary nature of Gawain's experience and thus does not contradict Robertson's views about the nature of medieval literature. Yet the poet realizes the full worth of Gawain's character and presents his theme in a larger dimension. Truly his unpatronizing, amused tolerance of Gawain's imperfections is Chaucerian, perhaps also rooted in the Christian equivalent of the ambiguous nature of the shadow: for evil to exist, it must exist in the good.[31]

[31] " 'Being and unity and goodness is all one,' explains Chaucer: and that is the essence of the strength behind his comedy" (Raymond Preston, *Chaucer* [London, 1952], pp. 289–290).

20

THE MEANING OF
SIR GAWAIN AND THE GREEN KNIGHT

Larry D. Benson

Sir Gawain and the Green Knight IS SO COMPLEX a poem that it
lends itself to many different interpretations, and ultimately
each reader must decide what particular meaning *Sir Gawain*
has for him. Yet there is a common basis for understanding
even so rich a work as this, for whatever deeper implications
a narrative contains, its readers should be able to agree on
answers to the more elementary questions of meaning: "What
is this work about?" "What is its subject and main theme?" That
readers of *Sir Gawain,* who can agree on so much else about
the poem, can not yet agree on these simple matters is partly
because they have seldom taken them seriously; like those
biblical scholars whom Hugo of St. Victor reprimands for leap-
ing directly to the *sententia* without first studying the *littera*
and *sensus,* critics have so concerned themselves with this
poem's deeper meanings that they have overlooked and some-
times obscured its simple subject and main theme.[1] But prin-

Reprinted from *Art and Tradition in Sir Gawain and the Green Knight*
by Larry D. Benson, pp. 207–218, by permission of Rutgers University
Press. © 1965 by Rutgers, The State University. All quotations from
Sir Gawain and the Green Knight are taken from Tolkien and Gordon's
edition (Oxford, 1930).

[1] As a sample of the variety of answers offered, see Charles Moorman,
"Myth and Medieval Literature: *Sir Gawain and the Green Knight,*"
MedStud, XVIII (1956), 158–172, in which the poem is regarded as a kind

cipally this disagreement arises because the poem has never been interpreted in the light of its literary context. Read apart from other romances, it is indeed obscure, and one cannot be sure what *Sir Gawain* is about nor whether it is ritual, religious allegory, or simple adventure. Within that context its simplest meaning is quite clear: The subject of this romance is romance itself.

The poet's style, his characterizations, and his changes in the beheading and temptation tales have the immediate effect of making his materials more emphatically romantic. Everything becomes superlative; Arthur is the "hendest," Gawain the "best," the Green Knight both the "myriest" and the "worst," and even his chapel is the "corsedest." The result is an enthusiastic intensification of the traditional qualities of romance, with the hero more courtly, the challenger more sharply opposed to knighthood, the lady more irresistible, and the beheading more ghastly than in any work in the tradition. In itself this is not significant, for every romance is about romance and every hero in this genre is a representative of chivalric virtue who must overcome obstacles that test the ideal he maintains. Every romance is also, like *Sir Gawain,* cast in the superlative; such tests require the greatest of heroes and the most difficult of obstacles.

In this sense, the *Gawain*-poet's treatment of *Caradoc* is simply a development of the process that began when the author of *Caradoc* adapted the Irish tale to the conventions of romance. What does significantly differentiate *Sir Gawain*

of *rite de passage* and the conflict as an initiation ritual; William Goldhurst, "The Green and the Gold: The Major Theme of *Gawain and the Green Knight*," *CE,* xx (1958), 61–65, regards the conflict as one between courtly civilization and nature; Joseph Eagan, S.J., "The Import of Color Symbolism in *Sir Gawain and the Green Knight*," *St. Louis Univ. Studies,* Ser. A, Hum. I, 2 (1949), 11–86, regards the conflict as essentially satiric, an attack on romance ideals; and George J. Engelhardt, "The Predicament of Gawain," *MLQ,* xvi (1955), 218–225, sees the conflict as mainly religious. I mention these works because, as my discussion will show, I have found them very useful. For a full summary of criticism of the poem see Morton W. Bloomfield's excellent *"Sir Gawain and the Green Knight,"* above, Chap. II.

from *Caradoc* and from other romances is that alongside these exaggerated traditional elements the poet introduces equally emphatic untraditional materials, such as the surprising conclusion, and unromantic points of view. They introduce another set of values, drawn from outside the framework of traditional assumptions within which the romance ideal is usually tested; the result is the testing of those assumptions themselves. When Gawain returns shamefaced to Camelot from an opponent who only laughs at him, we recognize that the poem has moved from pure romance to a gently satiric anti-romance, since even the reader cannot suppress a smile at the hero's expense, and comedy is not the stuff of which romance heroes are made.

The poem's theme, like its subject, is completely traditional, though significantly modified by the touch of comedy that places it in a new and nonromantic perspective. This is renown, the central ideal of chivalry and a universal topic of medieval romance, in which a concern for fame is the preoccupation of every good knight.[2] The poet carefully added this theme to each episode of the narrative, and the theme of fame more significantly than the bargains or the lace connects the beheading with the temptation and unifies the entire poem. It links the two most important subsidiary themes, the conflicts of courtesy with churlishness and of pride with humility, and unites with the plot even those episodes that the poet added to his sources and that seem to many to stand outside the essential structure of the work—Arthur's encounter with the challenger, the nonsexual elements of the bedroom scenes, the guide's temptation of Gawain, and the hero's return to the court.

Modern readers seldom recognize the importance of fame in *Sir Gawain* because that ideal and the vocabulary associated with it are no longer very meaningful. We are apt to associate fame with publicity rather than with virtue, thinking it an

---

[2] For a discussion of the romance ideal see M. A. Gist, *Love and War in the Middle English Romances* (Philadelphia, 1947). As Miss Gist remarks, p. 141, "The primary interest of every knight was his reputation."

"infirmity of the noble mind," controlled by chance rather than deeds. This attitude is found even in the fourteenth century, in *The House of Fame,* where Fame is a capricious deity, and in *The Speculum Gy de Warewyke,* where the converted Guy is brought to realize the difference between Heaven's meed and knightly renown. But the fourteenth-century reader could still think of fame as an ethical force, and unless we also appreciate that attitude we remain unmoved by lines like Gerames' call to battle in *Huon de Bordeux*—"Let vs there do as good knyghtys ought to do, to the entente that good songes may be made of vs"[3]—and we find it puzzling that a knight like Lancelot (in Chrétien's *Lancelot*) should be so concerned about simply riding in a cart. Some of us even find it difficult to sympathize with Roland when he refuses to sound his horn because he fears the loss of his fame ("En dulce France en perdreie mun los" [In sweet France by it I would lose my renown] v. 1054).

To a medieval reader Roland's motive was credible and even admirable, despite its touch of foolhardy pride, because he knew that fame is more than mere reputation. One earns it by strenuous and virtuous deeds, as did Bevis of Hampton, who was widely known for a doughty knight "In yche lond, that he rideth and goos,/ For to wynne price and loos" (vv. 21–22). Having won his fame, a knight is obligated to maintain it by acting in the manner for which he is renowned. As the young Alexander explains at the beginning of *Cligés,* renown and inaction do not go well together ("Ne s'acordent pas bien ansanble,/ Repos et los" [They do not go well together,/ Inaction and fame] vv. 157–158),[4] and constant knightly effort is required of the good man. To lose one's fame by a failure to act—or worse, by an unchivalric action such as riding in a cart—is to acquire shame, for chivalric deeds are a religious duty and to fail in their performance is a sin to be avoided at

[3] Quoted by Gist, p. 142.
[4] The entire passage, ll. 140–168, is an interesting statement of the importance of renown to knighthood.

all costs: "I had leuer be dismembered than to be shamed and blamed in this deed."[5]

Arthur and Gawain guard their fame as zealously as Roland and Alexander, but the nobility of their action is comically undercut by the relative triviality of the virtue for which they are famed, pure courtesy, and by the outcome of their conflict with the nameless churl who tests this fame, this pattern of noble conduct, and who finally demonstrates the limitations, even the slight absurdity of that ideal. Since this new theme was the *Gawain*-poet's most important modification of the tales he inherited, we can trace it most clearly in the passages he added to these tales in order to make their new function clear. So far we have only touched upon those additions; now that we know something of the poet's style and use of traditional materials we can reexamine the plot to define more clearly what the poem is about and why *Sir Gawain* is at once a brilliant affirmation and a comic rejection of the life that was romance.

RENOWN IN THE BEHEADING EPISODE

The poet's first thematic addition to the beheading tale is the Green Knight's speech explaining why he has come to Camelot. The challenger gave no such explanation in *Caradoc,* since his motive concerned the hero rather than the whole court. He therefore merely greeted the king and demanded a boon, though the later redactors added a few words of praise to the greeting: " 'Sire,' faict il, "je vous sallue comme le meilleur et le plus hault roy qui pour ce jour sur terre regne' " ['Sire,' he said, 'I salute you as the best and highest king who rules this day on earth']. In *Sir Gawain* this is greatly expanded, and the expansions change it from a speech of praise to a statement of the court's renown, not its virtues but its reputation for them:

> "Bot for þe los of þe, lede, is lyft vp so hyȝe,
> And þy burȝ and þy burnes best ar holden,

[5] Quoted by Gist, p. 179, from *Charles the Great,* p. 174.

299

Stifest vnder stel-gere on stedes to ryde,
Þe wyȝtest and þe worþyest of þe worldes kynde,
Preue for to play wyth in oþer pure laykeȝ,
And here is kydde cortaysye, as I haf herd carp."
(258–263)

The virtues are neatly bracketed within the important qualification that they rest only on hearsay so far as the challenger is concerned—"los . . . lyft vp so hyȝe," "as I haf herd carp." Bercilak then requests his boon, not simply asking it, as Éliavres did, but capitalizing on the fame of Arthur and his court and using it as the basis for his demand:

"Bot if þou be so bold as alle burneȝ tellen,
Þou wyl grant me godly þe gomen þat I ask
bi ryȝt."
(272–274)

Although neither Arthur nor Gawain realizes it, this speech rather than the challenge itself establishes the terms of the beheading test and the conditions for the action of the entire poem. The logic that the Green Knight employs here will reappear at crucial points throughout the adventure—when the lady wins her kisses and when the Green Knight urges Gawain to stand still and receive the return-blow. You are famous for bravery and courtesy, the Green Knight reminds Arthur. If that fame of which "alle burneȝ tellen" is deserved, you will act in the manner for which you are renowned. If you fail to live up to your reputation, your renown is but empty appearance, pride and "surquidré" rather than the virtuous substance of knighthood.

This is the issue in the whole adventure. The problem is not simply whether Gawain can keep the series of bargains he has made but whether he, the Round Table's representative, can live up to the fame of Arthur's court. The poet clearly states this essential fact in Bercilak's final explanation of Morgan's plot. There is no mention of the bargains; they were only the means:

"Ho wayned me vpon þis wyse to your wynne halle
For to assay þe surquidré, ȝif hit soth were

300

Þat rennes of þe grete renoun of þe Rounde Table;
Ho wayned me þis wonder your wytteʒ to reue,
For to haf greued Gaynour and gart hir to dyʒe."

(2456-60)

We have already noted the weakness of Morgan's enmity for Guenevere. It seems imposed upon the fabric of the poem, suggested perhaps by Éliavres' words to the queen in *Caradoc,* and it is probably here only to bring a completed cycle of action to the poem. The rest of the explanation is far more important, and *Caradoc* contains no suggestion for it; it grows from the logic of *Sir Gawain* itself, and it is clearly not imposed on the poem. Furthermore, Morgan is a good deal more successful in this part of her plan. Her emissary does manage their "wytteʒ to reue" when he comes to test the great renown of Camelot (for it is "folly" to undertake the adventure, as Arthur himself admits in line 324), and he does find that this renown is mere "surquidré," pride and boasting.

Therefore, when Bercilak taunts the Round Table with its failure to live up to its reputation, he is emphasizing the motive that underlies the entire action:

"What, is þis Arþureʒ hous," quoþ þe haþel þenne,
"Þat al þe rous rennes of þurʒ ryalmes so mony?
Where is now your sourquydrye and your conquestes,
Your gryndellayk and your greme, and your grete wordes?
Now is þe reuel and þe renoun of þe Rounde Table
Ouerwalt wyth a worde of on wyʒes speche,
For al dares for drede wythoute dynt schewed!"

(309-315)

In *Caradoc* the briefer reference to fame in the challenger's taunt was merely an insult, though it moves Arthur deeply to think that his reputation could be threatened. In *Sir Gawain* the reference to renown develops logically from the challenger's opening speech and from the assumptions of knighthood on which he had based it. The taunt moves Arthur not only to grief but to shame, anger, and action.

He seizes the axe, swings it about, and is just about to strike when Gawain interrupts with the request that he be allowed to take on the adventure. When Arthur, so fierce the moment before, meekly surrenders the axe to Gawain, it is apparent that the king has failed, for to take up an adventure that one does not finish is "surquidré," especially when one takes it up with so boastful an announcement of his intentions as Arthur makes. Yet it is also clear that Arthur has somehow failed the test even before Gawain's interruption and that Gawain must step forward not only to show his loyalty to the king but also to save the integrity of the court. Critics have given relatively little attention to this episode, but we can be sure the poet's audience scrutinized it carefully because of both the great symbolic importance of Arthur in medieval romance and the rarity of a situation in which he undertakes and then fails an adventure.[6] This is the sort of action that one expects from Kay, not the king (and, as we have noted, the author of *The Grene Knight* replaces Arthur with Kay). The episode fully deserves the attention its novelty draws, for Arthur's failure foreshadows Gawain's fall and defines success and failure in this poem. It shows that the bargains are not as important as they seem; Arthur fails not because he cannot keep the bargain but because he does not live up to the fame of Camelot as it is defined in the Green Knight's opening speech.

In that speech we are told that there are two aspects of Camelot's fame, each of which its champion must display, its famous bravery and its "kydde cortaysye." The frightened

[6] The incident is discussed and Arthur's failure is defined in varying ways by D. E. Baughan, "The Role of Morgan Le Fay in *Sir Gawain and the Green Knight*," *ELH*, XVII (1950), 241–251 (however, his interpretation is based on a misreading of l. 331; Engelhardt discusses this error in the article cited in note 1 above); Else van der ven-ten Bensel, *The Character of Arthur in English Literature* (Amsterdam, 1925), notes that this is a failure in courtesy, p. 138; Hans Schnyder, "Aspects of Kingship in *Sir Gawain and the Green Knight*," *ES*, XL (1959), 289–294; Albert B. Friedman, "Morgan le Fay in *Sir Gawain and the Green Knight*," *Spec.*, XXXV (1960), 260–274.

courtiers quickly disqualify themselves. They are famed as the "stifest vnder stel-gere" (260), but they are courtiers rather than warriors. They fail the test of bravery and look silently to Arthur, and the king, impelled by the rashness of his "young blood," accepts the challenge. He thus upholds Camelot's reputation for bravery, but in doing so he deserts what now becomes the most important aspect of its fame. He forgets that he is "þe hendest," and he becomes for the moment like the "methles" Green Knight, *démesuré* and churlish. This is the main point of this unusual episode. In it we are shown that in this poem manners are as important to the plot as the axe itself, for to live up to the reputation of Camelot, its champion must remain true to the courtesy that is central to that ideal. In it we are also shown the first of a series of varying scenes in which the knight and the churl face one another, each attempting to impose his own pattern of behavior on the other.

The episode begins with Arthur's elaborately courteous greeting:

> Þenn Arþour bifore þe hiʒ dece þat auenture byholdeʒ,
> And rekenly hym reuerenced, for rad was he neuer,
> And sayde, "Wyʒe, welcum iwys to þis place,
> Þe hede of þis ostel Arthour I hat;
> Liʒt luflych adoun and lenge, I þe praye,
> And quat-so þy wylle is we schal wyt after."
>
> (250–255)

Despite the challenger's hostile and frightening appearance, the king is neither fearful nor hasty (*rad* can mean either[7]). He courteously invites the stranger to act in the proper courtly manner—to alight graciously ("luflych") from his mount, to be entertained, and then afterwards to state his business. This is exactly the course followed by the courteous Gawain when he arrives at Bercilak's castle and by the courtly Bredbeddle in

---

[7] Editors gloss it as "fearful," deriving it from O.N. *hræddr,* but elsewhere in the poem the word means "swiftly"—1.862. Cf. OED, s.v. "rad."

The Grene Knight. However, our Green Knight abruptly refuses
Arthur's invitation and delivers one of his own, demanding that
the court's champion not only accept the challenge but that he
do so in the challenger's own fierce ("felle") and churlishly
vigorous ("lepe lyʒtly") manner:

> "If any freke be so felle to fonde þat I telle
> Lepe lyʒtly me to, and lach þis weppen."
> (291-292)

Arthur's failure is that when he does take up the challenge he
does so in exactly the churlish manner that the Green Knight
had demanded. His shame and anger lead him to forget his
famous courtesy entirely. He waxes "as wroth as wynde" (319)
—a simile from nature that suggests the beginning of a resem-
blance between the king and the churlish Green Knight. He
surrenders to his natural impulse ("bi kynde"), and he moves
away from the dais and "stod þat stif mon nere" (322):

> Ande sayde, "Haþel, by heuen, þyn askyng is nys,
> And as þou foly hatʒ frayst, fynde þe behoues.
> I know no gome þat is gast of þy grete wordes;
> Gif me now þy geserne, vpon Godeʒ halue,
> And I schal bayþen þy bone þat þou boden habbes."
> (323-327)

His speech, like his physical location, is now closer to that of
the Green Knight, rich in expletives ("by heuen," "vpon Godeʒ
halue"), insults ("þy grete wordes," "þou foly hatʒ frayst"),
and boasts ("I schal bayþen þy bone"). In the next line he
rushes forward to grasp the axe:

> Lyʒtly lepeʒ he hym to, and laʒt at his honde.
> (328)

The challenger had demanded, "Lepe lyʒtly me to, and lach
þis weppen," and Arthur has done exactly that. But whereas
he has capitulated to the challenger's demand, the Green
Knight remains true to his own churlish self. He alights not

"luflych," as Arthur had asked, but in the "felle" manner he had proposed:

> Þen feersly þat oþer freke vpon fote lyȝtis.
>
> (329)

The use of "þat oþer freke" and of "lyȝtis," echoing "lyȝtly" in the previous line describing Arthur's action, emphasizes the similarity between the king and the Green Knight. Arthur has become for the moment a churl. He seizes the weapon and,

> Now hatȝ Arthure his axe, and þe halme grypeȝ,
> And sturnely stureȝ hit aboute, þat stryke wyth hit þoȝt.
>
> (330–331)

Prior to these lines and those immediately preceding, the poet had paid little attention to Arthur's movement. Closely described violent movement, like violent speech, is characteristic of churls rather than gentlemen. Yet here the poet describes Arthur's actions by the technique of exact specification that he usually reserves for the Green Knight. He emphasizes every movement as the king leaps fiercely forward, grasps the axe and sternly swings it about, as if he, like the Green Knight in the final scene, intends first to terrify his victim. The courteous Arthur, who was never before "rad," has given way to "la fretta / que l'onestade ad ogni atto dismagha" [the rashness / which deprives every act of its dignity. *Purgatorio,* III, 10–11]. The Green Knight, on the other hand, is silent and slow-moving for the first and almost the only time in the poem, his cool deliberation contrasting markedly with Arthur's churlish haste: "He stroked his berde, / And wyth a countenaunce dryȝe he droȝ doun his cote" (334–335).

Arthur's action is so carefully justified by the dramatic situation (the shame and anger that he feels) and by the motivation that the poet provides in his characterization of the king ("his ȝonge blod and his brayn wylde") that we accept and perhaps even applaud this show of temper. But then Gawain interrupts with a long and ceremonial speech; it is a superlative display of the courtesy for which Camelot is famed, and it differs sharply from the manner that Arthur has adopted. Perhaps Gawain's speech reminds even the king of his obligation to courtesy, for his churlish ferocity immediately disappears. He now consults his barons and, with their consent, he delivers the axe with his formal blessing to the kneeling hero. The solemn and ceremonial tone of Arthur's surrender of the axe contrasts as markedly with the churlish haste in which he obtained it as Gawain's speech does with Arthur's angry words. The elaborate courtesy of this passage thus salvages some of Camelot's reputation at the same time it shows us that Arthur's failure in the challenge is a failure in manners. Then Gawain succeeds completely, and he saves the fame of Camelot by taking up the adventure with both the bravery and the courtesy for which it is renowned. Yet, since the king himself has failed, it is clear that the hero's triumph can only be temporary. The end will be heavy, Gawain will find himself unable to maintain his perfect character, and he too will desert his renowned courtesy to descend momentarily to the churlish level of his opponent. . . .

21

A REVIEW

John Gardner

Art and Tradition in Sir Gawain and the Green Knight. By Larry
D. Benson. New Brunswick, N. J., 1965.

THIS BOOK OF literary criticism will be useful to anyone teaching
medieval literature, whether in high school or in graduate school.
It is an interesting book, generally, though marred here and
there by lapses into the prissy, labored, or unconvincing. The
thesis is that to readers who do not know about medieval
romance and the Alliterative Revival the *Gawain*-poet "fre-
quently seems obscure when he is most clear, and simple when
he is most obscure." Understanding the poem, Benson says, is
largely a matter of putting the poem in the right context.

The thesis is a trifle pat. Both on romance tradition and on
the poet's artistry, however, Benson's study is good. He presents
a thematically oriented analysis of the evolution of the "behead-
ing game" down to the French prose redaction of the *Caradoc,*
a source very close indeed to *GGK,* as Benson shows (pp.
16–37 et passim; Benson prints this valuable text itself in an
appendix), and then comments on the more general relation-
ship of *GGK* and the *Yder.* He argues, convincingly, that the
Gawain-poet's modification of both the beheading and tempta-
tion stories follows from his change of theme. The *Gawain-*

Reprinted, by permission of author and editors, from the *Journal of
English and Germanic Philology,* LXV (1966), 706–708. The review, as it
appears here, has been slightly abbreviated by the author.

poet's focus is on courtesy and its outward effect, fame—an effect which, ironically, can produce a breakdown of courtesy, as it does in both Arthur and Gawain. Benson turns next to consideration of the general attitudes and expectations in romance tradition as a whole, among other things its regard for dignified restraint, its contempt for bustling churls, wild men, and strumpets, its characterization of Gawain as treacherous lecher. Glancing back at *GGK*, Benson discovers that the Green Knight is generally active and noisy, Gawain generally dignified and soft-spoken until, at the end, their characterization is virtually reversed. Part of the preparation for Gawain's change, Benson thinks, is the tension, built into the poem, between Gawain's traditional character and his present wish to remain continent and loyal, on the theory that virtue may save his head.

The third and fourth chapters are the best in Benson's study. The third, on rhetoric and the character of the alliterative half-line, makes the striking suggestion that the Alliterative Revival may have been set off by several poets' almost simultaneous discovery, in various parts of England, that alliterative meter was an ideal vehicle for the newly fashionable "high style" of the rhetoricians. Whether or not this guess is right (I believe it is well worth considering), Benson's analysis of rhetoric and alliterative form in *GGK* is excellent, and his discussion of the aesthetic and analytic functions of verbal variation here and elsewhere in the Alliterative Revival is a model demonstration that for good poets *amplificatio* did not mean mere dilation. The fourth chapter, on narrative and descriptive techniques in alliterative verse, distinguishes clearly (for the first time) between traditional narrative and descriptive techniques and techniques introduced by the *Gawain*-poet. In his final chapter Benson discusses the meaning of the poem. In Benson's words, "The subject of this romance is romance itself." The poem criticizes the romantic ideal, playing noble but rarefied Courtesy against vigorous, sometimes undignified Nature, that is, playing Arthur and Sir Gawain against the Green Knight.

For the most part Benson's argument is handsomely supported by close analysis of verbal texture and the larger structure of *GGK,* by perceptive treatment of the tension between romance and *fabliau* (in the temptation scenes), and by astute commentary on romance tradition. At times Benson's readings stand with the best New Critical studies, for instance his discussion of the imagistically "blurred" description of the Green Knight (pp. 58 ff.), or his Alain Renoiresque examination of point-of-view (pp. 185 ff.). . . .

Ultimately (though the question may not matter) one wonders how much a knowledge of romance tradition really illuminates. True, the subject is of interest in its own right, and comparison of the French prose *Caradoc* and *GGK* provides clues to the *Gawain*-poet's working method; but to the extent that critical interpretation depends on knowledge of the tradition, one is inclined to distrust the interpretation. *Pace* Benson, one does not really need to know romance tradition to realize that eyes "gray as glass" are beautiful, or that gentlemen are polite. Neither is it necessary to suspend modern assumptions to recognize that artifice, elaboration, and elevated style are legitimate values in poetry, for if it is today a law (as Benson tells us) that good style consists in brevity and an absence of artifice, the law is one Faulkner, among others, never heard of. Benson's discovery that the poem concerns courtly as opposed to common manners is not new, though presented in a new way; on the other hand, to read the poem as primarily about "romance itself" he is forced to pass over a good deal of interesting and suggestive criticism in silence. It is true that Speirs's mistakes have given the ritualistic theory a bad name; nevertheless, one must somehow account for the many details which call magic to mind, for instance the Green Knight's witchlike vaulting of the stream.[1] And though no one has as yet offered a convinc-

---

[1] On *GGK* as myth see, for instance, R. S. Loomis, *Wales and the Arthurian Legend* (Cardiff, 1956), pp. 77–90. Cf. John Speirs, *Medieval English Poetry, The Non-Chaucerian Tradition* (London, 1957), p. 234 et passim.

ing full scale reading of the poem as Christian allegory,[2] the poem's appearance with homiletic work apparently by the same poet in Cotton Nero A.x[3] lends credibility to the view that *GGK* may be, centrally, religious allegory. In short, if we grant that the poem should be read in the light of its tradition, we are left with the question, which tradition?

Moreover, I wonder whether the romance tradition known to the *Gawain*-poet and his audience is the same romance tradition we know. Benson speaks of the *Morte Arthure* in every connection but the one which is perhaps most important, its characterization of Gawain as noble though a trifle foolhardy, Arthur as dangerously proud. The influence of *Morte Arthure* on *GGK* has often been suggested, and William Matthews notes that, in the poetry that has survived, Western English and Scottish poets, in contrast to French poets and Malory, treat Sir Gawain as the model of knighthood, not treacherous or lecherous at all.[4] Benson's interpretation of Gawain's "fame" as sexual is not supported by the poem, which speaks only of chaste courtly manners, love-*talking*. This is not to say that the poem cannot be read as a treatment of fame in its relationship to pride; it is merely to say that possibly the romance tradition chiefly informing the poem is, except for a few shards, lost.

[2] The most recent speculation along this line is my own in the Introduction to *The Complete Works of the Gawain-Poet* (Chicago, 1965).

[3] Professor Benson agrees that the four poems in Cotton Nero A.x are by one man. See his article, "The Authorship of *St. Erkenwald*," *JEGP*, LXIV (1965), 393–405.

[4] See William Matthews, *The Tragedy of Arthur: A Study of the Alliterative "Morte Arthure"* (Berkeley and Los Angeles, 1960), pp. 144–150, 161–169, et passim.

22

GAWAIN'S FAULT IN
SIR GAWAIN AND THE GREEN KNIGHT

David Farley Hills

IT HAS BEEN pointed out that there seems to be a curious contradiction in *Sir Gawain and the Green Knight* between the fault (or faults) that Gawain confesses to and the fault as understood by Bercilak and the poet himself.[1] Mr. Burrow even goes so far as to suggest that we can only resolve the contradiction by discounting Gawain's view of the matter entirely. It is not, however, at all clear why the poet should cause his hero to misinterpret the facts, even supposing that he wished to show him as exaggerating his guilt; and to explain the contradiction in this way is to substitute one mystery for another.

Gawain's own view of the transgression is quite clear:[2]

> "Corsed worth cowarddyse and couetyse boþe!
> In yow is vylany and vyse þat vertue disstryeȝ. . . .
> Lo! þer þe falssyng, foule mot hit falle!
> For care of þy knokke cowardyse me taȝt
> To acorde me with couetyse, my kynde to forsake,
> Þat is larges and lewté þat longeȝ to knyȝteȝ.

Reprinted, by permission of author and the Clarendon Press, Oxford, from *Review of English Studies,* XIV (1963), 124–131.

[1] See J. Burrow, "The Two Confession Scenes in *Sir Gawain and the Green Knight*," *MP,* LVII (1959), 79: "He confesses three times to a sin which the poem twice authoritatively asserts that he did not commit."

[2] All quotations are from the edition of J. R. R. Tolkien and E. V. Gordon (Oxford, 1925).

> Now I am fawty and falce, and ferde haf ben euer
> Of trecherye and vntrawpe: . . ."
>
> (2374–83)

And so that we are in no doubt that this is Gawain's final inter-
pretation the poet makes him repeat the analysis when he
recounts his adventures to Arthur and the court at the end of
the poem:

> "Lo! lorde," quoþ þe leude, and þe lace hondeled,
> "Þis is þe bende of þis blame I bere in my nek,
> Þis is þe laþe and þe losse þat I laȝt haue,
> Of couardise and couetyse þat I haf caȝt þare;
> Þis is þe token of vntrawþe þat I am tan inne,
> And I mot nedeȝ hit were wyle I may last; . . ."
>
> (2505–10)

According to Gawain's own account, then, he was prompted
by cowardice to accept the green girdle and so to commit the
sin of covetousness, which led in turn to his breaking his com-
pact with Bercilak. There is no difficulty in concurring with
Gawain when he says he was prompted to sin out of fear, nor
in agreeing that he broke his compact with Bercilak and so
committed an "untruth," but why does he accuse himself of the
deadly sin of covetousness? It is the harder to understand
because no less than four times in the poem the poet goes out
of his way to reject the idea that Gawain accepted the present
for its intrinsic value. First, when the lady offers it she makes it
quite clear that, unlike the ring he has refused, which is "worth
wele ful hoge" (1820), it is a thing of little value (1848). Then
the poet himself, in a passage which at first sight seems largely
gratuitous, tells us:

> Bot wered not þis ilk wyȝe for wele þis gordel,
> For pryde of þe pendaunteȝ, þaȝ polyst þay were,
> And þaȝ þe glyterande golde glent vpon endeȝ,
> Bot for to sauen hymself. . . .
>
> (2037–40)

Bercilak echoes this when he tells Gawain he knew all about the gift:

> "Bot here yow lakked a lyttel, sir, and lewté yow wonted;
> Bot þat watȝ for no wylyde werke, ne wowyng nauþer,
> Bot for ȝe lufed your lyf; þe lasse I yow blame."

(2366–68)

And finally, when Gawain himself agrees to wear the girdle after Bercilak has offered it to him, he reiterates the same terms:

> "Þat wyl I welde wyth good wylle, not for þe wynne golde,
> Ne þe saynt, ne þe sylk, ne þe syde pendaundes,
> For wele ne for worchyp, ne for þe wlonk werkkeȝ,
> Bot in syngne of my surfet I schal se hit ofte,
> When I ride in renoun, remorde to myselven
> Þe faut and þe fayntyse of þe flesche crabbed,
> How tender hit is to entyse teches of fylþe;
> And þus, quen pryde schal me pryk for prowes of armes,
> Þe loke to þis luf-lace schal leþe my hert."

(2430–38)

The last of these quotations admittedly does not refer to his reasons for accepting the girdle in the first place, but it does seem to echo the terminology of the earlier explanations and somehow to suggest Gawain's concurrence with them.

It ought to be noted that no one in the poem expresses any sense of there being a contradiction between the two interpretations. Neither Bercilak nor Arthur disputes Gawain's interpretation, nor does Gawain challenge the other version. Indeed he seems, as we must infer from the behavior of the lady, to be most anxious not to fall into the sin of covetousness. Only the laughter of first Bercilak and then Arthur and his court would seem to suggest that their attitudes to the fault are not quite the same as Gawain's—but of that more later.

What is the explanation of this apparent contradiction? To answer this we must examine the medieval concept of covetousness. Covetousness (*cupiditas*) or avarice (*avaritia*) was regarded as one of the seven "deadly" or "capital" sins, as in

Chaucer's *Parson's Tale*.[3] Sometimes a distinction is made between covetousness and avarice by which the former refers to those possessions you want to acquire and the latter to those that you have and want to keep,[4] but quite often the terms are used synonymously. Among the seven Pride was usually regarded as holding chief place,[5] partly on the authority of Eccles. x. 15, "Initium omnis peccati superbia" [the beginning of all sin is pride]; but at the same time this had to be reconciled with 1 Tim. vi. 10, "Radix enim omnium malorum est cupiditas" [For the root of all evil is covetousness]. If avarice merely meant a love of riches it clearly could not be the root of all sin; therefore another, extended use of the word was established. This is how St. Thomas Aquinas explains it in the *Summa Theologiae*:[6]

. . . secundum quosdam cupiditas multipliciter dicitur. Uno modo, prout est appetitus inordinatus divitiarum. Et sic est speciale peccatum. Alio modo, secundum quod significat inordinatum appetitum cuiuscumque boni temporalis. Et sic est genus omnis peccati: nam in omni peccato est inordinata conversio ad commutabile bonum, ut dictum est. Tertio modo sumitur prout significat quandam inclinationem naturae corruptae ad bona corruptibilia inordinate appetenda. Et sic dicunt cupiditatem esse radicem omnium peccatorum, ad similitudinem radicis arboris, quae ex terra trahit alimentum: sic enim ex amore rerum temporalium omne peccatum procedit. (I. II. q. 84 a. 1)

[. . . according to some, covetousness can be variously understood. In one sense, it is an excessive desire for riches. And so it is a special sin. In another sense, it means an excessive desire for any temporal goods whatsoever. And so it is a type of all sins, for in every sin there is an excessive turning toward a mutable good, as has been said above. In still another sense, it can mean some inclination of a corrupt nature to excessively desire corruptible goods. And thus they

[3] E.g. Part 2, § 23: "the deedly sinnes, this is to seyn, chieftaines of sinnes."

[4] Ibid., *De Avaricia*, § 63.

[5] See Morton W. Bloomfield, *The Seven Deadly Sins* (East Lansing, Mich., 1952), pp. 74–75.

[6] Marietti edition, ed. P. Caramello (Turin and Rome, 1948).

say that covetousness is the root of all sins, by analogy with the
root of a tree, which draws its nourishment from the earth, for in
the same way all sin grows from a love of temporal things.]
Here we have a much wider use of the term than is covered
simply by a desire for riches. Avarice is not only the sin of
wanting money. It is also a sin against charity because it deflects
the soul from the love of God towards a love of corruptible
things; it is an inordinate love of anything other than God.

There are thus in medieval theology two distinct uses of the
word avarice (covetousness): in a special sense to denote love
of riches, and in a general sense to denote any turning away
from God's love. The special sense was, as we might expect,
the usual meaning we find in tracts and sermons throughout the
Middle Ages. A hint that the use of the term in the "general"
sense was essentially a learned use is given by Chaucer's Par-
son when he adds in parenthesis that he is going to use the term
"Avarice or Coveitise" according "to commune understond-
inge."[7] A less cryptic indication is given in one of Wyclif's Latin
sermons, where, referring to Ephes. v. 5, he says:

Vocat enim apostolus avarum more philosophorum et sapiencium
qui scripturam collegerant formaliter abstractive, illud quo homo
formaliter fit avarus, et ipsa avaricia secundum descripcionem pre-
dictam est ydolorum servitus, cum omnis talis preponderat tempo-
ralia supra Deum.[8]
[Adopting the abstract usage of the philosophers and scholars who
formally gathered together the Scriptures, the apostle (Paul) speaks
of avarice as that by which a man formally becomes avaricious; and
avarice itself, by definition, is described as the enslavement to idols—
that is, when all sorts of such temporal goods take precedence before
God.]

In this theological sense, then, covetousness came to be
regarded as the antithesis of charity, as Rousselot explains:

La "charité" et la "cupidité" se partagent le monde. Voilà, pour un
esprit nourri d'Augustin et encore malhabile à distinguer le domaine

[7] Part 2, § 23.
[8] J. Wyclif, *Sermones*, ed. J. Loserth, ɪ (London, 1887), 90.

315

de la philosophie d'avec celui du dogme, le point de départ néces-
saire, le supposé premier de toute théorie de l'amour, supposé pas-
sablement différent du principe néoplatonicien qui proclamait l'ap-
pétition de Dieu par toutes choses. Les conséquences suivaient, sinon
très rigoureuses, au moins très naturelles. Entre charité et cupidité
il y a antithèse absolue. Comme charité et grâce sont deux termes
équivalents, et comme *grâce* s'oppose à *nature,* on était tenté, dans
la langue courante, d'identifier nature et cupidité. On regardait celle-
ci, toute mauvaise qu'elle était, comme le fruit propre de celle-là, on
ne voyait plus qu'une différence confuse entre ces deux termes:
amour naturel et amour vicieux . . . on la sentait vaguement adé-
quate, et partout, dans les sermons, dans les traités ascétiques, les
lettres de direction, les effusions personnelles, on caractérisait cour-
amment la grâce comme l'amour de Dieu préféré à soi-même, et la
nature comme un égoïsme étroit.[9]

["Charité" and "cupidité" separate the world. For a mind nourished
by Augustine and still unused to distinguishing between the domains
of philosophy and dogma, this is the necessary point of departure,
the first supposition of any theory of love, presumed to be somewhat
different from the Neoplatonic principle which proclaims the desire
for God by all things. The consequences followed — if not very
rigorous, at least very natural. Between charity and cupidity there
is an absolute antithesis. As charity and grace are two equivalent
terms, and as *grace* opposes itself to *nature,* one was tempted, in
using the ordinary language of the day, to identify nature with
cupidity. One looked upon the latter, as bad as it was, as the natural
result of the former; one saw nothing but a confusing difference
between the terms: natural and unnatural love . . . one felt that this
was somehow inadequate, and everywhere—in sermons, in ascetic
treatises, in letters of guidance, in personal effusions—one ordinarily
characterized grace as love of God in preference to love of one's
self, and nature as narrow egoism.]

As Rousselot says, the idea was based on St. Augustine's view
of sin as a misdirection of love, which ought to be directed to

[9] P. Rousselot, *Pour l'histoire du problème de l'amour au Moyen Age*
(Beiträge zur Geschichte der Philosophie des Mittelalters, VI [1908]), app.
i, p. 88.

God, not to oneself.[10] And it was regarded as axiomatic that love of temporal things stemmed from a love of self.[11] The essence of this view of covetousness is that it offends against charity because one's own wishes are put before God's. Medieval theological writing often explicitly refers to this idea. Rousselot, for instance, quotes William of Auvergne (*De Moribus*, c. 41): "Pes cordis, dicit Augustinus, amor est, qui si rectus est dicitur caritas, si vero curvus dicitur cupiditas" [The foot of the heart, says Augustine, is love, which if it is virtuous is called charity, but if it is perverted is called covetousness]. And we find a similar view expressed a century or more earlier by Hugo of St. Victor: "Sicut igitur amor cum sit motus mentis naturaliter unus, secundum diversas qualitates diversa nomina sortitur; et dicitur aliquando cupiditas, quando scilicet ad mundum est; quando vero ad Deum est charitas" [And therefore love, as it is one natural impulse of the mind, is classed by various names according to its various qualities; it is called covetousness when it is obviously worldly, charity when it is Godly].[12] A work roughly contemporaneous with the *Gawain*-poet, the *Comprendium Theologiae* formerly attributed to Jehan Gerson, uses the same antithesis: "Sic cupiditas in suo esse dicitur radix omnium malorum ex inordinato amore, qui ex ipsa cupiditate habetur ad creaturam, qui inordinatus amor similiter afficit et attrahit animam, et a summo bono avertit" [Just as covetous-

---

[10] See, for example, *De Civitate Dei*, xiv. 28 (Migne, *P. L.*, xli. 436): "Fecerunt itaque civitates duas amores duo; terrenam scilicet amore sui usque ad contemptum Dei, coelestem vero amor Dei usque ad contemptum sui" [And so, by two loves, there were created two cities: the earthly one by love of self and indeed contempt of God, but the celestial one by love of God and indeed contempt of self].

[11] See, for example, Aquinas, *Summa*, i. ii, q. 77 a. 4: "Quod autem aliquis appetat inordinate aliquod temporale bonum, procedit ex hoc quod inordinate amat seipsum: hoc enim est amare aliquem, velle ei bonum" [The reason anyone excessively desires some temporal good derives from the fact that he excessively loves himself; because to wish anyone some good is to love him].

[12] *De Sacramentis*, ii. 13, Ch. 4 (Migne, *P.L.*, clxxvi. 527).

ness in itself, as it arises from excessive love, is said to be the root of all evil (which, because of covetousness, is extended toward creatures), so, excessive love likewise afflicts and pulls at the soul and diverts it from the greatest good].[13]

Any concern for the things of this world for their own sake appertained to the sin of covetousness. So a work wrongly attributed to St. Bernard explains:

> Nemo potest perfecte spiritualia bella suscipere nisi prius carnis edomuerit voluptates: non potest mens ad contemplandum Deum esse libera, quae terrena et transitoria huius mundi concupiscit: non potest videre oculus mentis alta, si eum claudit pulvis terrenae cupiditatis. Cupiditas grave peccatum est, omnium criminum materia est.[14]
>
> [No one is able to perfectly wage the spiritual battle unless he has first entirely subdued fleshly pleasures: the mind cannot be free to contemplate God if it desires the earthly and transitory things of this world; the mind's eye is unable to look on high if the dust of worldly desires closes in around it. Covetousness is a serious sin, the source of all misdeeds.]

Covetousness is the element in all sin which is due to loving oneself more than God and seeking, as Peter Comestor says, "consolation in transitory things"[15]—a consolation which is no consolation: "Quantumlibet ergo [animus humanus] contineat, nunquam est plenus, nisi Deus habeat, cuius semper est capax. Si vis ergo, o cupide, satiari, desinas esse cupidus, quia dum cupidus fueris, satiari non poteris" [So no matter how much (the human soul) contains, it is never full unless it hold God, whom it can always hold. O covetous man, if you wish to be satisfied, cease being covetous, because as long as you are covetous you cannot be satisfied].[16]

---

[13] Jehan Gerson, *Opera Omnia*, ed. du Pin (Antwerp, 1706), I, Chs. 326–327.

[14] *Liber de Modo Bene Vivendi*, Ch. XLV (Migne, *P.L.*, CLXXXIV. 1266).

[15] "Per avaritiam in transitoriis consolari." Sermon 44 (Migne, *P.L.*, CXCVIII. 1828).

[16] Innocent III, *De Contemptu Mundi*, Bk. II, Ch. VII (Migne, *P.L.*, CCXVII. 720).

Cupidity manifests itself in a constant worry about the things of this world, whereas we ought to trust in God's providence.[17] It is essentially a spiritual disease: "Avarus nec patientibus compatitur, nec miseris subvenit vel miseretur, sed offendit Deum, offendit seipsum, offendit proximum" [The avaricious man neither suffers with the patient nor succors nor pities the miserable; instead, he offends God, himself, and his neighbor].[18] It is not unusual to find love of wealth being used, as it were, as an example of this state of mind. The essential antithesis between *caritas* and *cupiditas,* for instance, appears in this extract from Peter Lombard's *Collectanea in Epist. S. Pauli:* "Qui veram fidem de Deo habet non cupit in miseriis fieri dives, nec pluris est ei mundus quam Deus" [Whoever has true faith in God does not long to be wealthy in adversity nor does the world mean more to him than God does].[19] Of course, to take this antithesis between the world and God to its logical conclusion would be to commit the heresy of the Manicheans. So it is usually stressed that it is an inordinate desire of a temporal good that offends against charity: "inordinatus amor sui est causa omnis peccati" [the inordinate love of self is the cause of all sin].[20] The *Gawain*-poet's contemporary, Wyclif, in Book III of the *Trialogus* discussing the sin of avarice (*avaritia*) says:

> Sed quantum ad avaritiam, potest dici quod ipsa descriptive ad nostram intentionem est inordinatus amor temporalium; et intelligo temporalia, ut sunt vulgariter intellecta, scilicet pro omni terrena substantia, quae potest esse de possessione hominis. Intelligo etiam per temporalia habitudines respectivas in rebus terrenis fundatas, quas homo irrationabiliter appetit, sicut dominia et honores mundanos, quae ex possessione talium oriuntur.[21]

[17] Ibid., Ch. x (c. 721).
[18] Ibid., Ch. xi (c. 721).
[19] Migne, *P.L.,* cxcii. 359–60.
[20] Aquinas, *Summa,* i. ii, q. 77 a. 4.
[21] *Trialogus,* ed. G. Lechler (Oxford, 1869), p. 190. Cf. Peter Cantor, *Verbum Abbreviatum,* ch. xx (Migne, *P.L.,* ccv. 73): "Avaritia immoderata est habendi cupiditas, quae non tantum est pecuniae, sed et

[But as for avarice, for our intentions it is possible to say that by its very definition it is the inordinate love of temporal goods; and by temporal goods, as they are commonly understood, I mean obviously all earthly things that can be possessed by man. And by temporal goods I also mean related possessions which are based upon earthly things and which are unreasonably sought by man, such as power and worldly honors which come from owning material goods.]

There is clearly, then, a long tradition among medieval theologians of interpreting *avaritia* to mean much more than merely the desire for riches. That it is not commonly met with in vernacular writing need not concern us, because most vernacular expositions of a theological nature are of the simplest and deliberately seek to avoid subtleties of definition. The idea, however, is clearly represented in this extract from Wyclif's tract on the seven deadly sins:

And so covetouse men ben aboute, as foolis, to turne þo ordynaunse of kynde þat God hymself hafs made; ffor God haves putte hymself hyeste of alle þingis, and aftir hym monnis soule, for þus þingis schulden be loved; and erthly þinges lowest, ffor þei schulden be leeste loved. . . . But þo covetouse mon dos al contrarye herto; and when he coveitis to be lord þus ageyns Gods wille, he forfeetis ageyne þo Lord of alle, and þus is made most pore mon. Ne vauntage herby haves he none oþer, bot by luf is drawen to helle, and þat is ferrist þing fro heven. Ffor loved þing drawes men to hit, as þo stoon of adamaunt drawes irne unto hym. And herfore God biddis men most love heven and hevenly þinges. And se we hou þo avarous mon coveytis unkyndely to fille his soule wiþ þing þat on no wyse may fille hit.[22]

Another English example of the use of "avarice" in this "learned" sense is found in *Piers Plowman*. In passus I and II

altitudinis et scientiae, cum supra modum sublimitas ambitur, imo etiam quaecunque res, cum supra quam satis est, appetitur, secundum Augustinum" [Avarice is having an excessive covetousness, not only for money, but also for eminence and knowledge—when sublimity is striven for beyond moderation, indeed, according to Augustine, whenever anything more than enough is sought after].

[22] Wyclif, *Select English Works,* et. T. Arnold (Oxford, 1869–71), III, 149 f.

especially a great deal is made of the contrast between truth, which is *deus caritas* (B 1. 85–87), and "mede," which in the beginning of passus II is shown as a personification to the Dreamer by Holy Church when he asks to be shown falsehood. But what now of the relevance of all this to *Sir Gawain and the Green Knight?*

Accordance to this "Augustinian" tradition *cupiditas* is a state of inordinate love for oneself, and it is just such a disposition that Gawain has shown in accepting the girdle to save his life. Clearly a strict respect for truth (which we might note in passing Langland equates with *deus caritas*) would require that Gawain should hand over the green girdle to Bercilak or perhaps refuse to accept it in the first place. In not doing so because he loved his life too much he was placing his love for himself above his love for truth and therefore God—a classical example of *cupiditas* in this "general" sense. Bercilak's assertion that Gawain was a little at fault (2366) because he wanted to save his life, and the poet's own reference to the girdle (2040), far from contradicting Gawain's own interpretation when he calls his fault "covetousness," actually help to define it more exactly for us. That we should find the *Gawain*-poet using a "learned" theological idea ought not to surprise us, I think; because not only is it clear from his knowledge of rhetorical usage, and the emphasis on Christian ideas that scholarship is beginning to reveal, that he was a man of some learning, but also, if he was the author of the other poems of the manuscript in which *Sir Gawain* is found, he clearly interested himself in theological problems.[23]

The supposition that the poet was using the term "covetousness" according to the "Augustinian" tradition makes sense of what would otherwise be nonsensical, but it does not quite account for all the details of the poet's treatment of Gawain's

---

[23] It is worth noting, too, how often he uses words of theological significance in the poem: e.g. 1774, 2433, 2436, 2488 (concerning sin), 897, 1876 ff., 2391 (concerning penance).

fault. We still have to ask why Gawain's attitude to his fault differs from that of Bercilak, Arthur, and the court. For Gawain clearly takes his slip very seriously while everyone else tends to laugh it off, though Bercilak does regard it as a fault (2366). I do not think we ought to make too much of this difference of emphasis; it is only fitting and in keeping with his moral scrupulousness that Gawain should be harder on himself than the others are. This would not only be a sign of true penitence, it would accord with the courtly requirement of *humblesse*. But it might be objected, I think, that if Gawain had committed the "deadly" sin of "avarice" a moral poem ought not to show most of the characters treating it lightly. Here again a look at medieval attitudes towards this kind of situation will help. The question here is not what is the nature of the fault that Gawain has committed, but whether there are any mitigating circumstances. Gawain, of course, could not with proper humility plead for this to be considered, but Bercilak and Arthur could, and they could have found such circumstances by considering the nature of fear.

St. Thomas Aquinas spends a good deal of time on questions relating to fear both in the *Summa* and elsewhere, and while he comes to the conclusion that worldly fear (*timor mundanus*) is always sinful,[24] he expresses a belief that fear is always an extenuating circumstance when a sin is committed:

> . . . timor intantum habet rationem peccati inquantum est contra ordinem rationis. . . . Et ideo quicumque, ut fugiat mala quae sunt secundum rationem magis fugienda, non refugit mala quae sunt minus fugienda, non est peccatum. . . . Si autem aliquis per timorem fugiens mala quae secundum rationem sunt minus fugienda, incurrat mala quae secundum rationem sunt magis fugienda, non posset totaliter a peccato excusari: quia timor talis inordinatus esset. Sunt autem magis timenda mala animae quam mala corporis; et mala corporis quam mala exteriorum rerum. Et ideo si quis incurrat mala animae, id est peccata, fugiens mala corporis, puta flagella vel mor-

---

[24] *Summa,* II. II, q. 19 a. 3.

tem, aut mala exteriorum rerum, puta damnum pecuniae; aut si sustineat mala corporis ut vitet damnum pecuniae; non excusatur totaliter a peccato. Diminuitur tamen aliquid eius peccatum: quia minus voluntarium est quod ex timore agitur; imponitur enim homini quaedam necessitas aliquid faciendi propter imminentem timorem. Unde Philosophus (Ethic. iii. 1) huiusmodi quae ex timore fiunt, dicit esse non simpliciter voluntaria, sed mixta ex voluntario et involuntario.[25]

[. . . fear is a matter for sin insofar as it is contrary to the rule of reason. . . . And therefore it is not a sin not to avoid evil which is less to be avoided in order to avoid an evil which, according to reason, is more to be avoided. . . . But if someone, through fear, avoids evil which according to reason is less to be avoided, and thereby incurs evil which according to reason is more to be avoided, he would not be able to be totally excused from sin, because fear of this sort would be excessive. But evil of the soul is more to be feared than evil of the body, and evil of the body more than the evil of external things. Thus if a person incurred evils of the soul—sins—by avoiding evil of the body (for instance, whippings or death) or the evil of external things (for instance, loss of money); or if a person sustained evil of the body to prevent loss of money—he would not be totally excused from sin. However, his sin would be diminished somewhat, because what is done out of fear is less voluntary; for some necessity of doing a particular thing is placed upon a man because of an approaching fear. Thus the Philosopher (*Ethic.* iii. 1) says that things of this kind done out of fear are not simply voluntary but a mixture of voluntary and involuntary.]

In the *Quaestiones Disputatae, De Caritate,* St. Thomas seems to go one stage further in regarding "natural" fear as an unavoidable condition of this life.[26] That fear of bodily harm called for a specially indulgent attitude is made very clear in Wyclif's sermon on the Feast of the Translation of St. Martin.[27] The

---

[25] *Summa,* II. II, q. 125 a. 4.

[26] Marietti ed., vol. II, *De Caritate,* art. 10, contra 4 et responsus: "Sed in hac vita non potest homo esse sine timore" [But in this life man is not able to be without fear].

[27] *Works,* ed. Arnold, I. 372 f.

connection between cowardice and covetousness is especially interesting here:

> For certis, among alle cowardisis, cowardise of richesse is þe moste. For many men þat have richessis dare neiþer seie a soþ, ne defende a soþ seid, for drede of leesing of þis richesse. And so men loven richesse more þan þei loven treuþe of þer God. . . . And unneþe ony riche man wantiþ clene þis cowardise. And þis is more þan cowardise of bodi, þat comeþ to man for drede of bodi; for a man shulde kindely love more his bodi þan his goodis, siþ goodis of kynde ben mouche betere þan ben goodis of fortune. But Crist telliþ ofte to his matirs, þat þei mai not be his disciplis but ȝif þei loven more him þat is treuþe þan loven þer owne liif. . . . And so men þat shal be saved maken þer tresour in God; for þis tresour is of oþer kynde þan ben þes riche men, and it is prescious good, for it is good of grace.

Bercilak's reaction and the reaction of Arthur and his court are what we should expect in accordance with this view of the situation. Gawain *has* "lakked a lyttel" because of his disloyalty to Bercilak stemming from the root sin of covetousness, but in the circumstances who would have behaved as well? One might almost say that from a layman's point of view the sin is a theological technicality, though it is a technicality which requires the fault to be expiated by a due sense of guilt. The whole question revolves round whether Gawain's fear was inordinate or not; from a theological point of view it was inordinate because it placed man above God, but from a lay point of view his fear was natural and justifiable. We ought also to remember that—at least according to St. Thomas—a capital sin was not necessarily worse than any other, but was called such simply because it gave rise to others.[28] That Gawain shows a sense of guilt in spite of the mitigating circumstances is a measure of his coming as near as is humanly possible to the ideal of Christian knighthood.

[28] *Summa*, I. II, q. 84 a. 4.

23

"CUPIDITAS" IN
SIR GAWAIN AND THE GREEN KNIGHT:
A REPLY TO D. F. HILLS

John Burrow

SIR:

I should like to comment briefly, if I may, on the main con-
tention of Mr. David Farley Hills's recent essay on *Sir Gawain
and the Green Knight,* in *RES,* N.S. xiv (1963), 124–131.
I agree, of course, that "cupiditas" ("covetise") had a general
sense in the Middle Ages ("any turning away from God's love")
as well as a special one ("love of riches"); and I agree too that
it is possible to consider Gawain's case as a case of "covetise"
in the general sense—indeed this seems a good way of bring-
ing out its moral seriousness. But I cannot agree that Gawain
himself uses the word in that sense. I think that the context in
the crucial passage beginning at line 2374, quoted by Mr. Farley
Hills, clearly requires one to take it in its more common "spe-
cial" sense. For one thing, "covetise" is set against "larges"
there, as "lewté" is set against "trecherye and vntrawþe"; and
"larges" is the traditional opposite of "covetise" in its special
sense, just as "charity" is its traditional opposite in the general
sense. ("Largesse gaine couaitise is sette," *Cursor Mundi,* 27404;
also *The Book of Vices and Virtues, The Castle of Perseverance,*

Reprinted, by permission of author and the Clarendon Press, Oxford,
from *Review of English Studies,* xv (1964), 56.

etc.) Can one say that "larges" is equivalent to Augustine's "caritas" here? Again, Mr. Farley Hills may choose to follow Augustine and speak of Gawain's disloyalty as "stemming from the root sin of covetousness," but this is not what Gawain himself says. In his account it is cowardice which comes first: cowardice "taught him," he says, to "accord" with covetousness and betray his host. There is no suggestion, either here or elsewhere, that "covetise" is more than one element—and that a secondary one— in the moral case.

I agree with Mr. Farley Hills that I was wrong to discount Gawain's references to "covetise" as mere exaggerations; but I think that one can make sense of them without resorting to St. Augustine. Everyone in the poem agrees that Gawain did not "covet" the green girdle, but the fact is that he did withhold it wrongfully, and such withholding is regularly treated by the manuals as a species or "branch" of covetousness (so in *Ancrene Wisse, Handlyng Synne, Cursor Mundi*). So one can take Gawain's confession to mean that cowardice led him to commit one of the traditional "acts of covetise." Morally, of course, it is not the "external act" but the "internal act of the will" which counts (*Summa Theologiae,* I. II, q. 18, a.6); but, as Mr. Farley Hills shows so well in the last part of his essay, Gawain has every reason to be hard on himself at this point.

I hope to consider these and related matters at greater length in a forthcoming study [*A Reading of Sir Gawain and the Green Knight* (London and New York, 1965)].

INDEX